Prophets as Performers

Prophets as Performers

Biblical Performance Criticism and Israel's Prophets

Jeanette Mathews

 CASCADE *Books* · Eugene, Oregon

PROPHETS AS PERFORMERS
Biblical Performance Criticism and Israel's Prophets

Cascade Books
An Imprint of Wipf and Stock Publishers
199 W. 8th Ave., Suite 3
Eugene, OR 97401

www.wipfandstock.com

PAPERBACK ISBN: 978-1-5326-8552-1
HARDCOVER ISBN: 978-1-5326-8553-8
EBOOK ISBN: 978-1-5326-8554-5

Cataloguing-in-Publication data:

Names: Mathews, Jeanette, author.

Title: Prophets as performers : biblical performance criticism and Israel's prophets / Jeanette Mathews.

Description: Eugene, OR: Cascade Books, 2020. | Includes bibliographical references and index.

Identifiers: ISBN 978-1-5326-8552-1 (paperback). | ISBN 978-1-5326-8553-8 (hardcover). | ISBN 978-1-5326-8554-5 (ebook).

Subjects: LCSH: Prophets. | Bible.—Prophets—Criticism, interpretation, etc. | Performance—Religious aspects. | Oral tradition. | Elijah—(Biblical prophet). | Ezekiel—(Biblical prophet). | Jonah—(Biblical prophet).

Classification: BS1505.2 M28 2020 (print). | BS1505.2 (ebook).

Manufactured in the U.S.A.   03/02/20

Contents

Acknowledgments

THE MAJORITY OF THIS book was written while I was on a six-month study leave period. I am grateful to my colleagues at St Mark's National Theological Centre for providing time and space for this project, and for covering my lecturing and administrative responsibilities in the School of Theology of Charles Sturt University during this time.

I want to acknowledge a Hebrew translation group that meets on a weekly basis at St Mark's but is largely made up of interested members of the Canberra community. Together we have translated and discussed much of the material that is included here. My special thanks go to Kevin Walsh, Alan Horner, Jen Rose, and Steve Prior.

David Neville has taken a great interest in this project and spent significant periods of time discussing it with me, aiding me in clarifying my ideas and encouraging me to find my own voice. I thank him for this. Thank you also to Dave Rhoads, Kelly Iverson, and Shé Hawke, who read the entire manuscript and gave some helpful and encouraging feedback.

Thank you once again to my husband, John Clark, and my family and friends for their love and support of me in my humble attempts to be creative, to offer commentary, and to find connections between the Old Testament and our own time and place.

Abbreviations

Abbreviations for biblical books follow *The SBL Handbook of Style, Second Edition*. Atlanta: SBL Press, 2014.

1QpHab	Qumran Pesher of the Book of Habakkuk
BCE	Before the Common Era (= BC)
CE	Common Era (= AD)
LXX	Septuagint: The ancient Greek translation of the Hebrew Bible
MT	Masoretic Text: The text of the Hebrew Bible developed by sixth to tenth-century CE Jewish scribes including vowel and chant markings based on inherited traditions
NRSV	New Revised Standard Version
v(v)	verse(s)
YHWH	Transliteration of the Hebrew word יהוה, one of the names for God used in the Hebrew Bible, often translated "LORD"

Introduction

Biblical Performance Criticism and Israel's Prophets

Performance and Scripture and Church

THIS VOLUME IS A contribution to the relatively new exchange between Performance Studies and Biblical Studies. Proponents of Biblical Performance Criticism suggest that much can be gained when we go beyond the act of private, individualized reading of the Bible in recognition that the earliest encounters with the biblical text were through performances of oral/aural media in the context of a communal setting.[1] As I have stressed elsewhere:

> The holistic and communal nature of performance, difficult to capture in mere words, encourages a focus not just on *what* is being said but *how* it is being said, attending to sounds and silence, visual images, the physical senses, appeal to the emotion, intellect, and experience.[2]

There is a sense in which Scripture has always been "performed." This assertion is literally true for the Israelite community and the early Church. The earliest transmission of biblical material was in an oral/aural context in communities where illiteracy was the predominant status. Even when these traditions were preserved as scripts, written copies were rare, necessitating communal contexts for them to be performed orally by lectors or orators.[3]

Throughout history until the present day we can still find examples of performance interfacing with Scripture in the church. The liturgical church tradition in particular continues to make use of communal recitation of

---

1. Iverson, "Oral Fixation or Oral Corrective? A Response," 200.

2. Mathews, *Performing Habakkuk*, 1.

3. See Iverson, "Oral Fixation or Oral Corrective? A Response" for a lengthier discussion of early transmission of Scripture.

1

psalms, canticles, and other Scripture, but these practices are also found in nonconformist denominations along with sung and dramatized portions of Scripture.[4] The Eucharist, at least in part, enacts the Gospel, and the sermon or homily is arguably a "performance" of Scripture with its improvisation of the message for contemporary audiences. Scripture readings continue to be included in the majority of church services. Although a few congregations benefit from a recitation of Scripture that has been internalized and performed, most often the Bible reading is by a lector from the written script, with understandably mixed impact depending on the quality of the performance.

Such "performance" of Scripture is important to acknowledge and celebrate, since, in Western society at least, experience of the Bible has become much more individualized due to increased literacy and ease of attainment of printed material along with an explosion in different translations and paraphrases since the mid-twentieth century. Refocusing on "performance" of Scripture reminds us that this ancient text continues to have the potential for embodiment in new faith communities, where its traditions may be reenacted in order to transform the world.

Prophets and Performance

It seems to me that the biblical prophets are especially open to an interface with Biblical Performance Criticism. This book will explore that interface via three case studies found in Chapters 4 to 6. To set the context, Chapter 1 gives an overview of the biblical prophets and a brief history of their interpretation, and Chapter 2 summarizes the ways in which Biblical Performance Criticism has been brought to bear upon the prophetic literature. Readers who are already familiar with Israel's prophetic traditions may wish to skip these introductory chapters. Chapter 3 proposes a new method of reading the biblical prophets with an emphasis on their many and varied performances.

Whatever can be hypothesized about staged prophetic drama in antiquity, we can say with certainty that the biblical prophets were engaged in performance. They spoke publicly before audiences. They mediated between God and their communities, including religious and political leaders. Sometimes they addressed their own communities, and other times came as outsiders to address a new community. Whether prophets

4. The church experience of my youth in the 1970s and 1980s was dominated by "Scripture in Song," and I have developed a more recent appreciation for the simple chants of the Taizé tradition that are predominantly a line of Scripture set to music.

of doom or hope, they spoke into "liminal" moments—a term borrowed from Performance Studies, which describes times of political and social crisis where normal cultural structures and activities are suspended, leaving the community open to critique or new vision. Prophets used symbolic action and invested meaning in ordinary objects and events. They were not merely channels for mediation but embodied communicators who were significantly impacted by their role.

Prophets most often framed their messages with the formula דְּבַר־יְהוָה (deḇar-YHWH), usually translated "word of the Lord." Indeed, it is claimed that "almost everywhere it occurs, debhar Yahweh is a technical term for the prophetic word of revelation."[5] The nominative דְּבַר (deḇār) is very common in the Hebrew Bible, and can be translated in a number of different ways, but the two main translations are "word" and "thing." This observation reminds us that prophets both *speak* the word and *do* the word of YHWH. The potency of God's word as event can be discerned in an oracle found in the book of Isaiah:

> so shall my word be that goes out from my mouth;
>> it shall not return to me empty,
> but it shall accomplish that which I purpose,
>> and succeed in the thing for which I sent it.
> (Isa 55:11, NRSV)

This concept of God's efficacious word is taken up by the witness of the New Testament where Jesus Christ is named the "Word of God" (John 1:1).

Scholarly studies of biblical prophets often distinguish between "pre-classical" and "classical" prophets, the latter sometimes referred to as "writing prophets." The preclassical traditions are predominantly preserved within Hebrew Bible narrative texts, while the majority of classical prophetic texts are poetic in style. Biblical Performance Criticism is a method that is equally effective for analyzing narrative and poetry, thus making it an ideal method to bring to prophetic traditions. Chapter 3 highlights features in narrative and poetic analysis that overlap with a performance critical approach.

Another way prophetic literature is differentiated is by the categories of Former and Latter Prophets, with the Latter Prophets being further divided into Major Prophets and Minor Prophets. This book assumes a continuity within the biblical prophetic tradition while respecting the diversity of prophetic expression and experience. It takes a case study from each subdivision: Chapter 4 analyzes performative aspects of the Elijah cycle from 1–2 Kings (one of the Former Prophets); Chapter 5 envisages the prophet

---

5. Schmidt, דָּבַר, *dābhar*, 111.

Ezekiel (one of the Major Prophets) acting as a performance artist with his unusual and attention-grabbing activity; and Chapter 6 offers a script of the book of Jonah (one of the Minor Prophets). In each case I have translated the relevant material from the Hebrew preserved in the Masoretic Text (MT).[6] It was while I was undertaking these translations that the uniqueness of each prophetic performance became evident. Indeed, if oral performance was the original foundation for written texts of Scripture, it makes sense to expect variation in style and expression. Richard Bauman, influential in the field of Performance Studies, recognizes the distinctiveness in folk oral literature that could be equally applied to prophetic literature:

> A further notable consequence of our deeper awareness of the artfulness of oral literature and the radical importance of performance as constitutive of verbal art has been the restoration of the work of oral literature to the individual artist who produced it and a recognition of the creative individuality of the performer's accomplishment . . . The ethnography of performance, attuned to the unique and emergent aspects of performance as much as to the traditional, conventional ones, presents us with . . . *unique works of literary creation, worthy of critical attention as such, as artists and works of art.*[7]

The Creativity of the Biblical Prophets

Translation of the prophetic traditions alerted me to the creative artistry of the original texts. Prophetic creativity in the biblical tradition is a combination of the compositional skill of the literary scribe and the underlying oral foundation. Careful translation alerts us to these underlying oral factors and elicits aspects of performance that might otherwise go unnoticed: repetition; wordplay; implied gestures; expectation of audience reception and involvement; use of ready-mades, pauses, and silence that intend to engage audiences. In some cases a dramatic structure can be discerned, so that the material divides easily into Acts and Scenes. Since prophetic literature is often presented with first-person address, with the prophet speaking on behalf of the deity or the community, a degree of ambiguity can arise that allows for different meanings and different reenactments to emerge from the foundational script.

---

6. Note that, unless otherwise indicated, all biblical quotations are my own translations.

7. Bauman, *Story, Performance, and Event*, 8–9 (italics added).

Performance Commentary on the Biblical Prophets

Biblical Performance Criticism as a method of inquiry includes many practitioners who prepare, internalize, and perform texts. Indeed, Peter Perry has claimed that it is this method that defines Biblical Performance Criticism.[8] My approach focuses on seeking the aspects of performance *inherent* in texts. My work thus aligns more closely with that of Shimon Levy[9] than with scholar-performers who have written on the method of Biblical Performance Criticism. The question that guides my commentary on prophetic material is, What do we gain if we consider the biblical texts as scripts for performance? Imagination becomes a key aspect to inquiry as I consider aspects such as the tone of delivery, the inclusion of a gesture, the intention behind a word that is now lost in translation. I also look for innovation with an understanding from performance analysis that all performance is reperformance.[10] Actors present memorized and rehearsed scripts in stage performance, but even in everyday interactions we draw on prior experience in order to use appropriate words and actions for the situation in which we find ourselves. "Reperformance" implies variation. Each time an ancient script is performed, the perspective, preference, and preconception of both reader and audience will result in subtle changes in interpretation. The ancient *biblical* script retains the authority inherent in its status as Scripture, yet faithful interpretation by church communities and committed scholars has an equally important role.

Connections between Biblical Prophets and the Twenty-First Century

A final element in this book is the attempt to find connections between these biblical prophetic performances and our own faithful activity within our place and time. Observing the uniqueness of each prophetic performance is a reminder that prophetic action in today's world can take on different guises. The performances described in this book include truthtelling, direct challenge, behind-the-scenes civic disobedience, miraculous acts of compassion, disturbance of the peace, silent protest, creative and provocative artistic installments, confrontational street theater, mystic visions, reluctant preaching, and simply being present within a community.

8. Perry, *Insights from Performance Criticism*, 21.

9. Levy, *The Bible as Theatre*. See Chapter 2 below for a longer discussion of Levy's work.

10. Schechner, *Performance Studies*, 34–36.

Thus the intention behind each of these performances can be improvised in our own settings if we are open to the leading of the Spirit of the same God who guided the Israelite prophets.

This study has been inspired by Dwight Conquergood's assertion that Performance Studies should pay attention to artistry, analysis, and activism (see Chapter 3 below). I have modified Conquergood's rubric to focus on *creativity*, *commentary*, and *connections* for each of the prophetic case studies I have undertaken in this book. I have tried to appreciate the original traditions in all their wondrous diversity and compositional merit (creativity); mine them for clues to original performance events (commentary); and remain alert to where contemporary hearers of these traditions are invited to participate in them by upholding, transmitting, and improvising these traditions for new settings in our own times and places (connections).

1

Israel's Prophets—An Introduction and Overview of Research

ANY BOOK ON ISRAEL'S prophets must begin by answering some basic questions relating to prophecy. Who were Israel's prophets, and what was their role in society? Did prophecy change over time? What is the relationship between the phenomenon of prophecy and the writings that came to be known as the prophetic literature? The first part of this chapter will address these questions.

Because this book proposes a new lens for approaching the prophetic literature, it will be helpful to provide an overview of interpretive approaches to the prophetic literature in both ancient times and more recently. I present this information in broad brushstrokes, bearing in mind that there are many fine introductions to the prophetic literature.[1] I direct readers to my bibliography for helpful recent books and articles that have informed this chapter.[2]

Who Were Israel's Prophets?

The simplest way to describe a biblical prophet is as someone who functioned as an intermediary between the human and divine worlds. They were charismatic individuals, both men and women, gifted to both receive and impart divine messages. Jewish tradition referred to forty-eight prophets and seven prophetesses, whose prophecies contained a lesson for future

1. See, among others, Heschel, *The Prophets*; Petersen, *The Prophetic Literature*; Sweeney, *The Prophetic Literature*; Redditt, *Introduction to the Prophets*; Lundbom, *The Hebrew Prophets: An Introduction*; Stulman and Kim, *You Are My People*; Troxel, *Prophetic Literature*.

2. For example, articles in the *Dictionary of the Old Testament Prophets*, edited by Boda and McConville; Hauser, ed., *Recent Research on the Major Prophets*; Jones, "The Seventh-Century Prophets in Twenty-First Century Research"; Tiemeyer, "Recent Currents in Research on the Prophetic Literature."

generations and thus were recorded.[3] A few non-Israelites were also recognized as prophets in the Talmud, such as Balaam (Num 22–24) and Job. The term "intermediary" stresses the two-way nature of the prophet's relationship with God. They received messages that were imparted to the human community but are often recorded as interceding on behalf of the community, or questioning the message, even arguing with God.

The Hebrew term נָבִיא (*nāviʾ*) and its feminine counterpart נְבִיאָה (*nᵉvîʾāh*) are possibly cognates of the Akkadian verb *nabû*, "to call," giving the meaning "one who has been called." This term came to be the standard term for classical prophets, and is the Hebrew word that is translated by the Greek word *prophētēs*, from which the English terms "prophet" and "prophetess" come.

Other terms used somewhat interchangeably in the Hebrew Bible are חֹזֶה (*ḥōzeh*) and רֹאֶה (*rōʾeh*), both meaning "seer," and אִישׁ הָאֱלֹהִים (*ʾiš hā-ʾĕlōhîm*), translated "man of God." First Chronicles 29:29 names the three prophets connected to David's court as Samuel the רֹאֶה (*rōʾeh*), Nathan the נָבִיא (*nāviʾ*), and Gad the חֹזֶה (*ḥōzeh*). חֹזֶה (*ḥōzeh*) is used most commonly in connection to the royal court (2 Sam 24:11//1 Chr 21:9; 1 Chr 25:5; 2 Chr 9:29; 12:15; 19:2; 33:18) so may have been the technical term for court prophets, but verses that use the term in parallel with נָבִיא (*nāviʾ*) (2 Sam 24:11; 2 Kgs 17:13; Isa 29:10) show that there is some fluidity in the way the titles were used.

In Israel's story, Abraham was the first person designated a prophet (נָבִיא, *nāviʾ*) because of his role as an intercessor on behalf of King Abimelech of Gerar (Gen 20:7); but Moses is portrayed as the one who instituted the office of prophecy (Deut 18:15–19). According to the narrative of Deuteronomy, members of the exodus community were afraid to approach God directly and asked for a go-between who would stand between them and the divine presence, conveying the messages of God to them (Deut 5:22–27).

Despite my description of prophets as charismatic "individuals," the text also refers to groups or bands of prophets, including the phrase "sons of the prophets," translated in the NRSV as "a company of prophets" (1 Kgs 20:35; 2 Kgs 2:3; 4:38; 5:22; 6:1; 9:1). Most of these references are from the Elisha narratives where Elisha is referred to as their "father," translated in the NRSV as "master." The presence of groups of prophets seems to be more characteristic of early prophetic forms described in the Deuteronomistic History. Reference to Deborah as a prophetess (Judg 4:4) and information from comparative ancient Near Eastern studies suggest that prophets were connected

---

3. Rabinowitz, "Prophets and Prophecy in the Talmud," 581. The seven prophetesses are Miriam, Deborah, Huldah, Sarah, Hannah, Abigail, and Esther.

to sanctuaries where they functioned as intermediaries and were consulted at times of military conflict. The story of Balaam (Num 22–24) indicates a role for prophets in pronouncing curses against foreign enemies. The bands of prophets mentioned in the books of Samuel and Kings are connected with the traditions of war against the Philistines. The establishment of monarchy in Israel also resulted in the introduction of court prophets, as mentioned above. In the Hebrew Bible prophecy and monarchy are so closely connected that some scholars argue prophecy ended with the demise of the Judean monarchy. The texts seem to make a distinction between professional prophets and independent figures working in isolation from official structures and critical of the state cult and officials. Nonetheless, the isolation of the prophet should not be emphasized too strongly in light of the toleration and acceptance implied in the fact that oracles were delivered in public areas and recorded, preserved, and reworked for future generations.

What Characterized Israel's Prophets?

If the etymology of the term נָבִיא (*nāviʾ*) as "called" is correct, the impetus for becoming a prophet or prophetess came from outside the individual. Another term that could be used is that the person is *chosen*, often against their will, to convey God's message regardless of whether it will be received or not by their intended audience. Indeed, the typical formula for a "prophetic call narrative" includes resistance to the call. This was not an easy role, yet it is portrayed as a privilege because the prophet had access to the presence of God and the divine council, and an insight into the mind of God.

For some prophetic books we have very little information about who the prophet was, conveying the sense that the prophet's *role* is of more interest than their biography. And yet, the prophets were not puppets. They retained their freedom, even to the point of engaging with God in challenging the message they were given. They were not philosophers or even theologians speaking *about* God. They were mediators conveying the message of God in their own speech and actions. It is significant that in the biblical prophetic traditions the prophets did not lose their individuality. The prophetic record reflects unique styles. There is great variety in how messages are conveyed: through poetry, prayers, sermons, pronouncements, drinking songs, symbolic performances, dirges, legal pronouncements, and other literary and performative genres.

Although the biblical emphasis is on the *word* of God as the source of prophecy, it is clear that dreams, visions, the working of wonders, and symbolic acts are all part of the prophetic repertoire. We even occasionally read of divinatory practices common to prophecy in other ancient Near East cultures and generally condemned in the Torah.[4]

This book has a particular interest in the performance of prophets, and many introductory books and essays acknowledge that dramatic acts were an important part of the prophet's role. Thus Shalom Paul and David Sperling note:

> [The prophets] often performed symbolic acts, which drama-tized and concretized the spoken word. Though the dynamism of the spoken word is considered to have a creative effect in and of itself, it is given further confirmation by this act, which is efficacious and actually plays a role in bringing about the event.[5]

The messages that the prophets conveyed generally involved exhort-ing their audience to live consistently with the Torah, whether it be kings who had ceased trusting in God's ability to protect them or members of the community who were not acting towards their neighbors in accord with the ethical requirements of the law. For the most part, the message of the prophets applied both to individuals and to the community as a whole. There does seem to be some fluctuation across the history of the proph-ets in this regard: individuals identified as prophets in the early story of Israel, such as Miriam, Moses, and Deborah, addressed their messages to the community as a whole. With the rise of monarchy, stories are recorded that depict prophets addressing individual leaders, sometimes publicly and other times in private. The "writing prophets" were predominantly addressing their words to the community as a whole, although again there are stories of individual recipients of oracles and even words and actions that appear to have no audience.

Biblical prophets were never merely predictors of the future, but no doubt aimed to shape the future by exposing and reforming the present. They were not aiming to utter universal truths, but were critical analysts of their own particular social and political situation, and were able to name possible future responses to those situations for their communities. In this respect they were creative. Walter Brueggemann speaks of "the power of poetic imagination" employed by the prophets. Despite speaking into politi-cal and social crises, they rarely offered policy solutions, but rather spoke in "images and metaphors [that invited] alternative perceptions of reality."[6]

4. For example, the use of hydromancy in Gen 44 and the consultation of a medium by Saul in 1 Sam 28.

5. Paul and Sperling "Prophets and Prophecy," 571.

6. Brueggemann, *Theology of the Old Testament*, 625.

Discussions of biblical prophecy often make sharp distinctions between preclassical and classical prophets. These categories are exacerbated by the four-part division in the Christian Old Testament as will be discussed further below, whereas the Hebrew Tanakh combines Former and Latter Prophets together in one section extending from Joshua to Malachi. The structure of the Tanakh reminds us of the continuity between the prophets of the narrative traditions and the classical prophets, whose names are given to the books of Isaiah, Jeremiah, Ezekiel, and the Twelve:

> Classical prophecy, like every other institution in ancient Israel, did not exist in a vacuum but came into being with an ancestry. The classical prophets were indebted in many ways to the heritage of their predecessors. The technical title *navi'* is applied to both. Both speak solely in the name of the God of Israel, who reveals His will directly to them. They are both sent by God, hear the divine word, and are admitted into His council; their messages are sometimes rooted in the Covenant . . . there was one continuous religious tradition.[7]

The Torah presents Moses as the greatest of the prophets:

> And he said, "Hear my words:
> When there are prophets among you,
>> I the LORD make myself known to them in visions;
>> I speak to them in dreams.
> Not so with my servant Moses;
>> he is entrusted with all my house.
> With him I speak face to face—clearly, not in riddles;
>> and he beholds the form of the LORD. (Num 12:6–8, NRSV)

It is possible that Deuteronomistic editing of the book of Jeremiah has deliberately aligned Jeremiah with Moses in order to either present Jeremiah as a new Moses or portray Moses and Jeremiah as the first and last of the great prophets. Common features include a similar call narrative, forty years of ministry, a heightened concern for Torah and covenant, intercession on behalf of the community, and conflict with those who did not accept the authority of the prophet.

The Deuteronomic Law also shaped the understanding of the authority of prophecy. According to Deut 18:9–22, Israelite prophets after the model of Moses would be raised up by God and given the word to speak. They were not to practice foreign modes of mediation (although, as noted above, there are occasional references to such practices elsewhere in the Hebrew

7. Paul and Sperling "Prophets and Prophecy," 572.

Bible), and the "test" that they were true prophets would be whether the word spoken in the name of YHWH would come to pass. Such a test gives rise to theological problems when noticing that prophets were not always heeded or vindicated in their own lifetime (see Jeremiah's complaints), or, in the well-known case of Jonah, that the word of doom announced did not come to pass due to the response by the Ninevites (Jonah 3). As we consider the biblical prophets, then, we should do so with an awareness that the collections were gathered and shaped to be relevant to later generations in the light of events that had already occurred.

Israel's Prophets: A Brief History of Interpretation

Inner-biblical Interpretation

The compositional growth of the prophetic literature took place over a long period of time and in a variety of contexts. Few of the individual books refer to other prophets or their writings, but it is evident that traditions were known and shared, even modified at times. Shared quotations and textual allusions between prophetic oracles suggest that later prophets reused the material of earlier prophecies either to connect their own material to an established tradition, or to reinterpret earlier material for a later time. A good example is the way Joel reused a common tradition. Isaiah 2:4 and Mic 4:3 both read:

> They [the nations] shall beat their swords into plowshares,
>   and their spears into pruning hooks;
> nation shall not lift up sword against nation,
>   neither shall they learn war any more. (NRSV)

Joel 3:9–10 [MT 4:9–10] reads:

> Proclaim this among the nations . . .
> Beat your plowshares into swords,
>   and your pruning hooks into spears;
>   let the weakling say, "I am a warrior." (NRSV)

The words in Isaiah and Micah were envisaging a future ideal characterized by peace among nations, but Joel reverses the imagery from peace to war, calling for battle among the nations rather than peace. In the book of Joel, the author's intention of calling the nations to account to be judged by God for abuses perpetrated against Israel resulted in modifying the words of a known prophetic oracle to serve a new purpose. This and other similar examples give the earliest evidence of interpretation of prophetic material.

God's messages conveyed to historical individuals in specific circumstances were understood as relevant to later times and places, but there was freedom to modify the words of the message to suit the new situation.

The Dead Sea Scrolls and New Testament

The writings from the Qumran community, known as the Dead Sea Scrolls and dated around the turn of the millennium, give further evidence that prophetic traditions were preserved and reinterpreted for later times. Among the scrolls are copies of the canonical prophetic books, *pesherim*[8] (commentaries) on several of them, and apocryphal works that expand on the themes of the prophets. The community evidently considered the book of Daniel prophetic—unlike the Hebrew Bible, which includes Daniel among the Writings. The Dead Sea Scrolls indicate that the community understood itself to have a particular calling to study Scripture in order to understand recent events or events soon to take place. Deliberate interpretive changes to the Scriptures and explanations in the commentaries show that the community even claimed to possess insights beyond the original writings. The Habakkuk *pesher*, for example, claims:

> Then God told Habakkuk to write down what was going to happen to the generation to come; but when that period would be complete He did not make known to him. When it says, 'so that with ease someone can read it,' this refers to the Teacher of Righteousness to whom God made known all the mysterious revelations of his servants the prophets.[9]

The interpretive focus of the Qumran commentaries includes recognition of the Teacher as authoritative, an expectation that they were living in the last days, that the Jerusalem priesthood would be judged and brought down, and that the Messiah would soon arise. The Habakkuk *pesher* and other *pesherim* identify enemies and nations referred to by prophetic writings as the "Kittim"—the Romans—and contemporary events are viewed as fulfilling the earlier prophecies.

Prophetic material is quoted frequently in the nonbiblical scrolls. When the scribe of the Damascus Document quoted Isa 40:3, "A voice cries

8. Berrin defines *pesher* as "a form of biblical interpretation peculiar to Qumran, in which biblical poetic/prophetic texts are applied to postbiblical historical/eschatological settings through various literary techniques in order to substantiate a theological conviction pertaining to divine reward and punishment" (Berrin, "Qumran Pesharim," 110).

9. 1QpHab VII, 1–5, quoted in Evans, "Dead Sea Scrolls," 148.

out, 'in the wilderness prepare the way of the Lord,'" this was understood as instruction for the community to live in the desert and prepare for the Messiah by studying the Law and the Prophets. Interpretation of the prophets by the Qumran community was therefore predominantly eschatological, allegorical, and existential.

An examination of the New Testament documents indicates that early Christian writers had a similar interpretive approach to prophetic material. They understood the prophets as forerunners of Jesus Christ (the Messiah), and understood their messages as directly relating to the events of Jesus's life, death, and resurrection. This assumption is underscored by the arrangement of the books of the Christian Old Testament. Even if the structure was influenced by the arrangement of books in the Greek Septuagint, Marvin Sweeney argues that the structure "plays a constitutive role in defining Christianity's theological reading of the Old Testament."[10] In the Christian Old Testament, the prophetic books compose the final section of a four-part division, following Pentateuch (the earliest history of creation and formation of Israel with its covenant), Historical Books (the history of Israel from the entry into the promised land to the Persian period), and the Wisdom Books (including the Psalms). The books of Lamentations and Daniel are added to the Prophets in the Christian Old Testament whereas both books are included in the Writings in the Jewish Tanakh. Sweeney quite rightly recognizes:

> Because the prophetic books contend that the sins of Judah and Israel led to their punishment and that YHWH intends to restore Judah and Israel following the period of their punishment, the Prophets occupy a key position in the Christian Bible. Appearing at the conclusion of the Old Testament and immediately prior to the New Testament, they point to the revelation of Jesus Christ as the means by which G-d's intended restoration of Israel at the center of the nations will be realized.[11]

The arrangement of the Jewish Tanakh reflects a different theological standpoint. The tripart division of Torah, Nevi'im (Prophets), and Kethuvim (Writings) places the prophetic literature at the center. The Torah comprises the same books as the Pentateuch and "represents the ideal construction of Israel as a holy people centered on the Tabernacle, a precursor for the Jerusalem temple."[12] The Prophets, including both Former Prophets (the books of Joshua through Kings) and Latter Prophets (Isaiah, Jeremiah, Ezekiel, and the Book of the Twelve) are concerned with the disruption of the ideal

10. Sweeney, *The Prophetic Literature*, 18.

11. Sweeney, *The Prophetic Literature*, 18.

12. Sweeney, *The Prophetic Literature*, 19.

and the possibility of its restoration. Thus they look forward to the third part of the Tanakh, which centers on holy life within creation and around the Temple. It is no theological accident that the Tanakh ends with Cyrus's decree for the rebuilding of the Temple in Jerusalem.

Jewish Approaches

The rabbinic understanding of the prophets in the Talmud could be summarized under two main principles: First, that Moses was the greatest and unsurpassed prophet in Israel with Isaiah given precedence over the rest; and second, the prophets were not responsible for any innovations or new doctrine, but expounded and clarified the Torah. When prophecy came to an end, the Shekhinah departed from Israel.[13]

The Greek-speaking Jewish translators of the Hebrew Scriptures whose work resulted in the Septuagint (LXX) can be viewed as early Jewish interpreters of the Hebrew Bible. Septuagint studies is an emerging field, with scholars debating the extent to which the translator(s) modified the source for theological purposes or under the influence of other texts. To give two brief examples, anthropomorphic descriptions of God may have been removed in the LXX Isaiah translation due to a heightened view of God in Second Temple Judaism, and the translator of Habakkuk understood the otherwise unidentified רוּחַ (ruah, "spirit") as the spirit of the Chaldean king, translating "then he shall change his spirit, he shall pass through, and make atonement [saying] this strength belongs to my God" (Hab 1:11). Perhaps influenced by the account of Nebuchadnezzar's conversion in Dan 4, the LXX version of Habakkuk transforms the terrible and fearful Gentile king into a proselyte!

Both Jewish and early Christian interpreters in the Greco-Roman period approached biblical texts with a hermeneutical method that understood the texts to have two levels of meaning: a literal or historical meaning, and a deeper spiritual, meaning. The interpretations differed in that Christians interpreted the prophetic texts through the hermeneutical event of Jesus Christ, while the hermeneutical event for the Jews was the reestablishment of a Jewish kingdom in the land of Israel. This two-level approach to biblical texts persisted through the medieval period until the time of the Renaissance and Reformation when new interpretive methods arose. Nonetheless, a few early writers such as Rabbi Abraham Ibn Ezra raised questions about authorship of books like Isaiah, straying into historical-critical areas that are typical of a much later period of scholarship.

13. Rabinowitz, "Prophets and Prophecy in the Talmud," 581.

According to Walter Wurzburger, modern Jewish philosophical thought views the prophets in one of two ways.[14] Some regard prophecy as a subjective experience—either a psychological delusion or a mystical experience. Others discuss prophecy as a supernatural phenomenon. An important component of prophecy in this view is the divine-human encounter in which the words of the prophet are an interpretation of a revelatory experience. Such persons had a special aptitude for moral and religious insight and were influential thinkers who developed Judaism from a mythical, tribal religion into a universal ethical monotheism comprising belief in one God and adherence to a moral law.

The Beginning of Historical-Critical Methods

A new interest in original languages of biblical texts arose following the medieval period, aided by the invention of the printing press. The Protestant Reformation placed emphasis on the authority of the Bible (*sola scriptura*) and gave greater access to the Scriptures through vernacular translations from the original Hebrew and Greek. On the basis of these original languages the Protestant churches made a division between original and apocryphal works. Commentaries on biblical books claimed the original text as the source of authority.

The Enlightenment period of the eighteenth century brought a challenge to the authority of the Bible when biblical texts were examined in the same way as other texts from antiquity. Questioning the sources, origin, authorship, purpose, and literary style of the biblical books was understood to be scientifically and historically responsible. At the same time, archaeological discoveries of parallel texts and traditions from the ancient world gave further impetus for treating the texts as literature and studying them in a scientific fashion. Evidence for figures with the same characteristics as the biblical prophets in neighboring regions, for example, provided new points of comparison for studies of the biblical prophets. These discoveries also undermined the popular perception of the prophet as a lone charismatic figure plucked out of obscurity to bring God's word when it was clear that in other ancient Near East contexts prophets were well-trained professionals with developed skills who functioned within recognized institutions such as temples and royal palaces. Questions raised by evolutionary theory brought further challenges to biblical authority, especially in relation to the creation accounts.

14. Wurzburger, "Modern Jewish Thought," 585–86.

These challenges gave rise to a conservative reaction that argued for and upheld biblical inerrancy—a backlash that continues to the present day—and yet the historical-critical methods of biblical research have come to characterize responsible scholarship. As will be discussed below, however, new methods continue to supplement the fruits of the Enlightenment.

Contemporary Interpretation of Israel's Prophets

Methods Focused on Establishing the Best Text

Foundational in any biblical interpretation is establishing the text that forms the basis for investigation. Renewed attention to the original languages of the Bible during the period of the Reformation challenged assumptions about the authority of Scripture and resulted in new and revised translations.

Few autographs (original scripts) exist for biblical materials, and when they do (for example, the Dead Sea Scrolls), variations between copies of the same material can be seen, and further variations are found among other ancient translations. The method for establishing the best text of Scripture is to compare the existing versions and apply basic rules to judge between them. One such rule relates to a preference for the shorter reading on the basis that it is more likely a scribe added to a text than removed part of it. In the case of the book of Jeremiah, however, the LXX version is about 12 percent shorter than the Hebrew Masoretic Text (MT). Knowing that the tenth-century Masoretes had a high view of the authority of Scripture belies the idea that so much could have been added when transcribing from the original. The discovery that the Jeremiah document from the Dead Sea Scrolls is closer to the LXX version than the MT leads to the conclusion that there are different Hebrew textual versions underlying the MT and the LXX.

Establishing the best original text was once considered the paramount aim of biblical scholarship. The example above, however, shows that such an aim is misguided if indeed there were more than one text considered authoritative circulating among faithful communities. In exploring variations in the texts of Ezekiel, Ashley Crane proposed that we should appreciate each textual variant for its own sake as evidence of the ways ancient Jewish and Christian communities understood and valued the Bible.[15] The emerging field of Septuagint studies takes a special interest in these textual variations.

Another pertinent method in establishing the text is preparing a translation that attends faithfully to the vocabulary, grammar, and structure of the

---

15. Crane, *Israel's Restoration*, 2.

original text. As any translator will attest, however, it is almost impossible to faithfully translate from one language into another or to prevent transcription errors. The many transcription errors that have been found among the ancient versions, both accidental and deliberate, make it very difficult to claim that any version of the Bible is free of error. The prophetic literature includes a substantial amount of poetic material, which adds a complexity to determining grammar and structure since Hebrew poetry is characterized by verbal transitions, person shifts, and removal of common particles (in particular, the definite article, the direct object marker, and the relative pronoun). Furthermore, there is a high number of *hapax legomena* (words that occur only once in the Hebrew Bible), resulting in significant variations of interpretation in translation. As will be argued below, a performance approach to the prophetic literature embraces such variations as appropriate responses when the script is enacted by new performers in new settings.

The "Worlds" of the Prophetic Texts

It is becoming more common to speak of the three "worlds" of the text: the world *behind* the text, the world *of* the text, and the world *in front of* the text.[16] These categories are helpful in outlining methods of research in prophetic literature. The "behind the text" approaches could also be described as methods focused on the history of the text. In general they are "author-centered" in that they answer questions such as Who wrote the text? Who were the original audience and what were their circumstances? What did the original author want to convey? The "world of the text" approaches are focused on the text itself as a literary composition. How was the message crafted? What structural or compositional influences are at play? What world has been created within the text? "In front of the text" approaches are typically newer hermeneutical questions that have been brought to the texts in the light of the reader's own experiences, perspectives, and concerns. These are sometimes referred to as "advocacy approaches."

"Behind the Text" Approaches to Israel's Prophets

A discussion of "behind the text" approaches to the prophets could be divided into two broad categories: historical-critical studies and social-scientific studies. Such approaches are now commonly referred to as "diachronic"

---

16. This way of speaking of the text was first attributed to Paul Ricoeur but has been taken up by Sandra Schneiders and others. See Schneiders, *Revelatory Text*, where the idea is applied to critical methods.

methods, since they study the way the biblical texts developed over time by examining their original components.

Historical-critical studies of the prophets have been interested in both the historical individuals identified as prophets and the history of the corpus of prophetic literature. There is, of course, some overlap between these categories since it can be argued that all of the prophetic books have at their core oracles delivered by historical figures in specific places and times.

Study of the prophets as historical figures has concentrated in several areas: the historical circumstances for the prophet's ministry, the relationship of the prophet to the cult, the relationship between the prophetic *persona* and the prophetic book, and the oral nature of prophecy.

Almost all of the biblical prophets are named, and sometimes a patronym is offered with the name, but it is common for there to be little corroboration elsewhere in the Hebrew Bible for that historical person. Some have attempted to scan the meaning of the prophet's name for information about the individual. Often the name is symbolically or directly related to their role (e.g., *Joel*, which amalgamates the two divine names, or *Micah*, meaning "who is like Yah?") A number of prophetic collections orient readers or listeners to a historical setting by giving specific details such as the reign of a king (e.g., Isa 1:1) or a chronological date (e.g., Ezek 1:1). In the absence of these details, scholars looked for clues within the material, even if scant. In the book of Habakkuk, for example, the only historical reference is to "the Chaldeans" (Hab 1:6), a name regularly used in the Hebrew Bible to refer to the Neo-Babylonian Empire, leading most scholars to assume that the setting for Habakkuk is the rise of this empire. Other material within the prophetic books helps to locate the prophet in time, place, and role. Books that have an emphasis on the Jerusalem temple and cult, for example, suggest that the prophets of those books were affiliated with the priestly leadership of the community, and therefore imply a postexilic perspective.

Nineteenth- and twentieth-century investigations of the characteristics of the prophets led to a view of the so-called classical prophets as radical, solitary figures who were isolated from the official cult. Yet the fact that their words were preserved and transmitted suggests that they were not as isolated as has been assumed. The diverse phenomena of biblical prophecy include "false prophets" (indicating that discernment was needed for prophetic authority), prophets who acted relatively independently and played a destabilizing role, and active prophets well integrated into the institutional cult.

As noted above, the biblical emphasis in prophecy is on the word of God as transmitted by the prophet. The prophets' words have thus been a focus of attention, especially in the light of the scant biographical information given about the prophets themselves in most cases. Prophets were recognized as delivering oral messages—short and well defined—that were subsequently collected, written down, and compiled. Two main areas of inquiry emerged: the study of those original messages (form criticism), and the way in which they were brought together (redaction criticism).

Orality studies have shown that traditions transmitted orally tend to follow common forms, themes, and patterns. Prophets drew on common traditions such as laments and curses and from sociocultural traditions such as legal forms and creation myths. Form-critical studies have not only identified traditions common across the prophetic literature, but have also examined the relationship between convention and innovation among the prophets. Intertextuality studies, discussed further below, have especially focused on the use, reuse, and modification of themes and traditions across the corpus.

Evidence of reuse of traditions as well as recognition of multiple settings, perspectives, or both within a single book has resulted in redaction criticism as a popular method of research among scholars of the prophetic literature. Scholarly attention thus moved from the original speaker to the redactor who gathered the material and shaped it to convey a particular message. Many of the prophetic books have a mixture of judgment and promise oracles that suggests the combination of individual speeches or smaller collections of oracles. In bringing them together, compilers have added explanations and updated the original material in the light of new circumstances. Much attention has been given to the book of Isaiah with its different perspectives (preexilic, exilic, postexilic). The book of Jeremiah is considered to have been redacted by a Deuteronomistic hand. Recent scholarship has revolved around questions relating to the compilation and redaction of the Book of the Twelve. Until relatively recently, the prophetic books that compose the Book of the Twelve were slotted into their appropriate historical settings and discussed in isolation from the remaining books in the collection. Recognition that the ancient witnesses viewed the books together gave rise to scholarship focused on finding the links between the books. James Nogalski has been a leading scholar looking for catchwords, common themes, and "seams" between books to argue that the Twelve is a compilation of smaller collections that have been deliberately brought together and expanded.[17] Debate has arisen, however, due to the following factors: the different ordering of the books when comparing the MT with the LXX; the fact that the individual books do not refer to each other; the recognizable, individual voice of each witness; and the fact that commonalities between the books in the Twelve are

17. Nogalski, *Redactional Processes in the Book of the Twelve*; Nogalski, *The Book of the Twelve*.

at least as significant as commonalities between those books and secondary material found outside of the Twelve, particularly in Isaiah, Psalms, and the wisdom books.[18] Attention to redaction criticism in the prophetic literature has demonstrated that the historical setting and social context of the later compilers of the prophetic books is equally important as determining the original events of prophecy.

While diverse in character, the common thread of social-scientific studies of prophecy is to apply insights from sociology, anthropology, and psychology to reconstruct the world portrayed in the texts and to understand the context in which the texts were produced.

From a sociological perspective, attention is given to institutional structures within society, especially to those that distribute power and wealth. The prophetic literature has been read against an understanding of ancient Israel as a tributary society in which the poor of the land were in danger of exploitation by more powerful groups with links to the local monarchic system, themselves under pressure due to their obligations to the more powerful empires of the region. Bearing in mind the geographical and climatic conditions of ancient Israel, those on the bottom rung of such a system were especially vulnerable so that formerly self-sufficient peasants became swallowed up in a "rent capitalism" model[19] where they lost ownership of their land or were forced into producing for others due to the requirements of the state or wealthy landowners. The indictment by the prophets of those who abused such a system for their own benefit is evident in texts such as Isa 5 and Mic 2.

More recent studies have questioned whether such stratification of society evidenced in the texts was a result of the growth of the Israelite monarchy or in fact developed and intensified during the period of colonization by the Persian Empire. Applying models of modern peasant societies to prophetic literature suggests that this literature reflects conflict between urban and rural dwellers and the pressures brought by a market economy in the postexilic era, resulting in debt and latifundialization (accumulation of land into large estates governed by a single landowner and worked by tenants). In such a context prophets denounced abuses of reciprocal patronage, unfair judicial systems, and forced debt slavery.

These debates highlight an issue faced by social-scientific research in biblical literature, namely, the reliability of the biblical text for sociohistorical reconstructions. Even for those who do not have a "minimalist" view of

18. See Ben Zvi and Nogalski, *Two Sides of a Coin*; Perlitt, *Die Propheten Nahum, Habakuk, Zephanja.*

19. See Lang, *Monotheism and the Prophetic Minority.*

the history behind the text, prophetic literature and the presentation of prophets in the Hebrew Bible are not uniform and thus resist definitive reconstruction of the texts and their original contexts. Much of the debate in current prophetic studies relates to the relationship between orality and literacy. Attention has long been given to the role of society in shaping the prophetic literature, but whereas focus on the eighth and seventh centuries of the divided monarchies of Israel and Judah was once assumed to be the background to the historical prophets, the focus (with notable exceptions) is now on the society in the Second Temple period in the fifth century. If the prophetic books were products of the scribal literati and were not fully compiled and edited until the Persian period, as many now argue, the social conditions presented in the texts may reflect the conditions of the postexilic period rather than earlier contexts.

Another area of scholarship that fits into the broad category of social-scientific studies was the attempt by form critics to determine the hypothetical *Sitz im Leben* ("setting in life") behind prophetic genres, especially in the original oral delivery of the forms. Various types of prophetic speech were postulated to have had their origins in concrete social locations. The woe oracle, for example, was thought to be drawn from a funerary context (see Isa 5:8–30; Hab 2:6–19). The original setting for the lawsuit or "rib" oracle (e.g., Mic 6:1–8) would have been the law court where the relationship between YHWH and the people of Israel was understood as a legal contract, mirroring the political climate of the ancient Near East where small states were able to maintain a relative independence by keeping treaties with larger political powers. Both sides had obligations in such treaties, and both knew there were penalties if the contract was broken. Rhetorical questions such as those found in Amos 3:3–9 reflected the wisdom tradition and suggested the prophet had connections with wisdom schools. These *Sitze im Leben* may have been relevant across a wide time span such that the question of *when* the prophetic literature came into being is not so important in appreciating the sorts of contexts that influenced such literature.

Anthropological and psychological studies included comparisons between biblical prophets and their ancient Near Eastern counterparts. Use of the term "intermediaries" in such studies indicate a desire to facilitate cross-cultural appraisals without privileging the Judeo-Christian prophets. By studying shamans, spirit mediums, medicine men and women, and other intermediaries, the role of prophets and social dynamics determining their functioning in society can be advanced. Points of connection and areas of contrast are mined in order to provide more information about biblical prophets. Common experiences of an atypical mental state characterized by abnormal behavior and an altered state of body and mind have given rise to application of psychological theory to the prophets. Ezekiel has been the most studied in this regard, and has more than once been diagnosed as suffering from paranoid schizophrenia due to his catatonic state, sexual regression, and delusions of persecution and greatness!

Theories of ethnicity and social identity have been applied to prophetic books in order to aid identification of redactional layers. To give just one example, Anselm Hagedorn proposed a three-stage growth in the book of Nahum, arguing that the changing perspectives toward the "enemy/other" gives evidence for the background of each layer, an idea informed by anthropological theory of how ethnicity functions socially. The writer of the first layer of Nahum perceives the other (that is, Assyria) as superior, so the so-called secular language is devoid of irony or taunting. The second level is situated in the Babylonian period after the fall of Nineveh, and the oracles reflect a religious dimension, presenting YHWH as superior to the foreign powers and enabling the writer to perceive the "other" as equal in status and so to incorporate condemnation and taunting. At the third layer the "other" is no longer determined by ethnicity but is identified in theological terms as the enemy of YHWH, who is the universal judge.[20]

This brief discussion has not covered all of the areas of scholarship in "behind the text" methods. What is evident when perusing recent scholarship, however, is that historical-critical and social-scientific studies exist among a plethora of other approaches to prophetic literature, leading Alan Hauser to introduce a discussion on recent research in the Major Prophets with this statement:

> The historical-critical consensus that dominated scholarship well into the 1970s no longer controls the agenda . . . it is clear that multi-faceted, interdisciplinary approaches to biblical interpretation are likely to be common for the foreseeable future.[21]

"Text Itself" Approaches to Israel's Prophets

Studies of the prophets via literary critical approaches place more emphasis on reading the texts for their own sake than on attempting to find out something about their compositional history. These methods read and appreciate the texts as literature and are referred to as "synchronic" methods since they focus on the final form of the text. They are interested in examining the intentional shaping of texts, including aesthetics and rhetorical effect.

20. Hagedorn, "Nahum—Ethnicity and Stereotypes."
21. Hauser, "Introduction and Overview," 1.

The biblical literature is broadly divided into prose and poetry, with the prophetic books comprising material from both categories but leaning more heavily towards the poetic. Some prophetic traditions are conveyed as stories and have been analyzed with the method of narrative criticism. Coherent plots that include an exposition, rising action, complication, crisis, falling action, and resolution or denouement can be discerned in the narrative presentations of Elijah and Elisha, for example, and in the narrative book of Jonah. As will be noted in my chapter on Jonah, however, the fact that the narrative of Jonah remains open-ended is a significant departure from the expected narrative arc. Narrative criticism pays attention to characterization, story time and place, and point of view. Features such as repetition and variation are noted.

Several scholars have applied the insights of narrative criticism to prophetic books other than those that are presented in obvious narrative form. Christopher Seitz, for example, shows how the structural unity of the book of Isaiah invites us to read the book with one message rather than dividing it into three parts with different emphases.[22] He has a similar approach to the Book of the Twelve and speaks of an "affiliated witness" such that, despite their individual differences, the books together form an overarching coherent plot.[23] Paul House also applies a narrative plot to the Book of the Twelve, recognizing an introduction (Hosea, Joel), complication (Amos, Obadiah, Jonah, Micah), crisis (Nahum, Habakkuk), falling action (Zephaniah), and resolution (Haggai, Zechariah, Malachi). Through this sequence of books the story is told of a protagonist (Israel) who descends to the depths of exile before being raised again to restoration.[24]

The scholarship of Brevard Childs was a key moment in Old Testament studies, including prophetic studies, with its "canonical critical" approach to Old Testament Scripture encouraging appreciation for the final form of the book.[25] Childs argued that even though prophetic books are made up of collections of smaller units that may have arisen in differing historical circumstances, we need to appreciate that the final redactors of the books deliberately shaped their material to convey a message of both judgment and restoration, with hope and promise usually having the final word such that God's promises are seen to be fulfilled. Moreover, the prophetic books

22. Seitz, "Isaiah 1–66: Making Sense of the Whole."

23. Seitz, *Prophecy and Hermeneutics*, 119.

24. House, *The Unity of the Twelve*.

25. Childs, *Introduction to the Old Testament as Scripture*. See also Childs, "The Canonical Shape of the Prophetic Literature." It is important to note that Childs himself was not comfortable with the designation "canonical criticism"—see Childs, *Introduction*, 82–83.

were edited with a view to their ongoing use by the community of faith. The thrust of Childs's work has been recently extended by scholars applying "theological interpretation" to the prophetic books (and other Old Testament literature), aiming to "listen for God's address" to the contemporary Christian chu ch.[26] Applying a "trinitarian hermeneutic," this method stresses a christocentric interpretation of the prophetic books, claiming to find coherent witness to God the Father and Jesus Christ within the prophets. In a sense, this approach is a logical extension of treating the text as the locus of study rather than the historical production of the text. The God of Israel, often referred to by the name YHWH, is a major character in those texts, and the revelation, intention, and character traits of that God are of deep theological interest. Such theological analysis also results in troubling interpretations—is God really to be understood as a warrior (Nah 1; Hab 3) or a cuckolded husband (Hos 2; Ezek 16)? Such questions raise the need for ethically based hermeneutics as will be discussed further below.

Attention to the poetic nature of prophetic literature has resulted in important studies from the perspective of rhetorical criticism. Rhetoric is an ancient art related to oral discourse. We know from Greek literature that individuals were schooled in rhetorical performance in order to enhance persuasive skills. Such skills could be transferred to written argument. Rhetorical criticism examines the ways words and ideas are arranged in order to convince the hearers or readers. Close attention to the structure of a composition including the use of repetition, chiasms, *inclusios*, and so on, reveal what was important to the author and what he or she wanted to convey to their audience. In the Hebrew poetic literature, evidence of oral delivery as well as literary composition can be found.

Phyllis Trible's analysis of the book of Jonah from a rhetorical critical perspective is an excellent example of this critical method at work.[27] Close attention to grammatical and lexical features of the text shows how the story and its theological message are emphasized by the structure of the book. For example, Jonah 1:3 has a chiastic structure framed by the repeated phrase "from the presence of YHWH":

> And/but-arose Jonah to-flee to-Tarshish from-the-presence-of
> YHWH,
>> and-he-went-down to-Joppa
>>> and-he-found a-ship
>>>> returning (to) Tarshish
>>> and-he-paid her-fare

26. See Bartholomew and Beldman, eds., *Hearing the Old Testament*.

27. Trible, *Rhetorical Criticism*.

and-he-went-down in-it
to-return with-them to-Tarshish from-the-presence-of
YHWH.[28]

As the verses proceed, the word "down" is used several times, accentu-
ating the desire of Jonah to remove himself from YHWH's presence. Yet in
verse 9 he answers the sailors' questions about his identity with a confession
of faith:

"And-YHWH, God-of the-heavens,
   I (am) fearing
who made the-sea and-the-dry-land."

By splitting a theological description of YHWH and placing his own
self-identification in the middle of it, "Jonah surrounds himself with the
God he is fearing."[29] The linguistic construction heightens the irony of the
message—a prophet of YHWH who attempts to flee from his prophetic calling and yet remains surrounded by the God he fears.

Another aspect of rhetorical criticism is the study of the art of persuasion, of how a speaker or writer has shaped the discourse to affect the
audience. There are many examples of prophets using extended metaphors
to stir emotions, or of prophets performing provocative acts to shock an
audience from complacency. More will be said about these characteristics of
the Israelite prophets in later chapters.

Studies of intertextuality between prophetic books have increased in
recent decades. Although such studies relate to compositional history, as
discussed above, often the focus is on the final form of the book and its
artful composition rather than on when and by whom the material was
composed. Reused words and themes across a particular prophetic book
or a collection of books, such as the "Day of YHWH" theme found in the
Book of the Twelve, suggest an intentional theological unity for the collection. Much attention has been given to the book of Isaiah, showing that
common motifs are integrated across the book, making it more difficult
to argue for a division of the book into three sections created by three
separate individuals.

Intertextuality studies of the prophetic books also examine the reuse of
earlier biblical traditions, especially the pentateuchal traditions. The book

---

28. Trible, *Rhetorical Criticism*, 129. Trible's iconic translation mirrors the Hebrew
sentence structure and hyphenates English words that together translate a single Hebrew word.

29. Trible, *Rhetorical Criticism*, 141.

of Ezekiel, for example, draws on laws from Leviticus and Deuteronomy but reframes them for an exilic audience.

Whereas historical-critical studies aimed to discover the identity of the original prophets behind the biblical traditions, even to the point of determining the *ipissima verba* (the precise, original words) that could be attributed to the historic prophet, literary approaches recognize that personification is common to all literature and so focus instead on the prophetic *persona*. The emphasis shifts from historical individuals and settings to the theological perspective or message of the book's compilers, which is presented through the prophetic *persona*. The prophet is usually presented as a model of faithful obedience to the call and covenant of YHWH (with Jonah as a notable exception!) As noted in my study on Habakkuk, "the prophet can be viewed as the character representing the drama of the book for both his own audience and later generations of faithful readers."[30] In other words, the prophet as literary *persona* does not need to be dismissed as a literary fiction, but is key to the ongoing impact of the original prophetic event.

"In Front of the Text" Approaches to Israel's Prophets

The approaches discussed in this section could be subsumed under the general heading of "reader-response criticism," a term used to highlight the role of the reader in the creation of meaning in a text. Unlike approaches that assume the original author encoded the meaning of the text, either by transmitting a concrete message for a specific time or by crafting the text in order to make a predetermined impact upon the reader, reader-response criticism acknowledges a multifaceted relationship between author, text, and reader. Each component contributes to the communication event, and multivalent readings can result from this. The readers bring their own experiences, perspectives, and concerns to the text and expect it to engage with these questions.

In recent scholarship the major issues that have been brought into conversation with the prophetic literature include concerns about the representation of female characters, concerns about representation of the earth in light of our environmental crisis, postcolonial perspectives, and trauma studies.

Feminist readings of the prophets have highlighted both positive and negative aspects of the presentation of God in the prophetic books as well as prophetic treatment of women. For example, Isaiah and Hosea both speak

30. Mathews, *Performing Habakkuk*, 178.

of God as a compassionate mother who would not forget the fruit of her womb (Isa 49:15; Hos 2:23), and eschatological visions in Jeremiah and Joel speak of God's connection with humanity in inclusive terms that allow for equal participation between men and women (Jer 31:31–34; Joel 2:28–29). The overarching prophetic concern for justice and on behalf of the power-less has been noted as helpful in the context of interpretation of texts emerging from a patriarchal society.

Feminist studies have emphasized the metaphorical nature of much poetic language while still accepting the power of metaphor to shape thought and interpretation. Another direction these studies have taken, therefore, has been to critique a dominant metaphor in the prophetic literature that likens the community of Israel to the daughter or wife of YHWH (Hos 1–3; Jer 3; Ezek 16, 23). In this metaphor the image of God is masculine and patriarchal, at times even abusive and violent towards the female character. In both sexual and nonsexual imagery, the faithless daughter/wife is stripped and publicly humiliated by her jealous father/husband to make her realize her sin of adultery (idolatry). It has been acknowledged that the intended recipients of such oracles were the male members of the Israelite community who, in a patriarchal society, would have been of-fended and shamed by being likened to female characters. Such metaphors were arguably shocking for an ancient Israelite audience, but today's female audiences are neither able to relate to such material, nor (especially in the current #MeToo climate) able to condone such material as authoritative Scripture. By bringing a uniquely female perspective to texts created by males, intended to be read and heard by males, and historically interpreted via masculine experience, feminist studies have raised new questions and thrown new light on the prophetic traditions.

In the light of current ecological concerns for the earth, another "in front of the text" approach to the prophets is to read them with an ecojustice perspective. Scholars debate whether the words of the prophets reflect a specific concern for environmental issues, or whether these issues are subsumed to human interests. John Barton claims "the prophets . . . are on the whole more concerned with social than with environmental ethics, and have their eyes fixed on the human rather than the natural world,"[31] whereas Kathleen O'Connor believes that, for Jeremiah at least, the fate of humans is inexorably linked to the fate of the earth.[32] In several of the prophetic books the earth bears the brunt of God's punishment of the people of Israel and Judah (e.g., Isa 24; Jer 3:23–27; Ezek 33:28–29; Joel 1–2; Hag

---

31. Barton, "Reading the Prophets from an Environmental Perspective," 55.
32. O'Connor, "The Prophet Jeremiah and Exclusive Loyalty to God," 134.

1:7–11). On the other hand, prophetic visions of an eschatological future often incorporate descriptions of a restored and harmonious natural world (e.g., Isa 11:1–9; 65:17–25; Mic 4:4). In legal traditions that are upheld by the prophets, Israel's relationship with the land is one of stewardship rather than ownership (Lev 25; cf. 1 Kgs 21).

In parallel readings with feminist hermeneutics, ecojustice readings raise the questions of whether the earth has a "voice" in the text, and whether it is possible to condone God's "abusive" actions towards the natural world. They ask whether the prophetic traditions can continue to have a formative value in the current environmental crisis, or whether they need deconstruction in order to be useful.[33]

Postcolonial criticism has become an important way to read the prophetic traditions as scholarship reaches greater consensus that the prophetic books were products of scribes and not fully compiled until the Persian period or later, hence were themselves products of colonized identity. This school of critical thought comes from the perspective of those who are or have been subjects of colonization. Like other "advocacy" hermeneutical methods, postcolonial criticism not only critiques interpretation from the perspective of those in power, it also analyses attitudes embedded in the text under the influence of social class and ideology. It asks what influence geopolitical power has had on the formation of texts. In relation to prophetic texts, it asks how the scribal class in Jerusalem related to the Persian administrators and Judean aristocracy of the Second Temple period, and how such relationships influenced prophetic compilations. Postcolonial readings are self-consciously from the perspective of the subaltern—a member of a group outside the hegemonic power structures.

As an example of a postcolonial reading of a prophetic text, Chesung Ryu has written on the book of Jonah. He noted that established readings of the book of Jonah criticize the prophet as the personification of a narrow-minded Jew and emphasize God's universal and inclusive love and mercy. Embedded in this universalistic inclusivity, however, is a working system of exclusivity that silences the voice of the weak. Ryu suggests an alternative reading for Jonah's anger and silence in 4:1–11. In the context of the power differential between the Israelites and the Ninevites, Jonah's silence functions as *resistance* on the part of the weak over against the rhetoric of the strong, the only resistance possible in such unbalanced power structures. From Ryu's perspective, a universalist message of God's love for the "other" ignores the basic injustice of hegemonic colonial oppressors.

---

33. See, for example, Habel, ed., *The Earth Story in the Psalms and the Prophets.*

Experiences in the twentieth century, including the Vietnam War and the Balkan conflict, have resulted in greater interface between theology and trauma studies in recent years. Some scholars view prophetic literature as examples of "survival literature," written from the perspective of the trauma of exile. By focusing on the *literature* of the prophets rather than the prophetic individuals, these studies are able to highlight the voices of hope that emerged from ongoing reflection on war and violence.[34] It is argued that written prophecy offers the perspective of the losers that dares to name the horror of war and disaster yet refuses to retreat into denial. In this the biblical prophetic literature stands out as different from other ancient Near Eastern literature and modern history accounts that usually present the perspective of the winners. It also self-consciously creates an interface between the ancient text and the contemporary community—the aim of all "in front of the text" approaches to the prophets.

Summary

This chapter has introduced the Israelite prophets as presented in the biblical texts, and has also reviewed the variety of methods scholars and people of Jewish and Christian faith have taken in interpreting them. It almost goes without saying, of course, that responsible scholarship embraces a diversity of approaches to the biblical texts. Historical, literary, *and* reception methods all shed light on prophetic traditions and their ongoing impact. James Nogalski reminds us that

> One must learn to read prophetic texts on multiple levels. One must learn to hear the individual speeches and to separate the speeches from one another. One must, however, also learn to hear these speeches within their current literary contexts and to recognize how they may have been adapted when they were incorporated into the context. Finally, though, if one wishes to interpret prophetic literature as Scripture, one must also learn to hear these texts as theological witnesses by ancient communities of faith that deserve responsible theological reflection for today's world.[35]

The next chapter will introduce another way of reading prophetic texts—from the perspective of Biblical Performance Criticism—that

---

34. See, for example, Stulman and Kim, *You Are My People*; Boda et al., eds., *The Prophets Speak on Forced Migration*.

35. Nogalski, *Interpreting Prophetic Literature*, 15.

contributes to the diversity of interpretive approaches to the Israelite prophets. Biblical Performance Criticism is a holistic method that broadly incorporates the three worlds of the text just discussed. The three case studies that follow will be introduced with a brief discussion of where the prophet is situated in the biblical tradition (the world behind the text), will then explore the prophet's creativity and provide commentary on performative aspects (the world of the text), and, finally, propose connections between the prophet and our own experience (the world in front of the text). My approach will take into account the importance of translation and analysis of literary and performative devices but will also highlight the potential in these texts to transform knowledge and praxis in the investigator, the faithful community, and the wider world.

2

A Review of Performance Critical Approaches to Prophetic Literature

READING THE PROPHETS THROUGH the lens of performance is not a unique idea, although it is surprising that the potential for reading prophets as performers has not been more readily embraced. This chapter will review some of the studies that have integrated prophetic literature and Performance Studies as well as noting limitations inherent in reading ancient scripts as sites of performance.

I have divided the studies discussed below into three broad areas. The first group are scholars who have read prophetic books as scripted dramas; the second have found links between Performance Criticism and Biblical Criticism when reading the prophets; and the third come to the prophets with the intention of illuminating performance aspects inherent in the text. I include my approach in this third category.

Initially, however, it is important to clear the way for this discussion by rehearsing the troubled relationship between performance and Judeo-Christian theology. An unease has existed between theater and theology for understandable reasons. The Hebrew text warns against making graven images and idols (Exod 20:4; Deut 27:15). The fact that Israel's God is such key character in the stories of faith suggests that "dramatizing" biblical narratives and discourse in any form runs the risk of portraying God as an "image;" at the very least reducing the "otherness" of the divine.[1] The modern Hebrew word *bamah*, meaning "theater," is derived from בָּמָה ("high place"). This word raises a warning signal for those with even a cursory knowledge of

---

1. In a recent study, Travis West challenges the notion that God could not be represented in ancient Israel. He claims, "Regardless of the specific way it was done, it seems clear to me that God was presented in *some* way, and biblical performance criticism offers the scholar tools to explore this theological and theatrical dynamic further." West, "The Art of Biblical Performance," 67 (note 61); italics original.

biblical laws and traditions since the "high places" often came under criticism as places where illegitimate worship was taking place.

From another angle of concern, rabbis in the Greek and Roman eras disapproved of attendance at theaters because it was there that sacrifices were offered to idols. It is thought that the earliest known writer of Jewish tragedies, Ezekiel of Alexandria, intended to divert Jewish audiences from attending pagan theaters by providing alternatives based on Hebrew Scriptures.[2] In addition to their connection with pagan religious festivals, Greek and Roman theaters were sites for ridicule and persecution of Jews and Christians.[3] Roman emperors passed laws that compelled all citizens to participate in official ceremonies on pain of death, and at the same time early church councils passed laws *against* attendance or participation in theater for church members![4] Early church theologians such as Tertullian (155–220 CE) and Augustine of Hippo (354–430 CE) denounced the theater as did the leaders of the Reformation. On the other hand, Meg Twycross discusses how the medieval church used liturgical drama along with stained glass windows and icons to communicate its stories to its largely illiterate congregations.[5] Although records indicate that performances based on biblical stories were spoken in Latin, Twycross asserts the valuable impact of the visual, auditory, olfactory, and kinesthetic aspects of the performance in communicating the stories. Without direct access to the Latin biblical texts, however, ordinary people were unable to compare Scripture passages with the dramas on offer. In addition, direct translation and quotation of the Bible into the vernacular was a punishable offence at the beginning of the Reformation period, so the dramatic works were "popular retellings" that drew on legendary and apocryphal material.[6] Twycross discusses how popular urban play cycles that were a collaboration between church and society became part of the dissension between Catholic and Protestant factions and were ultimately phased out in those areas where the Protestants became dominant, so that in England an Act of Parliament in 1605 spoke of "the great abuse of the holy name of God in stage plays, interludes, May games, shews and such like."[7] This Act demonstrates a renewed opposition to theater, since during the reigns of Elizabeth I (1533–1603) and James I (1603–1625) theaters had the support of the monarchy and became very popular, albeit always closed

2. Sowden, "Theater," 670.

3. Bruch, "The Prejudice against Theatre," 1–4.

4. Bruch, "The Prejudice against Theatre," 5.; Crystal, "Theatre," 209.

5. Twycross, "The Theatre."

6. Twycross, "The Theatre," 347.

7. Twycross, "The Theatre," 356–57.

for the period of Lent. Opponents were concerned that the theater adopted pagan festival practices, required men to dress in women's clothing in opposition to Scripture (Deut 22:5), and encouraged pleasure and recreation over work. Such Puritan sentiments became enshrined in law during the English Civil War under the Roundheads (1642) until the restoration of the monarchy in 1660. During this period theaters were demolished, actors considered rogues, and spectators fined.

This negative attitude towards the theater persisted despite "the very positive role [the Bible played] both as a source of dramatic inspiration and as an influence on content in all forms of theatrical representation,"[8] particularly in the West:

> In the first place it provided the starting point of modern theater in the medieval mystery plays, and secondly it continued to provide subjects and ideas to which playwrights, poets, composers, and choreographers have turned again and again.[9]

In his preface to *The Bible as Theatre*, Shimon Levy asserts that the Old Testament has had a long performative history:

> Ezekiel's oral prophecies or Deborah's Song were actually performed in the old days, and as such are clearly theatrical. Moreover, the Hebrew Bible has been read aloud in synagogues for hundreds of years, indeed as a holy ritual and an educational weekly event.[10]

Levy's seminars and workshops exploring the dialogue between theater and Scripture that began in the late twentieth century are indicative of the fact that in recent years the prejudice about theater has been waning, and biblical scholars have begun to draw on the language and theory of theater and performance as a substantive source for theological reflection and biblical interpretation.

Prophetic Books as Dramas

There is no firm evidence that anything like our concept of theater existed among the communities that gave rise to the Hebrew Bible, although, as discussed above, Israelite communities would have been aware of dramatic phenomena common in the ancient Greek Empire. Nonetheless, it is hard

8. Sowden, "Theater," 670.
9. Sowden, "Theater," 670.
10. Levy, *The Bible as Theatre*, x.

to dispute Levy's assertion that the Old Testament has performative aspects to it. Psalms and embedded songs immediately come to mind,[11] and several individual books have been treated as dramas.[12] It is the argument of this book that the biblical prophets are particularly suited to performance analysis since they were first and foremost oral performers.

The exact nature of the relationship between performance and the written scripts that were preserved as Scripture is a matter of lively discussion.[13] Early studies that focused on performance of texts argued that some psalms preserve fragments of "cultic drama" relating to Israelite festivals.[14] Sigmund Mowinckel specifically related ritual to cult when claiming particular psalms as "the text for a dramatically performed procession [comprising] different acts and scenes."[15] A key idea, of course, is that the drama is *cultic* or *liturgical*. Twycross discusses "liturgical drama" as aiming to strengthen faith and instruct "ordinary people" in the biblical stories,[16] and contrasts liturgical drama with "civic drama" although in the Middle Ages there would have been an evident overlap between church and civic bodies. Dramatic presentations of biblical material used within worship settings or cultic festivals are well characterized as liturgical drama, even though I will later discuss the potential for performances of prophetic material in contexts other than worship. For the moment, however, of particular interest for this study are the few scholars who have argued for deliberate dramatic shaping of prophetic books by their authors or redactors.

John D. W. Watts—Isaiah

Approaching Isaiah from quite an original perspective, John D. W. Watts has written a two-part commentary that does not conform to the tripartite division of Isaiah usually followed by scholars but divides the whole book

11. See Cousins, "Pilgrim Theology" for a performance reading of psalms; and Giles and Doan, *Twice Used Songs* as an example of performance analysis of songs embedded in narrative sections of the Old Testament.

12. To cite a few examples: Job (see Habel, *The Book of Job*; and Shelton, "Making a Drama out of Crisis?"); Song of Songs (Delitzsch, *Proverbs, Ecclesiastes, Song of Solomon*); Ruth (Giles and Doan, *The Story of Naomi*; Queen-Sutherland, *Ruth and Esther*).

13. See, for example, Niditch, *Oral World and Written Word*; Carr, *Writing on the Tablet of the Heart*; Doan and Giles, *Prophets, Performance, and Power*; Horsley, *Text and Tradition*; Ben Zvi and Floyd, eds., *Writings and Speech*.

14. Gunkel, *The Psalms*, 5–6; Mowinckel, *The Psalms in Israel's Worship*; Weiser, *The Psalms*, 23–35.

15. Gunkel, *The Psalms*, 5–6.

16. Twycross, "The Theatre," 338–39.

into a "drama" comprising a Prologue, six Acts and an Epilogue.[17] He divides the book as follows:

Prologue (1:1—4:6)

Part I: The Decreed Destruction of the Whole Land (5:1—33:24)

Introduction to Part 1 (5:1—6:13)

    Act 1: Jerusalem's Royal Heir (7:1—12:6)

    Act 2: The Burden of Babylon (13:1—27:13)

    Act 3: The Woes of Israel and Jerusalem (28:1—33:24)

Part II: The ריב of Zion: The New Order (34:1—61:11)

    Act 4: The Inheritance of the Nations and Israel (34:1—49:4)

    Act 5: The Inheritance of Jerusalem (49:5—54:17b)

    Act 6: The Inheritance of YHWH's Servants (54:17c—61:11)

Epilogue: For Zion's Sake—New Heavens and New Land (62:1—66:24)

Watts's dramatic structure partly results from his conviction that the book is a "conscious literary creation . . . not simply the end result of a process of tradition."[18] The decision to characterize that literary creation as drama is not fully explicated, although the dialogic style of discourse between YHWH/God and the people of Israel may be influential. The acts of the drama are divided in relation to historical circumstances with Part I relating to the late monarchy of Israel and Judah and Part II set in the Persian period directed to exilic and postexilic Israel in Babylon and Palestine. A feature of the book as a whole is the inclusion of believers of all races and nationalities in the new Jerusalem announced at the beginning of the book and fulfilled in the final vision. With greater attention to literary structure than to historical-critical issues, then, Watts's commentaries can be appreciated for their presentation of the book of Isaiah as a dramatic vision of God's involvement and intention in the history of preexilic and exilic Israel. In Watts's view, the overall purpose of the book of Isaiah is to announce to Israel that a new age is coming in which Israel will be characterized by servanthood rather than nationhood.

17. Watts, *Isaiah 1–33*; Watts, *Isaiah 34–66*. Watts may well have been influenced by the division of chapters in the Isaiah scroll found in 1QIsaa where a three-line gap between chapters 33 and 34 is found.

18. Watts, *Isaiah 1–33*, xliii.

John Eaton—Deutero-Isaiah

John Eaton, influenced by the work of Sigmund Mowinckel and Ivan Eng-nell, both of whom associated the Servant Songs of Deutero-Isaiah with liturgical drama,[19] developed the idea of Deutero-Isaiah as festal drama prompted by the Autumn Festival in preexilic Jerusalem. While acknowl-edging that the timing and duration of the "festival of Yahweh" in royal Jeru-salem are not certain, Eaton assumes that the festival sequence in question arose from the antecedents of postexilic celebrations of New Year (1 Tishri), Day of Atonement (10 Tishri), and the week of Booths/Tabernacles (15–22 Tishri).[20] He postulates an "outline for the royal drama"[21] on the basis of a number of psalms, concluding that the presentation of the Davidic office and the dialogue of God and people through the prophets are two impor-tant aspects of the drama. He then discusses how such a structure might have influenced the composition of Isaiah. Noting the interplay of voices and perspectives in Isa 40:1–11, Eaton suggests that the "rather dramatic form" mirrors the "liturgic voices" of priest or prophet.[22] Moreover, state-ments functioning like stage directions in the passage suggest the prepara-tion and acting out of a festal procession. As Eaton continues to analyze Deutero-Isaiah, he suggests that the combination of disparate forms in the composition is better explained by the author's drawing on a preexisting tra-dition in which the forms were already collected rather than by the author's adapting from the wide variety of secular and sacred situations to which the prophet had access. This included incorporating the content of the Servant Songs from the enthronement rites and the prophet's role in conveying po-litical change such that "the message of restoration could easily clothe itself in the language of the old liturgy."[23]

The particular contribution Eaton makes to viewing the prophets through a dramatic lens was his assertion that the prophetic work was transmitted through inherited liturgical patterns. In other words, liturgical drama was the basis for Jewish faith and for prophetic composition.

---

19. See Mowinkel, *He That Cometh*, 138–9; Engnell, "The Ebed Yahweh Songs," 56–57.

20. Eaton, *Festal Drama*, 9.

21. Eaton, *Festal Drama*, 25.

22. Eaton, *Festal Drama*, 28–29.

23. Eaton, *Festal Drama*, 118.

Klaus Baltzer—Deutero-Isaiah

In the introduction to his commentary on Deutero-Isaiah, Klaus Baltzer presents a thesis similar to Eaton's—that the work is a "liturgical drama," though not founded on festival rites as Eaton had proposed:

> The term 'liturgical drama' is intended to bring out the proximity of worship and the cult. The drama uses forms and subject matter already present in the liturgy, to the point when it itself may acquire a ritual function. This also implies that the performance can be repeated, and that the drama can be used at different places.[24]

Baltzer finds correspondences with examples of the dramatic genre in other parts of the ancient world, although he admits that differences also exist. He argues:

> For an understanding of DtIsa's work it is important to grasp that it was conceived in literary terms, but that as a liturgical drama it became through its performance literature for a (largely) non-literary public.[25]

While admitting that Deutero-Isaiah is dominated by speeches, Baltzer argues that the speeches include description of action, commands, and differing standpoints including audience reaction.[26] He therefore suggests they are better characterized as *scenes* and presents his commentary in six Acts, each of which has three Scenes, with identifiable actors and a chorus. Five of the six acts conclude with a hymn containing a plural imperative (e.g., "Sing!" "Rejoice!"). He speculates as to where and when it may have been performed, but emphasizes important aspects of performance: the "drawing in" of the audience, and the "repeatability" of drama by specifically linking it to the annual Passover/Mazzot spring festival.[27]

In using drama as an "umbrella" genre that brings together the smaller units in Deutero-Isaiah, a particular strength of Baltzer's commentary is his discussion of the use of time in the prophetic work:

> DtIsa uses all the potentialities of the theater in order to make past, present and future simultaneous in the time of the drama, so that they can be experienced in the context of the fiction ... the past is not simply finished and done with. It has to be

24. Baltzer, *Deutero-Isaiah*, 7.
25. Baltzer, *Deutero-Isaiah*, 14.
26. Baltzer, *Deutero-Isaiah*, 6.
27. Baltzer, *Deutero-Isaiah*, 22.

grappled with publicly if an understanding of it is to be arrived at; and here the festival offers an opportunity through the performance of the 'liturgical drama.'[28]

Other Studies of Isaiah

Several other scholars and commentators have recognized dramatic forms in Deutero-Isaiah, including Conrad, Berges, Nitsche, van der Woude, and Richtsje Abma, who notes, "Thus DI can be regarded at least as a text with traits of drama. It presupposes an audience (cf. the imperative forms and rhetorical questions), presents several speakers and contains a commenting chorus (cf. 50.10–11)."[29] Focusing specifically on Isaiah 49–55, Abma suggests the two locations in those chapters—namely, Babylon and Zion—represent two sets out of which the drama unfolds, with actors moving between the sets and the prophetic voice commentating on the action from outside of both locations. Abma's article argues for "lost stage directions"[30] in Isa 49–55, but unlike previous studies discussed, limits the drama to a specific audience at a specific time. Other studies of Isaiah's dramatic properties stress the possibility for reenactment, a characteristic that is crucial in performance theories.

John Wilks titles his short article "The Prophet as Incompetent Dramatist" to signal his skepticism that Deutero-Isaiah was ever "intended for the stage or cult in some way or other."[31] The suggestion of an underlying festival giving rise to Israelite liturgical drama reflected in the biblical texts is undermined by a growing lack of support for an Enthronement Festival in Israel, although Wilks does admit that there is evidence for entrance rituals that utilized the psalms. A second objection is the lack of specific information on practical aspects of staging a drama. Noting the overlap in language when discussing poetry and drama, Wilks notes that authors such as Baltzer have "misinterpreted the visual imagery so typical of a *poem* as a series of stage directions for a *drama*."[32] Benjamin Sommer makes a similar critique in his review of Baltzer's commentary, asking why readers should understand a given speech in Isaiah as drama rather than a poem.[33]

---

28. Baltzer, *Deutero-Isaiah*, 41.

29. Abma, "Travelling from Babylon to Zion," 4. For other authors mentioned see Utzschneider, "Drama (AT)."

30. Abma, "Travelling from Babylon to Zion," 28.

31. Wilks, "The Prophet as Incompetent Dramatist," 530.

32. Wilks, "The Prophet as Incompetent Dramatist," 539 (italics original).

33. Sommer, Review of Baltzer's *Deutero-Isaiah*.

Nonetheless, Sommer affirms the contribution that dramatic readings of Isaiah have made by drawing attention to the neglected aspects of rhetoric in Isaiah: "These chapters are full of sudden shifts of voice, references to movement, vivid questions, challenges, and responses. In short, they are dramatic, though not a drama."[34]

Paul House—Zephaniah

Paul House's commentary on Zephaniah, subtitled *A Prophetic Drama*, uses the term "closet drama" to address concerns such as those raised by Wilks and Sommer. He states:

> Many objections to speaking of biblical drama revolve around the historical concern of how, where, or if such a drama was staged. [Closet drama is] composed in dramatic style, but is written without the play ever meant to be staged. The author is thereby able to concentrate on poetry and content without worrying about how a play will affect an audience . . . the importance of closet drama for biblical studies is that its existence proves a literary piece need not be staged to be drama . . . its presence leaves open the possibility of exploring literature that has dramatic characteristics, plot, character, dialogue, etc., as drama.[35]

House begins with a genre discussion, distinguishing between lyric mode and dramatic mode. Lyric differs from drama in that the latter demands an audience. This emphasis is one that was noted by the scholars of Isaiah discussed above and one that will feature in my own methodology for reading prophetic texts as performances. It also forms a partial response to the critique that poetry is "misinterpreted" as drama. Drama is classically divided into tragedy and comedy, but House admits that it is difficult to classify the book of Zephaniah as either. He goes on to analyze Zephaniah via plot, characterization, and point of view, claiming that the seven sets of speeches in the book mark the divisions between Acts and Scenes. In Zephaniah the characters do not dialogue directly with each other but supplement and complement each other's words as in Greek drama.[36] The characteristics of classical drama—namely, exposition, complication, climax, falling action, and resolution—are applied to the book of Zephaniah.

34. Sommer, Review of Baltzer's *Deutero-Isaiah*.

35. House, *Zephaniah*, 50. Interestingly, the Puritan resistance to theater during the English Reformation could make an exception for closet dramas, especially if they included religious content, as long as live performances were not undertaken.

36. House, *Zephaniah*, 58.

House concludes that it can be established within a classical framework to have dramatic form. He summarizes:

> Zephaniah's structure is created by a series of alternating speeches ... Its plot has a definite conflict and resolution ... Its plot is shaped by an overwhelming emphasis on the 'day of Yahweh' ... An almost totally dramatic point of view pervades the book.[37]

Walter Dietrich—Nahum

Although his argument not as developed as House's characterization of Zephaniah as "closet drama," Walter Dietrich approaches the book of Nahum in a similar vein, suggesting that, given the overarching form of the book, it is fitting to view Nahum as a "dramatic text." While "certainly never 'performed' as a drama, the text could have been consciously formed in such a way that the readers or those listening to the reading could imagine a drama taking place within their imaginations."[38] Dietrich suggests breaking the book into a Prelude (Nah 1:1) and three Acts (Nah 1:2–2:1; 2:2–14; 3:1–19). He envisages different actors (the prophet, female figures depicting Nineveh and Judah, a messenger of peace, a "scatterer," a noblewoman and her maidservants, YHWH, the king of Nineveh), changing scenes, and audience involvement, noting that the book ends with a rhetorical question directed to the king of Nineveh but answered by the implied audience. He discusses the fact that subject matter of Nahum—the fate of Nineveh—is shared by the book of Jonah, which also ends with a rhetorical question. The placement of the two books as neighbors in the Septuagint highlights the "dialogue" between the books; but even in the Hebrew canon, thematic and compositional links (such as ending with a question for the audience) suggest interpretation of each individual book must be held in tension with the Book of the Twelve as a whole. Notable in this regard is the evidently dramatic nature of the book of Jonah, to be discussed further in Chapter 6 below.

Dietrich's commentary on Nahum incorporates both synchronic and diachronic perspectives. His proposal of a dramatic structure to the book is made in the initial "synchronic" section but is not returned to in his subsequent analysis (in either synchronic or diachronic sections), giving the impression that it is an idea "pasted on" to the book rather than integral to its composition, despite the assertion of conscious formation.

37. House, *Zephaniah*, 89.
38. Dietrich, *Nahum, Habakkuk, Zephaniah*, 22.

Helmut Utzschneider—Micah

Helmut Utzschneider's commentary on Micah (2005)[39] approaches the book as a "dramatic" or "performative" text structured in entries and scenes. He characterizes the text as "dramatic" on the basis of two primary traits:

> (1) by means of direct speeches and addresses, changing speakers, themes, and perspectives, they evoke the impression of actors' entrances; (2) the speeches visualize the scene of the entrances—in other words, they stage the location and other visual circumstances embodied in the speeches.[40]

In a later, unpublished paper, Utzschneider adds a third criteria in defining a performative text when he suggests it should have a coherent plot, indicated by a sequence of scenes held together by themes, story lines, or characters.[41] Such sequence of scenes can be thought of as "Acts." Utzschneider points out that modern dramatic texts announce the names of the actors by way of stage directions, but prophetic texts do not necessarily do so. In fact, it could be argued that a common characteristic in prophetic literature, particularly poetic texts, is ambiguity, arising from unidentified speakers and pronouns without antecedents. Yet Utzschneider argues that changes in pronouns, themes, or perspectives in prophetic texts function as entrance markers, giving a dramatic structure to the material. Mic 1:1–7, for example, can be recognized as a scene with three entrances. Verse 2 begins with an imperative addressed to an audience so clearly is an example of direct speech even though the speaker is not announced (Utzschneider regards the first verse in Micah as a "superscription" exclusively addressed to "real" hearers and readers—akin to stage direction, which are not part of the actual performance). This actor cannot be God since YHWH is referred to in the third colon of the verse. Verse 3 is the second entrance marked by the formulaic Hebrew words כִּי (*kî*) and הִנֵּה (*hinnēh*) as well as a change of theme. While this is still direct speech, it is no longer directly addressed to an audience but is rather a report of a theophany. Another change in theme and a back-reference in verse 5 marks another entrance, and this time the unidentified pronoun "I" must refer to God as the speaker. Utzschneider argues that these three entries are part of one scene, with a common location—the temple or entrance to the temple—holding them together.[42]

---

39. Utzschneider, *Micha*. Utzschneider has also written on Joel 1–2 as a performative text but I have not been able to access this paper.

40. Utzschneider, "Is There a Universal Genre of 'Drama'?" 67.

41. Utzschneider, "Drama (AT)."

42. Utzschneider, "Is There a Universal Genre of 'Drama'?," 67–69.

Utzschneider speaks of the interplay between narrative and speech within Hebrew literature, including the prophetic literature. But even without the presence of narrative, as is the case with the book of Micah, he argues that "clear connections with the historical narratives of the Old Testament can easily be found."[43] Past events and experiences narrated elsewhere in the Old Testament are telescoped into "flashes" of images in poetic form which would nonetheless be familiar to hearers or readers of the prophetic material. This "dramatization of [the] narrative tradition in prophetic speeches," he argues, "not only transported the experience of the past into the present for listeners but also updated these experiences with new interpretations."[44] An important theme of Performance Theory, namely, reenactment, is highlighted in this observation by Utzschneider.

Performance Approaches to Prophetic Literature

Dramatic Shape of Prophetic Literature

The classic dramatic classification of tragedy and comedy was applied to prophetic books by Norman Gottwald in an essay titled "Tragedy and Comedy in the Latter Prophets" (1984). Gottwald argued that in the overall shape of the prophetic books "there can be little doubt that it is the comic voice that subtends the tragic,"[45] despite the fact that the route to the comic conclusion may encompass suffering and catastrophe. He suggested that the mixture of genres, written over long periods that make up the prophetic books, means they cannot necessarily be read as coherent narratives but are nevertheless open to being analyzed under the headings of plot, theme, hero or protagonist, and social context. In his ensuing discussion Gottwald conceded that prophecy may be more like forms of tragicomedy where a double plot of both comedy (U-shape) and tragedy (inverted U-shape) is offered. In general, Israel's leaders who have brought ruin on the community are subject to the inverted U-shaped tragedy plotline while the community as a whole benefits from the U-shaped comedy plotline.

43. Utzschneider, "Is There a Universal Genre of 'Drama'?," 71.
44. Utzschneider, "Is There a Universal Genre of 'Drama'?," 72.
45. Gottwald, "Tragedy and Comedy in the Latter Prophets," 84.

"Prophetic Drama"

David Stacey's *Prophetic Drama in the Old Testament* was important in bringing the dramatic actions of the prophets to the fore. While acknowledging that forms of action such as dance, processions, sacrifice, and rituals play a part in Israel's cult, Stacey drew attention to the special emphasis on actions of prophetic figures. Unlike cultic practice repeated many times by different people, the prophetic actions were singular, aimed at gaining attention. He states:

> Prophetic actions must, therefore, be seen as a class by themselves. They were specific actions with a specific purpose, carried out by a peculiar kind of person, who believed himself to be, and was generally acknowledged to be, called by God, perhaps even from the womb (Jer 1.5), to this specific service.[46]

Stacey noted that dramatic incidents relating to prophets are frequently mentioned by commentators, often with an emphasis on the "strangeness" of the actions, but the focus has typically been on the words of the prophets rather than their actions. The general assessment was that prophets spoke oracles, and sometimes made the message more impressive by incorporating performed actions. Both pointed to future events, and once the words were spoken and the action performed, the event would come to pass. Although this sounds "magical," biblical prophets were Yahwists submitting to the will of their god rather than using words and actions to coerce the deities.

Stacey discusses some of the difficulties in analyzing these actions, particularly as the examples are "baffling" in their diversity. Some actions are deliberate, yet prophets could see significance in accidental actions and everyday scenes. Objects are sometimes used but do not seem to be essential in prophetic drama. Some actions were specifically directed to be seen by others, but elsewhere there is no specific mention of communication to others. Sometimes *lack* of action comprises the drama!

Rejecting some past theories that prophetic drama was due to a psychological imbalance (an "embarrassing" sign of an "overcharged psyche"[47]) or used as mere illustrations or visual aids, Stacey proposes that word, drama, and fulfilment are inseparable parts of the dynamic package that is the divine will.[48] He reiterates the "wisdom" of choosing the word *drama:*

---

46. Stacey, *Prophetic Drama in the Old Testament*, 62.

47. Stacey, *Prophetic Drama in the Old Testament*, 262.

48. Stacey, *Prophetic Drama in the Old Testament*, 279.

because of the complexity and elusiveness of the relation of all drama to reality. The drama stands over against reality; it holds up a mirror to it, it represents, it informs, it interprets; it heightens reality by highlighting it and revealing its inner nature; the drama affects the way that reality is experienced . . . Prophetic drama hovers around the reality and gives it further 'presence.' It is another form of manifestation of the reality itself.[49]

"Performance Artists"

Several scholars have used the term "performance artist" to describe the performative nature of prophets in the Old Testament. Hugh Page speaks of the prophets as "akin to present day *performance artists* and *public intellectuals* for whom preaching was an all consuming passion."[50] While acknowledging diversity, Page suggests that the common features of prophets are "logocentricity" and "artistry." He does not amplify his view of them as performance artists other than by making a reference to their being "totally absorbed by their vocation and even a bit eccentric,"[51] emphasizing rather the poetic nature of their performances. His motivation underlying his discussion is to encourage a greater affinity between Christian theology and the arts.

In other studies the prophets Hosea, Jeremiah, and Ezekiel have come under particular scrutiny with their identifiably dramatic actions. There has been a tendency to equate performance art's nature of protest or provocation with the purpose of the prophets as disrupters of their complacent contexts. In her editorial to a volume of the journal *The Bible and Critical Theory* titled "Prophetic Performance Art," Yvonne Sherwood pointed out the difference between performance art and the straightforward acts of conventional drama. She spoke of the deliberate use of sensation at the heart of prophetic language and performance: "Prophetic performers and speakers seem particularly, indeed peculiarly, dedicated to provocation and the ideal of turning the prophet and audience inside out."[52] She compared the categories of prophetic speech and wisdom literature in the Hebrew Bible to further emphasize her point: "Unlike Wisdom, Prophecy claims to be the direct word of God, and prophetic language and prophetic bodies reel in the

---

49. Stacey, *Prophetic Drama in the Old Testament*, 280.
50. Page, "Performance as Interpretive Metaphor," 49 (italics original).
51. Page, "Performance as Interpretive Metaphor," 49.
52. Sherwood, "Prophetic Performance Art," 1.1.

attempt to create a sense of words that, by definition, are not our words, and of actions that, by definition, are not 'our' own."[53]

In the same journal of essays Teresa Hornsby referred to Ezekiel "Off-Broadway" when she spoke of the prophet's tendency to take ordinary objects and actions into the public space for display, thus disrupting societal norms. In likening Ezekiel's actions to those of a performance artist she claimed:

> The performance would not get rave reviews for originality—the repetition, the excrement, the excessiveness, the presence of ordinary, private acts publicly performed are common fodder in the world of performance art. That Ezekiel's prophetic performances and performance art are so similar is not coincidence. Both seek to express concerns that emerge from the fringe and both offer direct resistance and, perhaps, attempt to subvert power centers.[54]

Similarly, Mark Brummitt showed that several incidents in Jeremiah that are conventionally understood as "symbolic acts" have greater impact when interpreted as "performance pieces," especially when viewed through the characteristic of performance art that could be described as a blurring of actor and spectator so that the audience finds themselves onstage.[55] For example, in the incident of the broken pot (Jer 19), the audience members become unavoidably involved in the performance and are no longer spectators.

Sherwood referred to Hornsby's essay on Ezekiel and Brummitt's analysis of Jeremiah as "attempt[s] to restage (in modern idioms) the audacity and strangeness of the original performance."[56] Using performance art as a framework is a better analogy than conventional theater in which there is a clear divide between "active performer and passive spectator-receiver."[57]

Sherwood was well-placed to comment on these essays given her own prior discussion of the possibility of comparing prophecy and performance art as intentionally provocative performances. Titling her essay "Prophetic Scatology,"[58] Sherwood argued that prophetic language is a *crudely* embodied discourse that frequently draws on elements of bodily discharge, sex, disease,

53. Sherwood, "Prophetic Performance Art," 1.2.

54. Hornsby, "Ezekiel Off-Broadway," 2.1 See my own case study of Ezekiel in Chapter 5 below.

55. Brummitt, "Of Broken Pots," 3.1

56. Sherwood, "Prophetic Performance Art," 1.3.

57. Sherwood, "Prophetic Performance Art," 1.3.

58. Sherwood, "Prophetic Scatology."

mutilation; using offensive words and imagery that are often sanitized in translation. She compared prophetic rhetoric and action to a contemporary exhibition of sensational "Britart" in the 1990s, concluding,

> it is clear that the desire to shock is as crucial to Yhwh and the prophets as it is to [contemporary] artists. True prophecy shocks, dislocates, refuses to pander to the eyes, produces un-bearable visions and unseeable spectacles. In the competition for 'truth', prophecy needs to legitimate itself in the here-and-now, needs to imagine a way for God to speak that will be suf-ficiently marked, sufficiently other, sufficiently *striking*.[59]

Shimon Levy (whose work will be discussed more fully below) referred to Ezekiel as "the holy actor" due to the "uniquely theatrical quality of some of this particular prophet's public performances."[60] Levy argued that as a proph-et-priest Ezekiel would have been experienced in public communication, al-though admitting that some of the material he was expected to communicate would have made him a reluctant, albeit committed, actor.

Among the range of metaphors and images employed by Ezekiel, Levy singled out "sex, food, and life" as the main ideas. Under the heading of "Erotic Theatre," Levy claims that Ezekiel's presentation of Jerusalem and Samaria (metonyms for the people of Judah and Israel) as prostitutes is the most erotically explicit material to be found in the Hebrew prophets. Eze-kiel's use of "blatantly sexual, often deliberately pornographic language"[61] was in order to gain his audience's attention and curiosity. Levy's discus-sion echoes Sherwood and others who have written of performance art's aim to shock for attention from an audience. Interestingly, Levy stated "In this case it is inconceivable that it [Ezek 16] was acted out in its time, but the suggestiveness of the spoken word and the imaginative power of the words created theatre in the minds of the listeners."[62]

Both Levy and Sherwood speak of God as the director of these pro-phetic performance artists. For Levy it is a "highly demanding director"[63] while Sherwood observes that where the contemporary artist/performer is "master of his own affliction and humiliation," prophets are voices and bod-ies "wielded by another,"[64] implying the offstage directorial deity.

---

59. Sherwood, "Prophetic Scatology," 211–12 (italics original).
60. Levy, *The Bible as Theatre*, 178.
61. Levy, *The Bible as Theatre*, 181.
62. Levy, *The Bible as Theatre*, 182.
63. Levy, *The Bible as Theatre*, 179.
64. Sherwood, "Prophetic Scatology," 215.

A pertinent issue when discussing performance art is the normalization of what was originally a dislocating experience into acceptable behavior. The nude body and bad language, even blasphemy, have become more and more acceptable in mainstream media. Clearly this critique is applicable to biblical prophetic performance also—the very act of canonization is a sanitizing process that normalizes the traditions. As discussed further in Chapter 3 below, translation that is performance-sensitive and appreciation of the embodied and kinesthetic aspects of prophetic performance can be employed to refocus attention on the confrontational nature of prophetic action.

Performative Speech Acts

Speech-act theory is a concept from the philosophy of language that examines the performative function of language. Based on terms developed by John L. Austin, "locutionary" acts are the performance of an utterance, while "perlocutionary acts" describe words that "perform" an action (for example, when a celebrant announces that a couple are married, or a judge announces guilt or innocence of a person on trial), and "illocutionary acts" are utterances that have a certain force in social settings (such as promising, ordering, warning, and bequeathing). Richard Briggs's review study showed how this theory has been valuable in biblical studies and should be of particular interest in a performance approach to biblical material, which is a "written form of communicative action."[65]

In his monograph *When Prophecy Failed* Robert P. Carroll spoke of the performative nature of prophetic speech:

> The general terms used to describe the prophetic preaching such as proclamation, announcement, threat, warning, opposition, pardon all indicate that the very core of prophetic language was performative. In behaving in such ways the prophets performed the tasks of challenge, indictment of community, repudiation of its behavior, conviction of crimes and offences, announced the people's guilt and passed sentence of death on it. On other occasions they commiserated with the community, pardoned it, promised it prosperity and blessed it. The perlocutionary aspects of their preaching may be seen in their encouragement and inspiration of the people, their persuasion

---

65. Briggs, "The Use of Speech-Act Theory," 265. It is surprising that there have not been more studies applying speech-act theory to prophetic speech.

of the people to act in certain ways and, on occasion, their deception of the community.[66]

Carroll links the "success" of the performance to the ability of the prophet to persuade his community to heed his words and act in an appropriate manner. As the title of Carroll's book implies, however, the prophets were by and large unsuccessful. Walter Houston challenges this view by distinguishing between the perlocutionary and illocutionary effects of prophetic words:

> The successful performance of an illocutionary act does not in general depend on the appropriate response of the hearers. It is necessary to distinguish, as Carroll has failed to do, between the illocutionary and the perlocutionary effects of an utterance . . . as long as the prophets' hearers understood that they were warning them, calling for repentance or whatever the particular speech act might be, and understood the content of the warning whatever it might be, then the prophets had done what they set out to do, even if they had not achieved the effect they had hoped for.[67]

Other authors who have applied speech-act theory to prophetic literature include Adams, who focuses on the illocutionary force of the Servant Song texts in Deutero-Isaiah, and Terry Eagleton, who has written a brief essay on J. L. Austin and the book of Jonah.[68] As these few studies show, potential exists for further dialogue between the proponents of speech-act theory and biblical scholars of the prophetic literature.

Performance and Power—Doan and Giles

William Doan and Terry Giles, professors of Theater and Theology respectively, have collaborated to explore the concept of performance in Biblical Studies in several publications. In their book *Prophets, Performance and Power* they focus on the performance of the prophets of the Hebrew Bible. The book examines the interplay between oral and written (scribal) performance, introducing the concept of power in the dynamics of performance— how a performer such as a prophet is granted social power, how that power operates on an audience, and how it is transformed and transferred by scribal

---

66. Carroll, *When Prophecy Failed*, 72.

67. Houston, "What Did the Prophets Think They Were Doing?," 177.

68. Adams, *The Performative Nature and Function of Isaiah 40–55*; Eagleton, "J. L. Austin and the Book of Jonah."

performance into a written text. Doan and Giles assume that "ownership" of the performance in antiquity is transferred from an original audience to a much smaller group of literati. Nevertheless, they envisage the process as a "continuity of performance, preserved through orality, repetition of the tradition, and the creation of the text, or script, through which the pattern of prophetic performance is preserved."[69]

Doan and Giles draw from both orality studies and performance theory in their analysis. They reject the once commonly held view of a school of prophets or disciples who preserved the oral words of the prophet in written form and instead explore the relationship between prophet and scribe with the aid of performance language. They speak of the relationship as akin to performer and script where the prophet is a performer who exercises social power through the immediacy of the performance. For the tradition to be preserved, however, the words must be recorded in a script, at which point the power of the prophet is curtailed and usurped. A script is a limitation on the performance because it controls the message. This observation is spoken of in terms of actor and character: "The scribes create prophetic *characters* out of the prophets themselves (prophetic *actors*), [characters that continue] long after the actor has left the scene."[70] The character becomes the locus of authority. The written text cannot replicate the actual experience of a prophet engaging an audience so instead creates an illusion of the prophetic experience, which Doan and Giles call "the prophetic drama."[71] In this way the message can continue to be transmitted, not only for a reading audience but also for a non-literate audience, and yet the message has been shaped by the scribe in the transmission. Doan and Giles argue this moves the power "from performer to playwright."[72]

In a more recent journal article, Giles and Doan set out in succinct fashion a proposed methodology composed of five "core principles" that help give Performance Criticism its unique contribution.[73] These principles are (1) "medium transferability," recognizing that a performance is an event rather than a genre and that the performative characteristics are retained when transferred to a new, written medium; (2) "act-scheme," the presentational structure of a performance that has a distinctive pattern and therefore is recognized by performers and spectators; (3) "audience formation" that occurs in the relationship between actor and audience as an event is presented

69. Doan and Giles, *Prophets, Performance, and Power*, 17.

70. Doan and Giles, *Prophets, Performance, and Power*, 23 (italics original).

71. Doan and Giles, *Prophets, Performance, and Power*, 29.

72. Doan and Giles, *Prophets, Performance, and Power*, 29.

73. Giles and Doan, "Performance Criticism of the Hebrew Bible," 278–82.

and the audience responds to shared or conflicting values; (4) "iconic" and "dialectic" modes of presentation in which patterns of activity pertaining to either being (iconic) or becoming (dialectic) can be recognized and reused in future performances; and (5) "explicit" and "implicit" activities that refer to the performative patterns embedded in biblical texts such as prophesying, singing, debating, and the implicit questions arising from these activities, such as tone of voice, gestures accompanying the speech, and so forth. Such questions provide a guide to understanding the oral and performed world of the Bible and thus influence how the text might be understood. As Giles and Doan admit in their article, the methodology is in its early stages but will become increasingly utilized in Biblical Studies.[74]

Discovering Performance Inherent in the Texts

Theater and the Prophets

Shimon Levy provides a broad exploration of the Hebrew Bible, particularly the narrative traditions, from a theatrical perspective. But rather than exploring the influence of the Hebrew Bible on drama, he wishes to discover the influence drama may have had on the stories of the Bible. Levy engages with secular theorists such as Richard Schechner and Marvin Carlson, playwrights Brecht and Ibsen, and directors Grotowski and Brooks in order to throw new light on biblical stories. He analyzes familiar texts with the lenses of characterization, dialogue, stage direction, scene design, props, costuming, and gestures. Moreover, Levy believes these features can sometimes reveal hitherto unnoticed revolutionary attitudes, especially with regard to the role of women in the Hebrew Bible.

Levy states that the postexilic Jewish community would not have presented its traditions in theatrical form like the surrounding Greek culture out of respect for their sacred nature, although he acknowledges that the sacred "found its expression in traditional rituals, never on a secular stage."[75] He therefore cautiously describes the biblical passages as "*potential* theatre" since "the way the message is portrayed is less prominent than the message itself."[76] Nevertheless, he explores a range of biblical traditions through the analytical framework of theater that is sensitive to words, gestures, the passing of time, and the significance of space.

74. Giles and Doan, "Performance Criticism of the Hebrew Bible," 284.
75. Levy, *The Bible as Theatre*, 3.
76. Levy, *The Bible as Theatre*, 15 (italics original).

Part 4 of Levy's five-part book is titled "Prophets as Performers" and highlights Elisha, Jonah, Daniel, and Ezekiel. Levy first reads the story of Elisha and the Shunammite woman (2 Kgs 4:8–37) as a play, with speaking parts and silent roles, identifiable locations and props.[77] Beginning with an "Exposition" in which "the playwright establishes an ongoing relationship"[78] between Elisha and the Shunammite, the play then unfolds in five Acts with the following divisions:

Exposition (4:8)

Act I: At the Shunammite's home (4:9–16)

Scene 1: The Shunammite woman and her husband (4:9–10)

Scene 2: Elisha, Gehazi and the woman (4:11–13)

Scene 3: Elisha and Gehazi (4:14)

Scene 4: Elisha and the woman (4:15–16)

Interlude (4:17)

Act II:

Scene 1: Wheatfield (4:18–19)

Scene 2: Carrying the sick child home (4:20a)

Scene 3: The child and his mother (4:20b–21)

Scene 4: The woman and her husband (4:22–23)

Act III:

Scene 1: The road to Mount Carmel (4:24–25a)

Scene 2: Elisha's place (4:25b–30)

Act IV:

Scene 1: Gehazi and the child (4:31a)

Scene 2: Gehazi reports back to Elisha (4:31b)

Act V:

Scene 1: Elisha and the child (4:32–35)

Scene 2: Elisha, Gehazi, the child and the Shunammite woman (4:36–37)

---

77. See Levy, *The Bible as Theatre*, 147–60.
78. Levy, *The Bible as Theatre*, 148.

No explanation is given for the division of scenes, which would ordinarily be marked by changes in actors, locations, or times. While the five acts are mostly set apart by new locations, Act II includes the wheatfield and the home as locations. We could infer from Levy's presentation that scene divisions are determined by the drama of the events themselves. For example, verse 31 becomes two scenes, the first of which describes the unsuccessful attempt at reviving the child by Gehazi, Elisha's servant, and in the second scene Gehazi reports his lack of success to the prophet. Recollection of Utzschneider's assertion above that speech determines entrances gives further insight into how 2 Kgs 4:11–16 could be divided into three scenes. Since verses 14–15 record dialogue about the woman in the third person, we can infer that she is no longer present after verse 13, enabling Levy to claim "at this point she leaves the room, an exquisite theatrical exit"[79] despite the lack of evidence in the narrative itself.

Levy's chapter on Jonah "examines the dramatic elements in the 'fantastic' text of the *Book of Jonah*, and the theatrical potential of actually staging it," describing it as a "'quest play' in which the hero goes through 'stations' on a road to self-discovery."[80] Discussing the book with a range of literary analogies, from ancient to very modern, Levy describes it as "an existentialist-Sisyphean philosophy, whereby the protagonist must yield to divine commands but at the same time maintain an inner freedom."[81] Levy divides the book into seven scenes on the basis of entrances and exits:

Scene 1 (1:1–2) God's call to Jonah

Scene 2 (1:3–16) Jonah's escape onto a ship and his ejection into the sea

Scene 3 (2:1–11)[82] Jonah's prayer in the belly of the fish and rescue from it

Scene 4 (3:1–2) God's second call to Jonah and entry into Nineveh

Scene 5 (3:3–10) The overthrowing of the prophecy (Levy notes that the prophecy parallels the function of the storm in chapter 1)

Scene 6 (4:1–4) The second prayer (a parallel to the first prayer)

Scene 7 (4:5–11) Exit from Nineveh

79. Levy, *The Bible* as *Theatre*, 150.
80. Levy, *The Bible* as *Theatre*, 161.
81. Levy, *The Bible* as *Theatre*, 163.
82. Levy follows the versification of the Hebrew Bible in his scene divisions.

Levy lists the props and costumes that can be readily seen in this drama, but notes they are "both 'real' things on stage and heavily charged items."[83] Likewise, lighting is "quite explicit in the auctorial text,"[84] ranging from extreme darkness to extreme light.

The main theme in the plot of Jonah as analyzed by Levy is the contrast between God's sovereignty and anthropological resistance. As a prophet, Jonah should be the mouthpiece of God, yet Jonah seems to be unwilling to be this. "In this respect Jonah, an actor in a divine show, refuses to act a text with which he does not identify."[85] Levy concludes:

> the mode of theatrical qua existential presentation of God is probably the most relevant point to be made in this drama: God is undoubtedly present here, in his words and deeds. It may be said that inasmuch as Jonah flees God, God is in pursuit of Man. From a Kabbalistic point of view, God needs man's willing participation. For the spectator/reader, this crucial issue remains unanswered at the end of Jonah's drama.[86]

The chapter on "Ezekiel: the Holy Actor" approaches the material a little differently as it contains a proposed script with Acts and Scenes for only one chapter of the book of Ezekiel (chapter 16). Levy begins his chapter with an evaluation of the use of "sacred space" in the book of Daniel, contrasting "real space" (Babylon), "dreamed space" (Jerusalem), and "visionary space" (insights into world politics). It is significant that both Daniel and Ezekiel are books set in and written from the perspective of exile:

> Exile, in mytho-poetic space-related terms, implies being bereft of 'proper' location. Persons in exile find and feel themselves in the wrong place. Exile is always 'the other' location or 'the others' space.'[87]

Setting is a key feature of performance, since to perform is to employ "a frame, a particular context or stage that sets the work apart from the ordinary stream of life and thus mark[s] it as art."[88] Hence the performance term *mis-en-scène* (literally: put in a frame). Levy argues that the specific socioreligious circumstances of exile give a peculiarly theatrical quality to Ezekiel's prophecies as it feeds on the tension between the strange and

83. Levy, *The Bible as Theatre*, 172.

84. Levy, *The Bible as Theatre*, 172.

85. Levy, *The Bible as Theatre*, 171.

86. Levy, *The Bible as Theatre*, 172.

87. Levy, *The Bible as Theatre*, 175.

88. Shusterman, "Art as Dramatization," 367.

unsuitable context and the audience's national-religious expectations. The *mashal* of the cooking pot (Ezek 24:3–14) provides a good example of this: by employing the ritual of a meat sacrifice offered in the Jerusalem temple while located in Babylon where sacrifice was not possible, Ezekiel was "invert[ing] the meaning of a ready-made" . . . "alienat[ing] the familiar" for his audience.[89]

The prophet Ezekiel was the recipient of God's word, which in this case (and in the case of prophetic books in general) can be interpreted as a performative word because they are not merely descriptions but effect action. But Ezekiel received the word in visions, and had to pass on the message to an audience who had not seen those visions. The description of the first vision with its many qualifiers (the words "appearance," "likeness," "something like" are used multiple times in the chapter) indicate how difficult it was for the prophet to express a basically inexpressible sight. Levy states:

> Employing theatrical means can therefore be seen as both an intrinsic component in the prophet's mission, and a necessary tactic to reach his audience. Ezekiel describes numerous attempts to manifest through verbal and non-verbal means of presentation what he has experienced spiritually in his visions. He is trying to turn his inner 'theatre of visions' into an external, publicly communicable theatre.[90]

The chapter on Ezekiel is detailed and engaging, discussing many examples of the metaphorical visions and "theatrical prophecies" in theater-related language, including (as noted above) in terms of performance art. One final quotation illustrates the way in which Levy discusses the difficult role this prophet was being asked to play as the embodiment of God's message for the exilic community:

> The characteristics of the theatre show about to begin and its prospective communicative parameters are hence: a highly demanding semi-offstage playwright-director, an unpopular harsh message ('lamentation, mourning and woe'), a lonely actor who has fully embodied the 'word', and an extremely hostile audience. This show is prophesied to become a flop even before its premiere.[91]

I have given a detailed summary of Levy's presentation of prophets as performers because it has been influential on my own approach to this

---

89. Levy, *The Bible* as *Theatre*, 185.

90. Levy, *The Bible* as *Theatre*, 192.

91. Levy, *The Bible* as *Theatre*, 193.

topic. Sharing with Levy the assumption that we cannot prove ancient Israel performed their traditions in staged productions, I am equally convinced that we can discover theatrical qualities within the texts, although I prefer to use the terminology of *performance* rather than *theater*.[92]

Levy's section on prophets as performers suggests that by the nature of their vocation prophets became performers, "embody[ing] the divine message and presenting it through [their] own body and soul."[93] He contrasts theater's "willing suspension of disbelief" with the common theme in biblical prophecy of "attempts to impose belief on the unwilling"[94] both on the part of the prophets and also the spectators to their prophetic performances.

Some of the helpful insights from Levy's studies include the distinction between "onstage" and "offstage" action; the role of silence in drama where "the highly dramatic effect of the unspeaking character is very powerful";[95] the frequent use of a "play within a play" technique; the dramatic form of dialogue so prevalent in biblical narratives; the importance in many stories of props, both real objects and metaphorically charged images; the dramatic characterization achieved through names in biblical accounts; and attention to the role of the audience.

Performing Habakkuk

My own previous work has been on the book of Habakkuk brought into dialogue with Performance Studies.[96] I have presented a "performance reading" of Habakkuk in an attempt to go beyond silent, individualistic readings to a communal exercise which focuses not just on what is said, but on how it is being said. Attention to performative aspects intrinsic to the text such as sounds and silence, visual images, rhetorical clues, and invitations to audience participation help bring the world of the text and the world of readers closer together so that present-day readers are able to perform the original script in improvised yet faithful reenactments.

By surveying contemporary literature of Performance Criticism, I was able to elicit five themes that are dominant in that literature:

---

92. Moreover, using the terminology of *performance* allows us to broaden our view of Israel's dramatic tradition beyond theatrical entertainment in order to consider its role in worship and ritual. See West, "The Art of Biblical Performance," chapter 2.

93. Levy, *The Bible as Theatre*, 179.

94. Levy, *The Bible as Theatre*, 10, 186.

95. Levy, *The Bible as Theatre*, 45.

96. Mathews, *Performing Habakkuk*.

1. self-reflexivity (the performer is aware of the separation between the self and the role)

2. universality (performance is a holistic means of communication and relevant to a broad range of experience)

3. embodiment (performance relies on actual bodies in a shared space with an audience)

4. process (the actual activity of the performance is as important or perhaps even more important than the completed event)

5. reenactment (all performance is based upon preexisting models, scripts, or patterns)

Each of these five themes could be discerned in the book of Habakkuk. Self-reflexivity is exemplified in the prophet's self-understanding as an intermediary between his God and his community. Members of the Israelite community are likewise encouraged to reflect on their own role in the drama of God's salvation history. The vague historical references that seem to deliberately obscure the original setting of the prophecies allow for a universal application of the material to many situations. Embodiment is a key feature of prophetic literature, distinguishing it from law codes, narratives, and historiography. The prophet embodies the word of God within his own being and experiences the revelation visually, audibly, and viscerally (see Habakkuk 3:16). Thematic and grammatical features in the book of Habakkuk, such as unanswered questions; changes in verb tenses that merge past, present, and future together; the lack of resolution; the last word of the book (prior to the colophon), which is an active verb; are evidence that the theme of process is readily applied. The performative psalm-like colophon invites reenactment, as does the book's adaptation of preexisting prophetic and psalmic formulae, forms, and themes.

In my analysis of Habakkuk as a performance I presented a translation that was attentive to dramatic aspects.[97] Otherwise disparate elements of the text could be brought together in a framework of two Acts of five and three Scenes respectively, supplemented by a prelude for each Act (1:1; 3:1), an interjection (2:14), an interlude (2:20), and a postlude (3:19b). A highly literal translation illuminated features such as changes in speaker and addressee, number and person of verbal forms, many conjunctions, presence and lack of particles, repeated words and ideas. When evaluating each Scene, I considered how the script had been shaped, who the actors were, whether an audience was present, features of setting such as lighting

---

97. See Mathews, "Translating Habakkuk as a Performance."

and props, and whether there was evidence of improvisation of traditions or "twists" in the script that surprise readers. Each of these aspects are critical in performance and, I argued, could highlight hitherto unnoticed or ignored elements of the text.

In the next chapter I will build upon this work but suggest a more streamlined approach to reading the prophets through the lens of performance. Naturally some of my work will overlap with the work of scholars discussed above. Nonetheless, I hope to offer some new insights and supplement the relatively low number of performance readings of prophetic literature with my three case studies (Chapters 4–6).

Limitations and Reservations

In the field of Ethnopoetics, researchers and scholars are developing ways to transcribe oral events "in such a way that the artistry of their oral performance is not lost."[98] Some advocate the necessity of audiovisual recordings to supplement written records.[99] But when working with ancient texts, many features of the original communication event are not accessible, especially extralinguistic features such as tone of voice, degree of volume, use of pauses or silence, intonation, gestures, facial expression, audience reaction, and so on. John Miles Foley used the term "Voices from the Past" in reference to literature that was originally orally performed but have become fixed in written text.[100] Foley was writing specifically about the Old English poem *Beowulf*, but his discussion applies to any analysis that attempts to retrieve the oral properties from written scripts. Although recognizing "the full experience of spoken and heard realities will remain forever beyond our reach" Foley claims "vestigial voices can still be heard—even if faintly—and we do these poems an injustice if we don't listen just as carefully as we can."[101] With an even greater focus on performance as the medium of communication, James Maxey assures us that:

> However limited, the written text still contains hints of performance. These hints can be overt when it comes to certain lexical themes and phonological alliterations. The text may also include stage directions that indicate the movement, vocal quality or emotional state of the performer—as well as the expected state

98. Bauman, "Folklore," 39. See Maxey, *From Orality to Orality*, 86–95; and Perry, *Insights from Performance Criticism*, 163–84 for examples of orally formatted scripts.

99. For example, Joubert, *The Power of Performance*.

100. Foley, *How to Read an Oral Poem*, 102.

101. *How to Read an Oral Poem*, 133.

of the audience. Nonetheless, the biblical texts that we have were not transcribed with all the details of a scripted performance that we might hope for . . . attempts are made to discover via the remnants of transcriptions the performance-directed text.[102]

The next chapter will not only outline a method for discovering these remnants of performance in prophetic texts, but will propose that reenactment, including improvisation, is an important aspect of reading Scripture through a performance lens. In other words, while establishing the original performance event as accurately as possible is a worthy goal, it is equally important, in my view, to recognize that a focus on performance includes openness to new performances of ancient materials.

---

102. Maxey, *From Orality to Orality*, 135.

3

Reading Israel's Prophets via Biblical Performance Criticism

> [Scholars of Performance Studies] are committed to a brac-
> ing dialectic between performance theory and practice. We
> believe that theory is enlivened and most rigorously tested
> when it hits the ground in practice. Likewise, we believe that
> artistic practice can be deepened, complicated, and challenged
> in meaningful ways by engaging critical theory.[1]

THIS COMMITMENT TO INTEGRATING theory and practice as expressed
by the late professor of Performance Studies, Dwight Conquergood, is
shared by many of those engaged in Biblical Studies. Scholarship that
intersects with ethical and liturgical practice is scholarship that serves
the church as much as the academy. As will become evident in the subsequent discussion, the emerging field of Biblical Performance Criticism has close affinities with the established discipline of Performance
Studies, itself an interdisciplinary field that includes theater studies,
cultural anthropology, linguistics, sociology, social psychology, ethno-
musicology, literary theory, and legal studies among others.[2] The common thread is the study of performance and the use of performance as
a lens to study the world.

---

1. Conquergood, "Of Caravans and Carnivals," 139.

2. This blurring of boundaries that characterizes Performance Criticism has been
embraced by proponents of Biblical Performance Criticism also. David Rhoads and
others have spoken of the fact that Biblical Performance Criticism is in partnership
with other critical approaches in Biblical Studies and secular methodologies, including
historical criticism, narrative criticism, rhetorical criticism, reader response approaches, theater studies, media studies, and so on.

Introduction to Biblical Performance Criticism

Volumes in the Cascade Books Biblical Performance Criticism series along with Peter Perry's study on Performance Criticism in the Fortress Insights series[3] have defined the method of Biblical Performance Criticism, so I will only make a few brief comments before explicating my own related approach to reading prophetic texts as performances. The phrase Biblical Performance Criticism is attributed to David Rhoads, whose long practice of performing New Testament texts has informed his research and teaching and has been articulated in his seminal publications.[4] This approach to Biblical Studies commenced and continues to develop under the auspices of relevant sections of the Society of Biblical Literature such as Performance Criticism of Biblical and Other Ancient Texts (PCBOAT) and the Bible in Ancient (and Modern) Media, including workshops and networking events at annual meetings. A website (www.biblicalperformancecriticism.org/) is dedicated to scholars in this field and disseminates information about relevant publications, conferences, and pedagogical tools.

An important motivation underlying scholarship in this area is the recognition that biblical communities were predominantly oral cultures so that communication events reflected in the Scriptures originally comprised oral performances before audiences. Biblical Performance Criticism thus attempts to get behind the written script to analyze the *whole* performance event and not just the aspects that have been transmitted in written composition. Drawing out remnants of oral performance can aid our interpretation of texts, because "the medium is part of the message, if not the message itself. Studying these texts in an exclusively written medium has shaped, limited, and perhaps even distorted our understanding of them."[5] Studying biblical literature as "performance literature—either as transcriptions of prior oral compositions or as written compositions designed for oral performance"[6]—entails looking for hints of the original performance in the text, including embedded stage directions, evidence of the performer's manipulation of tradition for effect, audience reaction and response, and so forth. Such analysis of prophetic texts as performance literature will be further elaborated below.

---

3. Perry, *Insights from Performance Criticism*.

4. See especially Rhoads, "Performance Criticism—Part I"; and Rhoads, "Performance Criticism—Part II."

5. Rhoads, "Performance Criticism—Part I," 126.

6. Rhoads, "Performance Criticism—Part I," 119.

Performance as Research

One of the identifying characteristics of Performance Studies is the application of practice-led or practice-based research.[7] Performance itself becomes a "mode of knowing [knowing-in-doing]—to the academy and to research."[8] Within Biblical Performance Criticism, scholars such as Rhoads, Perry, and others also argue for contemporary performances of biblical texts as a method of research. Rhoads claims:

> The experience of translating, memorizing, and performing these works has placed me in a fresh medium, an entirely different relationship with these texts than that of a silent reader and even quite distinct from the experience of hearers in an audience ... I enter the world of the text, grasp it as a whole, reveal this world progressively in a temporal sequence, attend to every detail, and gain an immediate experience of its rhetoric as a performer seeking to have an impact on an audience. I have gotten in touch with the emotive and kinetic dimensions of the text in ways I would not otherwise have been aware.[9]

Perry's exhortation is even more pronounced:

> In short, it is worth the time of every student and scholar of the Bible to perform. How can we ask the right questions of a text unless we get inside the primary way it is communicated? How can we reunite the text that has been broken down into its smallest parts? The process of preparing, internalizing, and performing a text allows us inside the communication of these traditions and unites the insights of many disciplines.[10]

While I am convinced that performance *as* research is extremely valuable, even essential, the contribution I have tried to make to Biblical Performance Criticism has a different starting point. I draw on insights and common themes that emerge when phenomena are studied with performance as the "lens" and show how biblical material can be similarly envisaged as performance. My analysis, therefore, is more informed by theoretical insights than practical insights, although I do share a commitment to translation for performance as discussed by Peter Perry and James Maxey among others (see

---

7. See Allegue et al., *Practice-as-Research in Performance and Screen*; and Nelson, *Practice as Research in the Arts*.

8. Nelson, *Practice as Research in the Arts*, 4, 9.

9. Rhoads, "Performance Criticism—Part I," 120.

10. Perry, *Insights from Performance Criticism*, 161–2.

below).[11] In my view, themes that are common to the broader field of Performance Studies have much to offer as we read biblical texts.

Performance as a Metaphor in Theology

It is important initially to differentiate my approach from a common way of using the language of performance, especially theatrical performance, as a formative metaphor in Christian theology and Biblical Studies. The Christian story has been likened to a drama comprising five acts, namely, (1) Creation, (2) Fall, (3) Israel, (4) Jesus, (5) The Church.[12] In this metaphor the fifth act has not yet been completed, but will be brought to its finale in the events of the Parousia. Drama is considered a good model for theology because of its emphasis on dialogue and its multiple voices and perspectives. The Bible has been regarded as the script or libretto of the drama, with its divine author, but the acting out of the drama in historical space and time allows for different interpretations. Such performative interpretation is envisaged variously as the preached word,[13] the liturgical festal cycle,[14] and the Eucharist.[15] Shannon Craigo-Snell uses the language of theater to describe the Christian experience: the church uses sets, costumes, lighting, and music to encourage an embodied response in a carefully chosen and adorned space; it relies on Scripture in the same way actors rely on a script; churchgoers and theatergoers alike desire and expect a communal experience shaped by members of the clergy on the one hand and members of the theater company on the other; Christians "perform" Scripture when they re-enact scenes from the life of Jesus, obey Scripture's commandments, and let Scripture shape their words and actions.[16] Kevin Vanhoozer views Christian doctrine from the perspective of theater, arguing that such an *analogia dramatis* illumines the nature and function of theology.[17] He speaks of God as the "playwright" and Jesus the "lead actor"; of the Bible as "script" of the cultural, social, and intellectual context of the church as the "stage"; of the Holy Spirit as "director"; of the pastor as "assistant director"; of the Christian believer as "engaged audience"; and of the theologian as "dramaturg"—the one

11. Perry, *Insights from Performance Criticism*, 68–69; Maxey, *From Orality to Orality*.

12. Wright, "How Can the Bible Be Authoritative?" 19.

13. Young, *The Art of Performance*, 162.

14. Williams, "The Literal Sense of Scripture," 126.

15. Lash, *Theology on the Way to Emmaus*, 45.

16. Craigo-Snell, "Command Performance."

17. Vanhoozer, *The Drama of Doctrine*.

advising both director and company. In his analogy the church is amateur theater performing for the love of it, drawing outsiders in and improvising for new settings. Christians have not "chosen" a role but are responding to the divine casting-call and aiming to "become" the role.

Vanhoozer admits to the danger of pressing a dramatic analogy too far so that it risks becoming a complex allegory.[18] Moreover, by discussing Christian experience and biblical interpretation in theatrical terms alone, envisaged as director-driven actors on a stage presenting a set script, other aspects of the broader understanding of performance are likely to be neglected. The practice-as-research model, for example, that emphasizes the need for rehearsal and refinement in performance does not fit well in this analogy. The ephemeral nature of performance does not easily correspond to the "grand narrative" way of understanding God's involvement in human history, nor does the open-ended emphasis I have described as "process," which I recognize as a dominant theme in performance. We need models that allow for these performance themes along with embodiment, audience involvement, improvisation, and reenactment.

Prophetic Literature as Narrative and Poetry

A particular strength of using Biblical Performance Criticism as a method for approaching prophetic traditions in the Hebrew Bible is that it is an approach that works equally well with prophetic literature in narrative and poetic forms.

Many aspects of Narrative Criticism and Rhetorical/Poetic Criticism are relevant when analyzing prophetic narratives, but reading them through the lens of performance highlights different dimensions. In this section I will take some of the major aspects of these critical approaches and indicate where Biblical Performance Criticism can offer new insights.

Narrative Analysis—Plot and Structure

Narratives depend on plots with discernible boundaries and, frequently, a pediment structure characterized by rising and falling action due to complication and resolution pivoting on a change to the opening conditions of the story. Narrative units are identified by criteria such as use of *inclusios* (repetition of material at the beginning and end of a unit), or a consistent style, or consideration of periods of time in which events occur. Hebrew narrative can

18. Vanhoozer, *The Drama of Doctrine*, 243.

also be identified by the characteristic *wayyiqtol* (narrative past) verbal forms that advance the plot. These verbal forms are rarely used in poetry.[19]

Disparate material that intrudes into narratives is often analyzed as superfluous to the narrative from the point of view of Narrative Criticism. Think, for example, of the prayer that constitutes the second chapter of the book of Jonah. It is possible and arguably preferable to read and interpret the narrative of Jonah without including the conventionally pious words of the poem because those words are at odds with the character of the prophet in the rest of the book. This material has been variously interpreted as coming from a different source or as inserted by a more pious redactor or as deliberate irony included by the author. From the perspective of performance, the verses could be read as a dramatic interlude, shifting the focus of the audience before the drama resumes where it left off.

Beginnings and endings are important in Narrative Criticism, as they determine the boundaries of the narrative unit.[20] Narratives in most cases open with an exposition, providing readers with the primary information and basic background to enter the story world. Prophetic literature, on the other hand, is focused on the intermediary role the prophet takes on behalf of the presence of God, so more often than not the prophet "bursts onto the scene" without any more introduction than his or her name.[21] The prophet Elijah is a good example of this, suddenly appearing in the midst of the "Regnal Account of Ahab ben Omri of Israel" (1 Kgs 17:1).[22] Whilst some prophetic traditions contain a plot with rising and falling action, the majority do not have discernible plotlines other than a broad movement from judgment to restoration. On the other hand, "crisis" is a characteristic background for prophetic material, which in itself could be understood as one large complication. Furthermore, prophets seek to engage their audience by developing suspense, offering scenarios with which their hearers could identify or distance themselves, and leading their audience to turning points in their thought and action.[23]

Yairah Amit uses theatrical language to describe the typical closure of biblical narratives: "The ending lowers the curtain, sends the players

---

19. Athas and Young, *Elementary Biblical Hebrew*, 73.

20. Amit, *Reading Biblical Narratives*, 33.

21. Matthews, *Social World of the Hebrew Prophets*, 54.

22. Sweeney's commentary *I & II Kings* divides according to the regnal accounts of the kings of Judah and Israel.

23. In his discussion of New Testament texts as first-century performances, Rhoads understands these characteristics as plot within performance. See Rhoads, "Performance Criticism—Part II," 166. I maintain that in prophetic performances a plotline is not always evident.

off the stage and behind the scenes, to another place and event, or, in the case of a concentric ending, back to where they came from."[24] And, yet, prophetic literature is rife with open-ended conclusions. Rarely do we hear of the death of a prophet, and the description of Elijah's departure on a fiery chariot is ambiguous enough to build the Jewish legend of his return to herald the Messiah. The book of Jonah famously concludes with a rhetorical question, inviting ongoing conversation. The penultimate chapter in Jeremiah concludes "Thus far are the words of Jeremiah" (Jer 51:64b, NRSV), prompting readers to expect a sequel!

Narrative Analysis—Narrator and Characters

In Narrative Criticism the narrator is understood, in general, to be omniscient and reliable. Amit describes the narrator as "an unnamed, abstract figure who mediates between us and the story, [who] tells us what happened and informs us which characters are speaking, from God to the humblest servant."[25] The narrator is usually outside of the story and is the source of information for what God says, does, and thinks. Original biblical audiences did not experience the narrator in this way, instead "the narrator was always the flesh and blood performer."[26] In prophetic performance in particular, the prophet offers God's words and thoughts in first-person speech and so combines the narrator and character within the prophetic *persona*. Moreover, the prophet offers prayers, complaints, questions, and commentary *to* God alongside the words *of* God, thus displaying a high level of self-reflexivity, a characteristic that is uncommon in a narrative world. Jeremiah's "confessions" (chapters 11–20), for example, are so characteristic of the prophet's prophetic discourse that tradition has attributed the book of Lamentations to his authorship.

Characterization from the perspective of performance highlights the importance of embodiment, a crucial factor in the presentation of the prophets themselves. Prophetic speech can be described as performative speech-acts, in that the words are intended to bring about the message in the very speaking of them. But the prophets who often embodied their message were clearly more than orators. Embodiment is shown sometimes in highly provocative performances and often within the prophet's own life experiences. The call stories of prophets commission them to *act* in various ways: Jeremiah is told "to pluck up and break down . . . to build

24. Amit, *Reading Biblical Narratives*, 36.

25. Amit, *Reading Biblical Narratives*, 94.

26. Rhoads, "Performance Criticism—Part II," 166.

and to plant" (Jer 1:10) and Isaiah is commissioned to "make the heart of this people fat and dull their ears and smear over their eyes" (Isa 6:10). The prophets were performers engaged in what might be termed poetic drama. Whether prophets of doom or of hope they spoke into "liminal" moments: times of political and social crisis for the Israelite community. They used symbolic action and invested meaning in ordinary objects and events. They were not merely channels for mediation but embodied communicators. So Habakkuk's visceral response to a vision of God is described as "my belly is in turmoil . . . my lips tingle, decay comes into my bones" (Hab 3:16). Ezekiel is asked to eat the scroll on which the message for the house of Israel was written (Ezek 2:9—3:3). Often the prophet's message had lifelong implications: such as the marriage of Hosea, parenting children with symbolic names as we see in both Hosea and Isaiah, Jeremiah's commission to remain celibate (Jer 16:1–4) and his economic land-purchase transactions (Jer 32:6–15), and Ezekiel's commissioned stoicism in the face of his wife's death (Ezek 24:15–24).

In addition, the concept of embodiment alerts us to a range of actors including offstage performers, nonhuman creatures and entities that are given voice and agency. The stories of Elijah and Elisha include hundreds of prophets that are not often acknowledged because they do not have names. As well as the prophets of Baal and the prophets of Asherah (1 Kgs 18:19) there are numerous other prophets of YHWH mentioned in those stories (1 Kgs 18:4, 13; 2 Kgs 2:3; 4:1 etc.) The ravens in 1 Kgs 17 and the fish and the worm in the book of Jonah are characters to whom God speaks and through whom God acts.

Dialogue is a feature in some prophetic narratives, but a significant difference when compared to other biblical narratives is that God becomes a character with whom the prophet is in dialogue. This raises a difficulty in that there is a necessity for characters in a performance to be gendered. This is a positive step when envisaging nonhuman actors, as discussed above, but offers difficulties when God is understood as a character. The Hebrew text uses masculine verbs and adjectives for YHWH and Elohim, so I will portray YHWH as a masculine character in my performance translations. This concession should make us even more alert to the instances in the Hebrew Bible where God is portrayed with feminine characteristics.[27]

27. See my discussion in Chapter 1 in the section "In Front of the Text" Approaches to Israel's Prophets" (27–30 above).

Narrative Analysis—Time and Space

Narrative Criticism speaks of two aspects of time to be considered when analyzing a narrative: the time taken to read the narrative, and the "narrated time" or passage of time that passes within a narrative. Narrated time can be sped up or slowed down by different techniques. In biblical narratives the most common techniques for slowing time are repetition and dialogue. The narrator frequently announces what will happen, then describes the events using very similar words. In the second technique, time passes as "real time" when characters converse because the time taken to say/read the words mirrors the actual conversation.

Both of these techniques can be seen in prophetic narratives. It is common enough to see the prophet's actions repeating the same verbs as the Lord's instructions so that it stands out when this doesn't occur, as seen in the following examples:

> The word of YHWH came to him [Elijah], saying, "Get up (קוּם), go (הלךְ) to Zarepheth in Sidon . . . And he got up (קוּם), and he went (הלךְ) to Zarepheth" (I Kgs 17:9)

> The word of YHWH came to Jonah son of Amittai, saying, "Get up (קוּם), go (הלךְ) to Nineveh . . . And Jonah got up (קוּם) to flee (ברח) to Tarshish" (Jonah 1:1–3)

There is also a *timelessness* that is characteristic of prophetic literature. The merging of past, present, and future within the same book is conveyed by interspersing oracles of judgment and hope, by the use of imperatives and present-tense verbs, and by leaving material open-ended.

In relation to use of setting and space in biblical narratives, there is widespread agreement that locations are important unless the story is intended to be fictional (such as parables), yet descriptions of locations are quite minimal so that the main aspects of the narrative are what the characters say and do, rather than what they look like or what their environment is like. Nonetheless, some locations are significant for the message of the story, and this is true of prophetic traditions also. Elijah spends formative periods in the wilderness where God provides for him and is revealed to him, linking Elijah's story with the foundational Israelite story of Moses and the wilderness wanderings. Jonah's sea voyage illustrates that God's power cannot be escaped but is evident even at the bottom of the ocean. Ezekiel's location by the River Chebar among the exilic community and his visions that transport him to and from Jerusalem are highly significant. The inward spiraling of place names in the first three chapters of Amos, beginning with the names of distant foreign city-states and moving to neighboring nations with kinship ties and finally to Judah, the nearest neighbor, before zeroing in on Israel clearly uses those place names quite deliberately. On the other hand, some prophetic accounts seem to be at pains to ensure that the prophet's time and location are not identifiable. Some have argued (and I would agree) that there is a purposeful blurring of historical detail and narrated time so that prophetic oracles can be applied to new times and places.[28] Performance themes of process and reenactment are thus enhanced in prophetic literature.

When considering the concept of space from the perspective of performance rather than narrative, descriptive elements, though sparse, can be viewed as significant stage directions relating to movement, costumes, and props. Several prophetic stories are fully dependent on the props that are central to the story—think of Jeremiah's earthenware jug (Jer 19), linen loin-cloth (Jer 13), and yoke of iron (Jer 28); or Ahijah's new garment torn into twelve pieces to signify the division of the United Kingdom of Israel (1 Kgs 11:26–40). Indeed, Shimon Levy contends that some biblical excerpts:

> can be performed verbatim, since the biblical 'stage-instruc-tions' pertaining to time, space, movement, costumes, props, lighting and other theatrical components, are often built-in. Though completely verbal in a written text, notions of costumes and props, for instance, serve as non-verbal 'biblical stage-directions' when performed.[29]

Prophetic Poetic Discourse

Prophetic literature in general is unmistakably dramatic in that it is focused on a *persona* who speaks scripted lines and invites audience reflection and participation. When written in poetic form, however, the literature is terse and complex with little plot development, as noted above, and ambiguity in relation to actors and settings.

Poetic Analysis—Setting/Scene Division

While the concept of plot is not readily available to structure prophetic literature, a dramatic lens allows for division into scenes and acts. A classic

---

28. For example, Childs, *Introduction to the Old Testament as Scripture*, 453; O'Brien, *Nahum, Habakkuk, Zephaniah, Haggai, Zechariah, Malachi*, 62; Mathews, *Performing Habakkuk*, 167.

29. Levy, *The Bible as Theatre*, 5.

definition of a theatrical scene is given by Alan Downer: "a portion of the total play in which the stage is occupied by an unchanging group of players."[30] This definition is not easily applied in prophetic literature with its paucity of dialogue and lack of clarity of actors. We can usually assume an audience, but sometimes the audience are mere onlookers and at other times they are drawn into the action. It could be argued that the goal of prophetic literature is the transformation of the prophet's audience into actors, and this introduces a fluidity to the actors on stage.

Jack Lundbom uses three criteria to determine divisions between individual oracles that are gathered together in prophetic literature.[31] He first pays attention to the section markings, the *setumah* (ס) and *petuuah* (פ) that are found in the Hebrew text, and that have been shown to be ancient, as they are found in texts of the Dead Sea Scrolls and the Samaritan Pentateuch. These diacritics mark the end of units to aid in recitation. The second criterion is the messenger formulas found among the prophets, such as "Thus says the LORD God." The third aspect that can mark divisions in the prophetic texts is the use of *inclusios*. Along with these criteria we can divide scenes on the basis of observable changes in actors, location, and time, paying particular attention to "entrances and exits."[32] Scenes that share a common theme can be considered an "Act" in the drama.

Poetic Analysis—Actors and Characterization

Character analysis is particularly complex in prophetic poetic literature. The first-person voice is frequently used, more often than not representing the prophetic *persona* speaking on behalf of the deity. Conventions for introducing direct speech that are common in narrative literature, however, are often lacking. This can result in ambiguity when we attempt to identify the actors. The first chapter of Habakkuk, for example, is analyzed by most commentators as a dialogue between the prophet and his God, with the prophet speaking in verses 2–4, YHWH in verses 5–11, and the prophet again in verses 12–17. But this division of the text is not necessarily supported when the text is carefully read. The following is my translation, noting that all punctuation is a result of my own judgment. Question marks are

---

30. Downer, *The Art of the Play*, 170.

31. Lundbom, *The Hebrew Prophets*, 162.

32. Levy, *The Bible as Theatre*, 164. Note that Levy's division of Jonah into seven scenes varies from my own division (see Chapter 6 below—197–201), as I include prologues, an interlude, and an epilogue.

placed where there are interrogatory words or particles, and exclamation marks are used to denote imperative verbs:

Habakkuk 1

[1]The revelation that Habakkuk the prophet saw:
[2]How long, YHWH, shall I call and you not hear?
I cry out to you 'violence' and you do not save.
[3]Why do you make me look at sorrow?
And to trouble you pay attention.
And devastation and violence are before me
and there is strife, and contention carries on.
[4]Therefore Torah is paralyzed
and justice never goes forth.
For wickedness surrounds the righteous one.
Therefore crooked justice goes forth.
[5]All of you, look at the nations! and pay attention!
And be profoundly astounded!
For a work is being worked in your days
—you would not believe it if it was recounted.
[6]For behold, I am raising the Chaldeans,
that nation hurtful and hasty,
the man who marches across expanses of earth
to possess dwelling places not his own.
[7]Terrible and fearful is he,
from himself his justice and his dignity go forth.
[8]And swifter than leopards are his horses,
and keener than wolves of the evening.
And they gallop his gallopers and his gallopers.
From far they come, they fly,
Like a vulture he hastens to eat.
[9]Every one comes for violence,
the eagerness of their faces goes forward.
And he gathered captives like sand.
[10]And as for him, at the kings he scoffs
and rulers are an object of derision to him.
As for him, at every fortress he laughs.
And he heaped up dust and he captured her.
[11]Then he swept through [as] wind,
and he passed by and was guilty.
This is his strength for his god.
[12]Are you not from old, YHWH?
My God of holiness, you will not die.
YHWH, for justice you set him;
and Rock, for rebuke you established him.

¹³Your eyes are too pure to look at evil.
And you are not able to pay attention to trouble.
Why do you pay attention to those who act treacherously?
You keep silence when wickedness swallows [the] righteous one.
¹⁴And you made humankind like the fish of the sea,
like a lowly sea creature with no one ruling over it.
¹⁵Every one he has brought up with a fishing hook,
he drags him away with his net,
and gathers him with his fish trap.
Therefore he is glad and rejoices.
¹⁶Therefore he sacrifices to his net,
and offers smoke to his fish trap.
For with them his portion grew rich,
and his food was fat.
¹⁷Shall he therefore empty his net
and continue to slay nations without mercy? ס

Verse 1 is a narrator or announcer's voice in the third person. The paucity of independent pronouns in the Hebrew means the identity of the speaker
is largely determined from verbs that include gender and number within their
forms, and pronominal suffixes that likewise identify gender and number. The
Hebrew text does not help us decide where divisions should be, as there are
no section markings prior to the *setumah* after verse 17. The vocative YHWH
in verses 2 and 12, however, suggest the prophet is addressing his God, and
second-person singular verbs as well as the content of the complaints, including reference to holiness and purity and the ability to create, support this assumption for verses 2–4 and 12–14. The plural imperatives in verse 5, while
indicating a different speaker, are not obviously addressed back to the prophet.
Are we to infer an audience? Furthermore, the verb forms include participles
where the subject of the verb is not obvious: who is "working the work" (v 5)?
And who is describing the Chaldeans in verses 6b–9 and the Chaldean king
in verses 10–11? Do verses 15–17 also refer to the Chaldean king, or are they
a continuation in sardonic fashion about the creative power of YHWH?

While rehearsing for a performance of this script, Peter Perry became
convinced that the identity of the speakers in this verse should be reassigned,
so that other than verse 1 and 5a, the entire chapter should be understood as
speech of the prophet. Here he outlines his thought process:

> God's speech is usually taken to continue until [verse 11] . . .
> The problem is that God's introduction is positive. God calls
> the audience and the nations to attention. God invites them to
> be astounded, which sounds like they will be impressed with

the solution. God announces that this is a 'work being worked in your days,' as if it is a satisfactory response to Habakkuk's complaint. God sounds like a carnival barker ready to unveil the great attraction. And then: it is the Chaldeans! After building up the audience's expectation of a positive solution to injustice in Judah, I had trouble announcing the Chaldeans as 'hurtful and hasty' (1:6b) . . . Instead of a statement, I made 1:6b into a rhetorical question the prophet speaks in shock to God's revelation that God had raised up the Chaldeans.[33]

Perry's script divides the speakers in this way:

> *The LORD to the audience:*
>
> All of you, look at the nations and pay attention!
> And be profoundly astounded!
> For a work is being worked in your days
> —you wouldn't believe it if it was retold.
>
> For behold, I am raising the Chaldeans!
> *The prophet to the LORD:*
> That hurtful and hasty nation?
> the Man who marches across expanses of earth
> to take possession of dwelling places that are not his own?
> He is terrible and fearful,
> from him, his justice and his dignity go forth.[34]

I have found Perry's analysis convincing and would now change my own script of Habakkuk accordingly.[35] This example illustrates that identification of characters in poetic prophetic literature can be ambiguous. Even when the prophetic voice clearly changes within the same book (such as Isaiah or Zechariah), the change is made without comment, enabling the inference that the same prophetic *persona* is being presented.

Named actors need not be the only characters in prophetic literature. It is widely acknowledged that metaphor plays an important role in the poetry of the Hebrew Bible. From the perspective of performance, metaphors can be regarded as personified entities that have a role in the script. The following examples illustrate the broad range of personified metaphors that could be understood as actors in a drama in prophetic poetic traditions. In Habakkuk Torah is "paralyzed" (Hab 1:4), a vision "breathes" (Hab 2:3), a stone "cries out" and a rafter "answers" (Hab 2:11). Earth itself

---

33. Perry, *Insights from Performance Criticism*, 96–97.

34. Perry, *Insights from Performance Criticism*, 165.

35. See Mathews, *Performing Habakkuk*, 89–96 for my original division of the script.

is an entity that is capable of knowledge and devotion (Hab 2:19–20). In Joel locusts act at the behest of God (Joel 2), stars withdraw their brightness (3:15 [MT 4:15]), mountains drip with wine and hills flow with milk (3:18 [MT 4:18]). Trees and plants bring forth their own vegetation, not only in Gen 1:24 but also according to the prophets (Ezek 34:27; Joel 2:22; Hag 2:19). In Isaiah, gates "wail" and the city "cries" (Isa 14:31). Indeed, cities are personified in Isaiah, Jeremiah, Ezekiel, Amos, Micah, Jonah, Nahum, and Zephaniah. Special attention is given to Daughter Zion as the personification of the nation of Israel.[36]

The prophets envision God's judgment being carried out by independent destroyers—sometimes human armies but also nonhuman entities such as wild animals and plagues. Ezek 14:21 specifically refers to God's "four judgments of evil: sword, and famine, and evil beasts, and pestilence." Habakkuk 3 mentions pestilence (דֶּבֶר, dāber) and plague (רֶשֶׁף, rešef) as part of the retinue accompanying a theophanic vision, but portrays them as entities capable of independent volitional movement: "before him Pestilence marches and Plague goes forth before his feet." This perhaps reflects the use of an older mythological poem in which the destroyers are themselves deities, and the Hebrew names in fact are names of Canaanite deities Deber and Resheph and are often thus left untranslated by commentators. Likewise in the subsequent verses, the names for Rivers (נְהָרִים, nehārîm), Sea (יָם, yām), Deep (תְהוֹם, tehōm), Sun (שֶׁמֶשׁ, šemeš) and Moon (יָרֵחַ, yārēaḥ) are all names used for deities in other ancient Near Eastern cultures and can be understood as actors in their own right, especially when we hear them "giving voice" or see them "raising their hands."

Audience

The importance of the audience is a particular focus of Biblical Performance Criticism that has not traditionally been considered in Narrative Criticism or Rhetorical Criticism. Narrative Criticism and Rhetorical Criticism, of course, are interested in the effect on the *reader*, betraying the text-focused and individualized nature of those critical methods. Biblical Performance Criticism emphasizes the interaction between performer, the composition, and the audience where the performance event itself is the "site of interpretation."[37]

36. See, for example, Isa 1:21–26; 22:1–14; 52:1–2; Jer 4–6; 8–10; Amos 5:1–3, 16–17, 18–21; Mic 1:2–16; 4:9–10; Zeph 3:14–20.

37. Rhoads, "Performance Criticism—Part I," 128. The emerging field of Perspective Criticism, of which Gary Yamasaki is a leading voice, is an audience-oriented

As noted by William Doan and Terry Giles:

> One of the dynamics investigated by performance criticism is the interplay among spectator, actor, and character. A powerful outcome of the interaction among these three is the formation of a social identity or the propagation of a shared belief that becomes owned by a spectator. The power of the performance is often judged by its ability to move an audience, to enable the audience to think, believe, or act differently.[38]

Unlike individual readers of texts, audiences are communal in nature. Two conclusions can be drawn from this observation: first, audiences respond to performance collectively; and, second, audience members influence one another's responses. The social location of the audience is thus influential in interpretation. On the other hand, audiences are not homogenous but can comprise people from different backgrounds with different interests. A single performance will not have a single meaning, therefore, and members of an audience may respond in different ways.

Biblical Performance Criticism, therefore, helps us see that the same text can have different meanings, both when performed in a single iteration and when performed in different settings to new audiences. But audiences of biblical performances are never merely spectators. I noted above that attention to plural imperative verbs in the Hebrew script will alert us to the expectation for audience involvement. When we are reminded that Scripture originated in living bodies and was transmitted through historical communities in the context of live audiences, we are encouraged to interpret and live out the message of the prophets in our own concrete contexts.

Language in Biblical Prose and Poetry

There are some characteristic compositional features of biblical narrative and poetry that impact upon analysis from a performance perspective, particularly as they remind us of the oral origin of Scripture. Biblical narrative is often described as paratactic and repetitive. Episodes are strung together with a concentration of *wayyiqtol* (narrative past) verbs at the beginning of phrases. Many translations mask this style as the conjunction at the beginning of the verb is often ignored, but for a narrative that is heard, the repetition of the conjunctive *vav* is rhythmic and obvious. When translated

---

narrative approach, developed in recognition that the earliest audiences of biblical narratives were hearers rather than readers. See Yamasaki, *Perspective Criticism.*

38. Doan and Giles, "The Song of Asaph," 35–36.

literally there is a sense of ongoing movement reflected in the text.[39] Repetition is another characteristic, again sometimes masked in translations that strive for a more pleasing aesthetic by using a variety of words. Repetition is common in oral delivery as an aid to both storyteller and audience. When flipping back the page to read it again is not an option, repeated words and themes keep audiences tuned in to the message. By the same token, any variation to an expected pattern will draw attention. Hebrew narrative, as noted earlier, is often described as sparse in detail, with little description of characters and settings. The plot is moved forward by narration, speech and dialogue, and the actions of the characters.

In poetic forms the language is terser, with fewer particles and verbs doing double duty that can lead to ambiguity. Poetry can be much more descriptive, however, with parallelism, similes, and metaphors used regularly. There should be no real difficulty in translating these features well. Hebrew poetry is also characteristically full of puns and wordplay of both words and sounds. These are less easy to translate into a new target language but can be very significant in performance. A translation of Mic 1:10–15 attributed to Clyde T. Francisco for a graduate seminar at the Southern Baptist Theological Seminary illustrates a wonderful attempt to capture the puns of the original Hebrew:

> Tell it not in Gath,
>   in Weepville do not weep.
> In Duston, roll in the dust.
>   Pass over Beautytown in nakedness and shame;
>   the people of Rescueville have not rescued;
>   the lamentation of Helpvillehouse has taken from you its help.
>   The people of Bittertown are longing for sweet,
>   for evil from YHWH has come to the gate of Jerusalem.
>   Hitch your chariots to a *reckesh* (horse), people of Lachish.
>   The beginning of sin to the daughter of Zion,
>   for in you has been found the apostasy of Israel.
>   Therefore you shall give a parting dowry to Bridesburg.
>   The houses of Snaretown are a snare to the kings of Israel.
>   Therefore the owner has come to you, Ownapolis.
>   The glory of Israel shall go into oblivion.[40]

39. See my translations in Chapters 4, 5, and 6, where I have retained the conjunctive *vav*.

40. Quoted in Redditt, *Introduction to the Prophets*, 272–73. Eugene Peterson's *The Message* is similarly creative in replicating the wordplay.

Despite the use of puns and wordplay in poetic language to draw attention, all oral communication is reliant on the use of conventions, and so departure from what is expected will also be noticed by an audience.

The Prophetess Deborah in Prose and Poetry

Comparing the prose and poetic versions of the story of the prophetess Deborah (Judg 4–5) highlights some of the issues I have been discussing in this section.

In Judg 4 (the prose version) a story is told with a double plotline that overlaps. The Deuteronomistic introduction and conclusion (Judg 4:1–3; 23–24) provide a clear beginning and end, although the final Deuteronomistic formula "And the land had rest for forty years" is placed at the end of the poem in Judges 5:31b, conveying the editor's intention that both versions (prose and poetry) are to be read together. The prose unit has two expositions: the first introduces Deborah as a prophetess and judge (Judg 4:4) and the second introduces Heber the Kenite (Judg 4:11), providing information that is important later in the story to help explain the actions of Jael, Heber's wife. There are also two complications: the first being Barak's lack of courage, and the second the intrusion of Sisera into Jael's tent. Both plotlines depend on rising and falling tension. The first describes the lead up to the battle between two tribes of Israel and the army of an oppressive Canaanite king led by Sisera (Judg 4:6–10, 12–14), the turning point where the Lord throws the enemy army into a panic (Judg 4:15), and the description of Israel's victory (Judg 4:16). Though attributing the victory to the Lord, the story makes it clear that the human warriors of Zebulun and Naphtali were the ones to execute the deed.

The second plotline covers the fate of the escaping Sisera, who mistakenly expects to find protection in the tent of his master's ally but instead meets his death there at the hand of Jael, the wife of Heber the Kenite. Told dispassionately by a narrator, the narrative is nonetheless full of irony. Jael seems to offer hospitality, even going overboard by giving milk rather than the water requested. Sisera accepts her ministering and is relaxed enough to fall asleep. Within the interior space of a woman's tent, she acts like a warrior by decisively assassinating him with a blow through the temple. Without any description of her physical appearance, her speech and actions identify her as a powerful, resolute, loyal Israelite. The scene ends with Barak finding that the man he has been pursuing has been felled by a woman, ironically fulfilling Deborah's prophecy that the glory for Israel's victory had "fallen into the hand of a woman" (Judg 4:9). The kinship ties between the husband of Jael and the house of Moses mentioned in verse 11 give a possible explanation for Jael's loyalty being for Israel rather than her husband's Canaanite ally.

The poem preserved in Judg 5 is dense, difficult to translate and interpret.[41] The problems presented to translators are often explained by the antiquity of the composition, as it is thought to be one of the earliest poems preserved in the Hebrew Bible. But even if we must speculate about its precise meaning, we can observe that its composition is quite unlike the prose chapter despite the common subject matter.

Elements in the poem that might provide a plotline do not begin until well into the body of the song, and even then are marked by repetition, metaphorical language, and parallelism. The description of Sisera's fate is both truncated in detail and expansive in expression. With little introduction to Sisera or any explanation for how he was able to be overcome by Jael, his death is described with a series of parallel verses using no less than eight verbs of destruction (identified in italics):

> Blessed among women is Jael, wife of Heber the Kenite, //
>   among women in the tents, blessed.
> Water he asked, milk she gave //
>   in a bowl of nobility she brought curds.
> Her hand to the tent peg she sent /
>   and her right hand to the hammer of workers //
> And she *struck* Sisera, she *crushed* his head /
>   and she *shattered* and *pierced* his temple.
> Between her feet / he *sank*, he *fell*, he *lay still* //
>   between her feet he sank, he fell /
> where he sank / there he *was slain*.[42]

The phrase "bless the LORD," found at the end of verses 2 and 9, forms an *inclusio* for the theophanic poem here in Judg 5, exhibiting mythical elements along with parallelism and repetition. Characterization is strong: a much greater cast of actors is identified and described with colorful adjectives: "mother of Israel" Deborah, valiant Barak, faithful Issachar, timid Reuben, brave Zebulun, "most blessed" Jael, the wise ladies, and so on. Yet it is not possible to identify the singer, who uses first-person language and vocative verbs, directly addressing kings, YHWH, Deborah and Barak, the

41. See Mark Biddle's comments on the "enigmatic" song of Deborah in *Reading Judges*, 62–72.

42. Judges 5:24–27. The slashes mark the disjunctive accents in the Hebrew poetry: a double slash marks the *athnach*, the main pause in the verse, and a single slash marks the *zaqef qaton*, which subdivides the longer unit.

Israelite clans, and the anonymous "you who ride on white donkeys" (Judg 5:10). The language is emotive, praising some clans for participating and castigating others for not joining forces. One who is especially cursed is the mysterious tribe Meroz (Judg 5:23), not known elsewhere in the Hebrew Bible. The description of the battle itself is brief, and dominated by metaphorical language similar to the theophanic poem here in Judg 5, so that natural elements (stars and torrents of water) are fighting against the enemy on behalf of Israel. Irony is also present in the poem, especially in the last scene (Judg 5:28–30) where the haughty mother of Sisera waits in vain for spoils of war in her latticed house, unaware that her son has been murdered by a humble tent-dweller.

A major characteristic in the poetic version of the story is the invitation to participation. Songs, "meant for public performance . . . function to evoke a public response."[43] A number of imperatives demand attention and action from those hearing: "bless the LORD" (Judg 5:2,9); "hear, give ear" (Judg 5:3); "Tell of it" (Judg 5:10); "Awake, awake, utter a song. / Arise" (Judg 5:12); "March on, my soul" (Judg 5:21); "Curse [those who] did not come to the help of the LORD" (Judg 5:23). The use of the first person throughout the song brings its performance into the sphere of the audience in much the same way that the psalms do: inviting the reader or hearer to make the words their own. Despite, or perhaps due to, its celebratory tone, in its original setting the song must have functioned to motivate willingness to join in battle against Israel's enemies. But the liturgical tone and the fuzziness of historical indicators show that it has continued to have significance beyond the intention of the original composer.

As has become clear in this section, Narrative Criticism and Rhetorical/Poetic Analysis are obvious partners for Biblical Performance Criticism. While there are evident areas of overlap, however, there are also enough distinctive emphases in Biblical Performance Criticism to suggest it is a particularly apt way to read prophetic traditions. Moreover, it is a holistic method that can be applied to both prose and poetry, and has analytical insights for all three of the methodological groupings discussed in Chapter 2—namely, "behind the text" methods, "the text itself" methods, and "in front of the text" methods.

---

43. Biddle, *Reading Judges*, 63. See also Giles and Doan, *Twice Used Songs*, on the fundamentally performative nature of biblical songs.

Biblical Performance Criticism as Creativity, Commentary, and Connections

Dwight Conquergood, quoted at the beginning of this chapter, sets an agenda for Performance Studies that I intend to emulate in my reading of prophetic texts as performances. By way of introduction, he rehearses the division that grew between academics and practitioners that privileged written texts with their claim to objectivity and "empirical" knowledge and simultaneously disqualified nonwritten knowledge and experience as illegitimate. He describes this as the contrast between "propositional" and "participatory" knowledge.[44] Unless fixed, measureable, and recorded, knowledge is not valued. Such a hierarchy exists even within first-world academic institutions, but the dichotomy has been greatest in communities where subalterns experience texts as instruments of power and control. Illegal immigrants in the United States, for example, are referred to as "undocumented" immigrants.[45] Proponents of Biblical Performance Criticism have similarly lamented the emphasis on text alone that has predominated in the academic discipline of Biblical Studies.

Conquergood compares two different domains of knowledge: the "official, objective, and abstract" domain characterized as "the map"; and the "practical, embodied, and popular" domain characterized as "the story."[46] As we have already noted, embodiment is a key concept in performance, marking a shift from abstract knowledge to grounded, embodied knowledge. It is this second domain that includes extratextual dimensions such as intonation, silence, gestures, emotion—all aspects of oral performance! In any communication event meaning will be present that is not overt: this is why Biblical Performance Criticism aims to go beneath the surface text to discover the "whole performance event" that is hidden there.

When we apply this contrast between "map" knowledge and "story" knowledge to Scripture, we *should* be concerned if Biblical Studies takes

44. Conquergood, "Performance Studies," 146.

45. The hegemony of the written document was underscored for me when I supported a refugee to Australia who wished to change the legal surname of her children to match a new surname she had chosen for herself. The family had arrived in a refugee camp with no papers and were registered under the woman's father's name. As an adult, my friend was entitled to change her own surname but in order to change the surname of her dependents (which had only ever existed on paper) we had to attend the Supreme Court and establish to the judge's satisfaction that the children no longer had communication with their biological father, a man who had abused and abandoned them. The existing surname of the children was not even *his* name, but his permission was still required under registration laws. Happily, our case was successful.

46. Conquergood, "Performance Studies," 145.

its approach from within the first domain with its distanced and objective perspective. Scripture is performed communication: between God and humanity, between faithful scribes and their readers, between communities of faith and subsequent generations for whom and to whom they preserve and pass on their traditions and convictions. Moreover, Scripture aims to transform its addressees, enabling them to embody the script and re-enact it in their own settings. For the faithful community, theory (theology) *must* become practice (praxis)!

Conquergood claims that Performance Studies is a field of academia that aims to "pull the pin" on this false dichotomy between theory and practice:

> We can think through performance along three crisscrossing lines of activity and analysis. We can think of performance (1) as a work of *imagination*, as an object of study; (2) as a pragmatics of *inquiry* (both as model and method), as an optic and operator of research; (3) as a tactics of *intervention*, an alternative space of struggle. Speaking from my home department at Northwestern, we often refer to the three *a*'s of performance studies: artistry, analysis, activism. Or to change the alliteration, a commitment to the three *c*'s of performance studies: creativity, critique, citizenship (civic struggle for social justice).[47]

I have found it helpful to adopt Conquergood's threefold focus in approaching biblical texts from the perspective of performance, but am proposing the triad of creativity, commentary, and connections. In brief summary, to be further elucidated below, my application of these categories to prophetic traditions will entail (1) recognizing the *creativity* of the individual prophet's performance highlighted through performance-sensitive translation; (2) providing *commentary* on the prophets as performers in their own settings and on their literature as "performance literature"; and (3) exploring the *connections* between the Hebrew prophetic traditions and our own contexts. Investigating how the text has been shaped to invite reenactment is a worthy goal of biblical study, given that transformation of our world in line with divine love and justice witnessed to in Scripture.[48]

---

47. Conquergood, "Performance Studies," 152 (italics original).

48. I am aware that Peter Perry has adopted Conquergood's triad to his performance criticism method also, except that he uses the terminology of "imagination, inquiry, intervention." Broadly speaking, he equates "inquiry" with the world behind the text, 'imagination' with the world of the text, and 'intervention' with the world in front of the text. See Perry, *Insights from Performance Criticism*, 34–39. My emphases are slightly different.

Reading Prophetic Texts as Performances

The *Creativity* of the Biblical Prophets

I have referred above to many of the rhetorical aspects of prophetic literature, including the use of metaphor, open ended questions, direct address
to the audience, wordplay and other ear-catching devices—each of which
could be understood as emblematic of the creativity of the prophets. David
Rhoads reminds us that the ancient world valued the artistry of *speaking*:

> The choice of words, the arrangement, the patterns of repetition
> with variation, the pleasantness of sound to the ear, the memo-
> rable nature of sayings and images, and the developing power
> of persuasion—all these worked together to produce riveting
> experiences for ancient audiences.[49]

The way that we can most readily access these are through performance-
sensitive translation of the Hebrew texts. If prophetic texts were composed
to be heard, they were composed as "scripts." Although we cannot be certain
of the original pronunciation in ancient times, merely reading the Hebrew
text aloud can alert us to soundplay, rhythm, rhyme, repetition, and so on. It
is essential, therefore, to notice the elements that are effective to the ear and
do our best to replicate these in our own translations. Translation takes place
along a continuum from formal translations, with a literal word-for-word
approach, to "functional" translations based on dynamic equivalence, which
seeks to replicate meaning for the receptive culture. I would argue that in
order to elicit embedded performative aspects of texts useful for reading
them through the lens of Biblical Performance Criticism, we need to lean
to the formal end of the spectrum. I therefore choose to use highly iconic
translations that are perhaps even more focused on word-for-word equivalence than one would normally find. Even if this results in a translation that
does not sound smooth, it will be useful for highlighting creative aspects of
the performance that might not otherwise be noticed.

The areas that I pay attention to are these:

- Translation of the same Hebrew word or root with the same English
  word wherever possible. This allows for the repetition of sounds and
  ideas that the original audience would have heard to be conveyed to a
  new audience.

---

49. Rhoads, "The Art of Translating," 38.

- Careful translation of syntactic forms that reflects the use or absence of particles, the presence of independent pronouns, and clear delineation of number and gender of verbal forms (which are not necessarily distinguishable in English). Similarly, when verbs shift between persons, such as from third person to second person, these should be translated faithfully. I have already commented on the way second-person verbs invite audience participation.

- Replication of gender and number of nominal forms if possible (Hebrew, like other languages, has gendered nouns with no neuter form). It is common for English translations to replicate the English language, which uses a greater number of neutral terms. But giving objects and entities their Hebrew gender helps highlight the "actors" in the drama.

- Word order, especially if different from what might be expected in common Hebrew syntax. This might include fronting pronouns and positioning verbs in relation to subjects.

- Replication of wordplay where possible, including alliteration, assonance and consonance, onomatopoeia, paronomasia, and ideophones.[50]

- Divisions in the Hebrew text such as the *athnach*, *petuuah*, and *setumah* that suggest which ideas belong together and how the text might be divided into scenes.

Commentary on the Biblical Prophets

Working with a performance-sensitive translation, my commentary on the prophetic traditions will highlight performative features embedded in the texts. What clues can be found to the underlying oral event behind the written text? Does the text easily break into scenes and acts? Are there "stage instructions" relating to time, space, action, costumes, and props?

I will highlight the performances that are already present in symbolic acts of prophets, but will ask what sort of performances are on show. Is the

---

50. I disagree with the assessment I read in one discussion of wordplay in prophetic literature where it was argued that such techniques are impossible to reproduce in English translation. With thought and imagination one might find suitable translations. In Isaiah 5:7, for example, the Hebrew words מִשְׁפָּט / מִשְׂפָּח // צְדָקָה / צְעָקָה might be translated as "outpouring of justice/outpouring of blood// outpouring of righteousness/ outcry of distress" or even "righteousness/routed// righted/rooted" whereas the NRSV reads "he expected justice, but saw bloodshed; righteousness, but heard a cry" with no wordplay at all. Similarly, Jeremiah's "almond tree" (שָׁקֵד) that is "watching" (שֹׁקֵד) could perhaps be translated with the words "almond" and "omen" for the same effect (Jer 1:11–12).

prophet supplementing words with action or does the performance itself constitute the message? Is the performance akin to street theater (with the simple aim of drawing attention), or is the prophet engaging in performance art (seeking to actively involve the audience in the performance)? How important is the concept of embodiment in this performance?

I will investigate which characters, both human and nonhuman, are active and serving as models for faithful reenactment. I will draw out evocative metaphors and colorful visions where visualizing and experiencing the material is more than just reading it. I will examine whether the innovative use of familiar formulas might cause the audience, whether ancient or contemporary, to reassess their understanding of the prophetic word in their own unique situation. I have adopted the term "ready-mades" from improvised performance as shorthand for the terms or phrases that have connection to other parts of Scripture that in their use evoke other settings and potentially reshape the conventional meanings of those words and phrases. Such ready-mades are clues to the improvisation of traditions by new performers in new settings (see excursus below).

Performance is dynamic: characterized by immediacy and open-endedness. I will assess whether such characteristics are evident in the prophetic traditions under analysis, including any implications arising from those conclusions.

In short, my commentary on the biblical prophets will determine whether understanding them as performers adds any insights to our interpretation of their message.

Connections with the Biblical Prophets

This third area for examination reminds us that Scripture can be understood as a script for faithful reenactment by engaged audiences. A script is not fully realized until it is performed. Rather than just words on a page, embodied performance means that real bodies in real time will act out the truths of the tradition. Whatever insights are gained from analyzing the prophetic traditions need to be faithfully reenacted in our own times and settings.

Focusing on the role of the audience will thus be an important emphasis when Biblical Performance Criticism engages with the biblical prophets. Rather than a group of spectators, however, we will expect an engaged audience that unites with the performers and the script "by identification with shared or conflicting values and beliefs . . . [T]he transformation of a spectator into an audience occurs when spectator and performer meet in that imagined realm of performance."[51] Terry Giles refers to audience formation as a major component of performance criticism.[52] Conquergood's inclusion of "activism" as a key component of performance criticism exposes his concern that the discipline should not remain purely an academic exercise but should have an impact within the public arena. He uses a variety of descriptives to express this:

> Activism, outreach, connection to community; applications and interventions; action research; projects that reach outside the academy and are rooted in an ethic of reciprocity and exchange; knowledge that is tested by practice within a community; social commitment, collaboration, and contribution/intervention as a way of knowing: praxis.[53]

Audience transformation due to performance is a goal of faith communities who continue to use Scripture as inspiration. Careful reading of the prophetic "scripts" will help draw out connections between performative aspects already embedded in the text and the inherent hermeneutical possibilities that allow for faithful reenactments.

Summary

Dwight Conquergood challenged the field of performance studies to reach beyond the academy and embrace a threefold emphasis on the object of study, the method of inquiry, and engagement with the world. I have productively applied this method to the biblical prophets by focusing on the three components of creativity, commentary, and connections. Paying attention to prophetic *creativity* means replicating, as much as possible, the compositional choices reflected in the original text via performance-oriented translation. It also involves recognizing the uniqueness of each prophetic performance. My *commentary* combines methods sensitive to performance with historical-critical and literary methodologies in order to draw out both the historical and theological issues underlying the original prophetic compositions and their ongoing impact in new settings. *Connections* ("hitting the ground in practice") reminds us of the importance of reenactment of Scripture's prophetic traditions that enables these ancient texts to continue to have impact on today's audiences.

---

51. Giles, "Performance Criticism," 580.
52. Giles, "Performance Criticism," 580.
53. Conquergood, "Performance Studies," 152.

Coming to Israel's prophets with the lens of Biblical Performance Criticism will help us to see the value of each individual prophetic performer. "Prophetic literature" is not a uniform genre. Instead, the prophets have a specific response to their own circumstances, conveyed through their unique personalities. Having examined Habakkuk as a performer in my previous monograph, I now turn to three different case studies from amongst the prophets: Elijah from the narrative traditions of the Deuteronomistic History, Ezekiel from the Scroll of the Major Prophets, and Jonah from the Scroll of the Twelve.

Excursus: "Ready-Mades"

As far as I can determine, the term "ready-made" was first used in relation to the arts by Marcel Duchamp, who selected ordinary manufactured objects ("ready-mades") and repositioned them to create artworks; this is exemplified by a porcelain urinal titled *Fountain*.[54] "Ready-made" is a term also used in forms of musical performance that highlight improvisation, such as Irish jigs or many forms of jazz. Skilled musicians add embellishments and decorations to standard tunes, often making use of stock patterns already in their repertoire ("ready-mades"), while maintaining the original tune's basic theme. Many of us can recognize "riffs" played out of context, or well-known portions of music used in advertisements to create a particular emotional response from viewers. The term has also been used in linguistics to denote memorized clauses and clause-sequences that come "ready-made" in constructed discourse. Ian Mackenzie argues that, in both speech and writing, linguistic performance does not involve composing sentences out of a store of thousands of known words and grammatical rules, but rather deploys "prefabricated, institutionalized, and fully contextualized phrases and expressions and sentence heads, with a grammatical form and lexical content that is either wholly or largely fixed."[55] In other words, our speech is mostly formed by reliance on prepatterned phrases than by the generation of sentences from scratch. These prepatterned phrases can be described as "ready-mades." The success of improvised stage performance depends on the actors making use of cultural knowledge and references that are shared with other actors and the audience as the scenario unfolds.[56]

54. http://www.tate.org.uk/art/artworks/duchamp-fountain-t07573/.

55. Mackenzie, "Improvisation," 173.

56. Improvisation can also be worked effectively into scripted performance, as shown in the ever-popular Gilbert and Sullivan operettas, in which staging, lyrics, and sets often reflect scenarios and issues relevant to contemporary audiences.

As Mackenzie argues, written literary composition shares its properties with spoken language and relies on a store of institutionalized utterances. By producing variations on what is expected, an author can create surprise or humor for readers and listeners.[57]

I have come across the term "ready-mades" in Hebrew Bible Studies on two occasions. Wilfred G. E. Watson used the term in relation to stock expressions and fixed word pairs in Hebrew poetry:

> Hebrew poets had to hand two different sets of traditional fixed components: stock expressions and the fixed pair, both fitting the requirements of the formula. That is to say, both were (a) *ready-made* and already existing in tradition; and (b) *useful* as particularly suited for the composition of poetry.[58]

As noted earlier, Shimon Levy writes of "this ready-made, basically pleasant memory" when discussing Ezekiel's "cooking pot show" (Ezek 24:1–14).[59] According to Levy, the incongruity of performing the ritual of cooking meat with its sacrificial overtones while located in exile in Babylon would have drawn in the audience but overturned their expectations: "The estrangement of the theatrical act therefore ensues from the vast gap between the familiar content and the unsuitable circumstances under which the action was performed."[60]

Similarly, I use the term "ready-made" to include any word or phrase that relies on the audience's stored knowledge and expectations in order to engender elements of surprise or disquiet when heard in new or unexpected situations.

57. McKenzie, "Improvisation," 175.
58. Watson, *Classical Hebrew Poetry*, 137. Author's italics.
59. Levy, *The Bible as Theatre*, 185.
60. Levy, *The Bible as Theatre*, 186.

4

Case Study 1: Elijah

Elijah in the Context of Israel's Prophetic Tradition

THE ELIJAH NARRATIVES ARE found in the books of 1 and 2 Kgs that are included in the Former Prophets in the Hebrew Bible and the Historical Books in the Christian Old Testament. The books of Joshua, Judges, Samuel, and Kings set out the history of the Israelites from settlement to exile and are often referred to as the Deuteronomistic History by biblical scholars because they tell the story from a particular theological perspective aligned with the book of Deuteronomy. The literary style of the Elijah material shares this theological perspective, but is different enough to suggest an independent source lay behind the narratives, which were then shaped and integrated into the larger history.

The prophet Elijah belongs in the group of preclassical prophets in that there is no book named after him. Like other preclassical prophets, he is remembered more for his deeds than his words. There are only five and a half chapters devoted to his ministry, yet he is considered a major figure in Jewish and Christian tradition, being one of only a few Old Testament prophets named in the New Testament literature. The portrait of Elijah is drawn with Moses in mind, and the two characters become exemplary for the "Law and the Prophets" in early Christian thought (Matt 17:3–4; Mark 9:4–5; Luke 9:32–33). His sudden appearance and dramatic departure provided an aura of mystery that resulted in an expectation that Elijah would be the forerunner to the Messiah. The prophetic corpus of the Hebrew Bible concludes with a reference to Elijah:

> Lo, I will send you the prophet Elijah before the great and terrible day of the LORD comes. He will turn the hearts of parents to their children and the hearts of children to their parents, so that I will not come and strike the land with a curse. (Mal 4:5–6, NRSV)

Elijah's historical setting is the ninth century BCE during the reigns of Ahab (869–850 BCE), Ahaziah (850–849 BCE), and Jehoram (849–843 BCE), kings of the Northern Kingdom.[1] Ahab was the son of Omri (876–869 BCE) and is one of the few biblical kings for which extra-biblical evidence exists. The Assyrian king Shalmaneser III (858–824 BCE) records a battle between himself and a coalition of smaller kingdoms at Qarqar on the Orontes River in Syria in 853 BCE. There Ahab, the ruler of Israel, is said to have supplied two thousand chariots and ten thousand soldiers.[2] The biblical text tells us that Ahab reigned for 22 years in Samaria, the capital of the Northern Kingdom built by his father, Omri (1 Kgs 16:29). During this time the significant city of Jericho was reestablished. Ahab's wife was Jezebel, daughter of King Ethbaal of the Sidonians, attesting to an alliance with neighboring Sidon (Phonecia). Political treaties with Tyre, Syria, and Judah are also known from the Omride dynasty. It was the first significant dynasty of the Northern Kingdom, and in extrabiblical sources the Northern Kingdom of Israel is sometimes referred to as the Land of Omri or House of Omri. The Annals of Mesha, ruler of Moab, record Omri's invasion of Moab during his father's reign, its continued subjugation under Ahab, and Mesha's subsequent battles with Israel in order to recapture his Moabite territory.[3] There is a hint of this conflict in the Elijah cycle: "And he revolted—Moab—against Israel after the death of Ahab" (2 Kgs 1:1). Mesha of Moab enters the story again in 2 Kgs 3, when Ahab died, but it is Elijah's successor, Elisha, who advises the armies of Israel and Judah during that battle.

Despite this evidence that Ahab was a relatively powerful and influential leader, the portrait painted in the Deuteronomistic History is of an "evil" Northern king who worshiped foreign gods, building altars and erecting sacred poles within Samaria (1 Kgs 16:29–34). The editor lays the blame for this apostasy on Ahab's foreign wife, who had presumably brought her own cultic practices to Israel. The Deuteronomic law forbade both marriage to Canaanite peoples (Deut 7:3–4) and worship of other gods (Deut 5:7–10). By marrying a foreigner and building altars to Baal and Asherah, Ahab opened himself to criticism by Deuteronomistic editors and, especially, a devoutly Yahwist prophet Elijah whose name, appropriately, means "My god is Yah."

When Elijah enters the drama he simply appears without introduction or explanation. There is no typical "prophetic call" recorded, simply the claim that he "stands" before the YHWH, the God of Israel (1 Kgs 17:1). Walter Brueggemann speaks of him interrupting the regnal history

---

1. Dates taken from Petersen, *The Prophetic Literature*, 229.
2. Matthews and Benjamin, *Old Testament Parallels*, 179.
3. Matthews and Benjamin, *Old Testament Parallels*, 168–69.

of Judah and Israel as a "prophetic counterforce" enacting "the raw, un-filtered power of Yahweh that lies completely beyond the command of the royal houses."[4] The Elijah episodes are interwoven with the story of Ahab and Jezebel, and are dominated by motifs of drought, true worship of YHWH, and loyalty to the covenant.

Elijah as a Performance

In reading Elijah as a performance, I have envisaged the material as a series divided into four episodes, each of which represents significant events in the story of Elijah. Each episode has several scenes, with a narrative voiceover introducing each scene. As will be discussed further below, I characterize Episode 3 as a prequel in the chronological story. A cliff-hanger of sorts concludes the fourth episode, leaving the expectation of a new spin-off series starring Elisha. Elisha is a character briefly introduced in Episode 2, who becomes more prominent towards the end of the Elijah Series.

While translating this material I was struck by its character-driven nature. Several characters are present in most of the scenes, or, if not present, remain important behind-the-scenes forces driving the action.

The episodic and character-driven Elijah narratives lend themselves to pieces of ensemble drama in antiquity—drama that enables each new community to remain connected to their God through these ancestral traditions. My aim here, however, is not to re-create a drama as it may have played out in ancient Israel, but to creatively exploit the dramatic qualities of the material by translating and analyzing it through the lens of performance. As with any contemporary drama series, I imagine a script that aims to engage the interest of an audience and keep it coming back for more. I will begin by introducing the *dramatis personae* prominent in the episodes before presenting translations of each episode followed by a discussion of creativity, a commentary on the performative aspects of the episode, and suggestions of connections that can be made with each episode. Episode-specific characters will be introduced as appropriate.

---

4. Brueggemann, *1 & 2 Kings*, 207.

Major Characters

Voiceover Narrator

The narrative voiceover, while not a major actor, introduces each scene and is ubiquitous in the series so deserves description. As in much Hebrew Bible narrative, the narrator is omniscient and largely matter-of-fact. Allowance for individual interpretation can be discerned in the script. For example, a tone of surprise could be given when announcing, "she ate: she, and he, and her house, for days!" (1 Kgs 17:15); or, "the fire of YHWH fell and she ate the offering, and the sticks, and the stones, and the dust! And the waters that were in the trench she licked up!" (1 Kgs 18:38). Other than tone of voice, however, it would be difficult to judge from the script alone what the narrator's view of events is. As Brueggemann states, the narrator exhibits "no curiosity."[5]

This script has been incorporated into the larger Deuteronomistic History, and the narrator cannot help but make a negative value judgment of Ahab and Jezebel (1 Kgs 21:25-26). Deuteronomistic influence is also seen in the epilogue to the first scene in Episode 4: "And the rest of the words of Ahaziah which he did, are they not written in the book of the words of the days of the kings of Israel?" (2 Kgs 1:18).

No comment is made about Elijah by way of character assessment—all that we learn about Elijah comes from his own mouth—but there *is* a narratorial description of the prophet Obadiah's faith and actions that indicates admiration for that prophet since it preempts that character's own self-description:

> Now Obadiah was fearing YHWH greatly. And it happened when Jezebel cut off the prophets of YHWH, he took—Obadiah—a hundred prophets and hid them—fifty men in the cave—and sustained them [with] bread and water. (1 Kgs 18:3b–4; cf. 18:12b–13)

Other asides serve as explanations to the audience: a reminder that there were originally twelve tribes in Israel (1 Kgs 18:31), and the information that Ahaziah had no son to succeed him after his death (2 Kgs 1:17–18).

Repetition and brevity convey a laconic tone occasionally:

> they prophesied until the offering of the oblation, but not any voice, and not any answer, and not any response (1 Kgs 18:29)

---

5. Brueggemann, *1 & 2 Kings*, 211.

> And a spirit—great and strong—tearing away mountains
> and breaking cliff before the face of YHWH. But not in the
> spirit was YHWH. And after the spirit an earthquake. Not
> in the earthquake was YHWH. And after the earthquake,
> fire. Not in the fire was YHWH. And after the fire a sound
> *demāmāh daqqāh* (1 Kgs 19:11–12)

Despite the distanced impression given by this narrative voiceover, liberal use of הִנֵּה (*hinnēh*), translated "behold!" indicates the narrator's interest in the story and desire for the audience to remain engaged (see 1 Kgs 17:10; 18:7; 19:5, 6, 9, 13; 2 Kgs 1:9; 2:11).

Gods: YHWH and the Baals

Much of this Elijah Series is focused on a "Battle of the Gods,"[6] giving justification for listing YHWH and Baal as major characters. Baal, in various manifestations, is only ever offstage, but is a potent character nonetheless, motivating much of the action.[7] It could be argued that Elijah's raison d'être is to confront the influence of Baal on the king of Israel and therefore the nation of Israel, motivated by his own fierce allegiance to YHWH. Both deities, therefore, have central roles.

The motif of drought and rain underlies the rivalry. There is a well-known backstory to the series in that both cultic systems lay claim to being in control of rain and fertility. Baal never appears on stage to make this claim directly, but YHWH does so in an emphatic speech at the beginning of Episode 2: "I will set rain upon the face of the ground" (1 Kgs 18:1). When the rain does come, however, no word of YHWH accompanies it. The actions of the prophet Elijah and an enigmatic "spirit" bring about the downpour (1 Kgs 18:42–45). In this performance, moreover, although we have the impression that YHWH is in control of events, he most often manipulates the action through other actors: ravens (1 Kgs 17:4, 6); a widow-woman (1 Kgs 17: 9, 15); a spirit (1 Kgs 18:45); and a messenger (1 Kgs 19:5, 7; 2 Kgs 1:3–4, 15).

YHWH, therefore, has an enigmatic role in these episodes, being hardly active in some scenes. John Olley comments on 1 Kings 19:

> Most surprisingly, after the opening phrase nowhere is YHWH
> the subject of any word or action in the whole chapter! The

---

6. This description is used in Rofé, *The Prophetical Stories*, 183.

7. In a similar manner to speaking about the character Godot in Beckett's *Waiting for Godot*.

closest is when 'the fire of YHWH fell' (v. 38), not an expected 'and YHWH heard Elijah's prayer and sent fire' (contrast 17.22).[8]

The personality of YHWH is likewise enigmatic. He seems to be caring towards his prophet by providing sustenance (1 Kgs 17:4, 9; 19:6, 8), heeding Elijah's prayers (1 Kgs 17:22; 18:38), and sharing thoughts with him (1 Kgs 21:28). The attention Elijah receives from YHWH and his messengers leads Frieda Clark Hyman to suggest he was "the most coddled of all the prophets of the Tanakh."[9] On the other hand, communicating with Elijah through messengers suggests a deliberate distancing at times by YHWH. His judgment of Ahab is harsh (1 Kgs 21:19), yet he is open to showing mercy when a display of repentance is offered by Ahab (1 Kgs 21:28). In the condemnation of Ahab and Jezebel, Elijah speaks *for* YHWH without an introductory formula (1 Kgs 21:21–24), giving the impression that the characters share one mind. Similarly, Elijah claims that dew and rain will come at the behest of his own word (1 Kgs 17:1). And yet YHWH's self-revelation at Mount Horeb is inconclusive and does not seem to impact Elijah greatly, as will be discussed further below. YHWH acknowledges the existence and impact of the Baals without ever addressing the other god(s) directly (1 Kgs 19:18; 2 Kgs 1:3, 6, 16).

Baal is the generic name for deities outside of Israel and so the name appears in this script predominantly as "the Baal/s." The proper name Baal Zebub, identified as the god of Ekron, is used in Episode 4 (2 Kgs 1:2, 3, 6, 16). Although a powerful force motivating the action, there is no character development as the Baals neither act nor speak in the series.

Fascinatingly, Elijah is also described as a "Baal" by Ahaziah's messengers (2 Kgs 1:8).

Elijah

Elijah is present in every episode and appears in most scenes and is definitely the star of the show! Nonetheless, he is a flawed hero with a dark side. He is introduced as "Elijah the Tishbite of the 'Tishbe' in Gilead" (1 Kgs 17:1, NRSV). Most translations retain "Tishbite" as the demonym but frequently translate "Tishbe" according to the dictionary meaning of "sojourner, i.e. resident alien, (temporary) inhabitant . . . settler."[10] The common root supports my translation of "Elijah the Settler from the Settlers of Gilead."

8. Olley, "YHWH and His Zealous Prophet," 35.

9. Hyman, "Elijah: Accuser and Defender," 290.

10. Clines, *Concise Dictionary of Classical Hebrew*, 485–86. Clines notes a consonantal connection to the verb יָשַׁב, *yašab*, "to sit."

The lack of mention of father, wife, or children allows him to be a true zealot (1 Kgs 19:10, 14), unhampered by "mortal bonds."[11] Unlike Elisha, who comes after him and is often accompanied by a companion Gehazi and the "sons of prophets," Elijah seems to prefer to work alone. His relationship with Elisha as a commissioned successor is terse. His response to Elisha's first question with the words "What have I done to you?" (1 Kgs 19:20) seems ill-mannered, and three times he entreats Elisha to remain behind as he is making his last journey around the country (2 Kgs 2:1, 4, 6). Although Elijah invites a last request from his persistent disciple, Elijah's response is one of exasperation; he describes Elisha's request as "difficult" (2 Kgs 2:10). Another potential disciple is Obadiah, who refers to Elijah as "my master" (1 Kgs 18:7) but is brusquely answered, "go tell your master" (i.e., Ahab) "that Elijah is here" (1 Kgs 18:8). Twice Elijah is accompanied by a "lad" (1 Kgs 18:43; 19:3), but the lad is left behind on both occasions. The only emotional relationship evident in the series is between Elijah and the widow-woman's son over whose life he pleads with YHWH.

A loner, then, but a forceful and arrogant personality. Frieda Hyman describes him as "stern, demanding, even autocratic."[12] From the beginning he claims to be "standing" before the face of YHWH (1 Kgs 17:1), not falling on his face as other prophets do in the presence of God. His speech is full of imperatives, although we should note that in his engagement with those who serve him—the widow-woman of Zarephath, his lad, and Elisha—he tempers imperatives with the modifier נָא ("please") (1 Kgs 17:10, 11; 18:43; 2 Kgs 2:1, 4, 6). As far as the audience is concerned, the interaction with the prophets of Baal on Mount Carmel is Elijah's own idea—certainly we never hear YHWH commanding it—and is full of chutzpah, with a "bring it on" attitude at the beginning, savage mocking at their lack of results, and exaggerated actions to heighten the impact of his own performance. He is prepared to use the power available to him in a destructive way, commandeering Israelites to help him slaughter the prophets of Baal (1 Kgs 18:40) and calling down fire from heaven on the troops sent by Ahaziah (2 Kgs 1:10, 12). Several times he claims to be the only real YHWH worshiper left in Israel (1 Kgs 18:22; 19:10, 14), despite the presence of Obadiah, Elisha, the hundred prophets of YHWH hidden by Obadiah (1 Kgs 18:4, 13), and the seven thousand who have not "bowed down" or "kissed" the Baal (1 Kgs 19:18). As noted earlier, Elijah speaks for YHWH at times, and in the judgment speech against Ahab extends the indictment to include Ahab's wife and descendants in YHWH's condemnation.

11. Hyman, "Elijah: Accuser and Defender," 288.
12. Hyman, "Elijah: Accuser and Defender," 283.

Elijah's arrogance is mitigated by his actions following the success on Mount Carmel and the coming of the rain that ended the drought. Elijah, threatened by a message from Jezebel, makes a hasty retreat into the desert where he expresses a desire for death (1 Kgs 19:1–4). In fact, private inner doubts are expressed several times in the series. In Episode 1, when confronted by the widow-woman's anger and grief over her dead son, he removes himself from her presence before crying out to YHWH (1 Kgs 17:19). In Episode 4 he has to be reassured by a messenger from YHWH that no harm will come to him when going down to meet King Ahaziah, even though he had been confidently calling down firebolts on Ahaziah's troops (2 Kgs 1:15). In the speech he makes before YHWH on Mount Horeb he sounds alone, desperate, and defensive (1 Kgs 19:10, 14). The fact that this speech is repeated exactly, word-for-word, *after* YHWH's theophanic presence indicates that Elijah gained little assurance by YHWH's self-revelation.

This assessment of Elijah's character suggests that he is a typical introvert.[13] Bold when performing but reserved in one-on-one interactions and needing to withdraw for renewal of energy. Despite coming across as self-assured, brave, and boastful, goading when put in the public spotlight, his lack of inner confidence, fears, and self-doubts come to the fore in his private moments.

Elijah's character is reminiscent of Moses—another reluctant performer who nonetheless was able to put on a good show when thrust into the center of attention. Moses performed miracles, confronted a king, took flight into the wilderness when threatened, relied on YHWH for sustenance in the wilderness, parted waters, encountered YHWH at Mount Horeb, handed over the mantle to a new leader chosen by YHWH, and mysteriously departed from earthly life in the Transjordan across from Jericho (see Deut 34:1). As noted earlier, however, there is no narrated voiceover assessing Elijah's character as we hear for Moses (Deut 34:10–12). The audience members are left to make their own assessments from the portrait emerging in the series.

In most biblical scripts, little instruction is given for the characters' appearance or costuming. Unusually, then, we are given a physical description of Elijah: "A man—a Baal of hair and a girdle of fur girded on his loins" (2 Kgs 1:8). Since *baal* can be translated "lord," "husband," or "master," the phrase seems to imply a man dominated by hair. Elijah's cloak (אַדֶּרֶת, *'aderet*) is a significant prop in two other episodes (1 Kgs 19:13, 19; 2 Kgs 2:8, 13, 14), but a different word is used on those occasions. Elijah's hairy appearance

---

13. More often this character assessment is equated with a depressive personality. See Olley, "YHWH and His Zealous Prophet," 38 for references to several commentaries that argue this line.

became a key part of his identity, as shown in later biblical allusions (Zech 13:4; Matt 3:4). Undoubtedly because he came to symbolize Jewish messianic expectations, Elijah was used as a ready-made for the depiction of John the Baptist (Matt 3:4; Mark 1:6; John 1:21). The gospel portrait of Jesus also owes much to the story of Elijah. Obvious parallels include the raising of a child from death; forty days' journey in the wilderness where sustenance came at the hands of angels; calling of disciples and an expectation of radical commitment; confrontation of injustice by the powerful against the poor; and an ascent into heaven.

Elijah is a larger-than-life character. He operates largely outside of normal relationships and societal constraints. He dresses oddly (2 Kgs 1:8), exhibits peculiar behavior (1 Kgs 18:42), spurns would-be disciples (1 Kgs 18:8; 2 Kgs 2:1, 4, 6), performs superhuman physical feats (18:46; 19:8), has the powers of heaven at his disposal (1 Kgs 17:1; 18:38, 45; 2 Kgs 1:10, 12), and ultimately vanishes in a whirlwind of fire (2 Kgs 2:11). Although flawed by arrogance and self-doubt, he is a formidable force and displays undisputed star quality.

Jezebel

Like the Baals, Jezebel is a major force in the series despite her infrequent appearances and few lines. Her adherence to Baal is evident in her name, likely to have been pronounced "Itha-baal" ("woman of Baal") in her native Phoenician.[14] The distorting of her name to "Jezebel" (meaning "where is honor"[15] or, with alternative vowel pointing in the Hebrew, "heap of dung"[16]) reflects Deuteronomistic influence on the 1–2 Kgs account. Although not popular with her original audience of Israelite YHWH adherents, Jezebel is a character who commands attention and admiration.

First and foremost, she is a foreign-born princess who becomes queen in a new context. She brings what she knows about royalty from her own background and imposes it in the new context, perhaps without understanding how much that conflicts with Israelite traditions. Or maybe she does understand but has greater ambition for her royal house, hoping to influence it into being more like royalty in neighboring nations. Hence her statement to Ahab, "You, right now, are making a kingdom over Israel" (1 Kgs 21:7).

---

14. Hazleton, *Jezebel*, 2.

15. Sweeney, *I & II Kings*, 206.

16. Meyers et al., eds., *Women in Scripture*, 100.

The reference to the "prophets of the Baal—four hundred and fifty—and prophets of the Asherah—four hundred—the ones eating at the table of Jezebel" (1 Kgs 19:19) shows how influential she has been in bringing her cultic practices into Israel. In doing so, she becomes *the* rival for Elijah, whose driving zeal is for worship of YHWH alone. The tension between them is heightened in an improvisation in the Septuagint, where in 1 Kgs 19:2 words of Jezebel via her messenger are inserted: "If you are Elijah, I am Jezebel." If Elijah had showed chutzpah before the prophets of Baal, she is defiantly showing it back to him. In the Masoretic Text, however, the two characters are never together onstage—their words to each other are conveyed by messengers (1 Kgs 19:2; 21:23[17]). Nonetheless, the words that are in our script at the beginning of Episode 3 put her on an equal footing with Elijah. Just as he had been an instrument for YHWH's action, Jezebel was prepared to be an instrument for the vengeance of her gods: "Thus let the gods do and thus let them add to what they do if by this time tomorrow I [have not] put your breath like the breath of one of them" (1 Kgs 19:2).[18] Elijah had already proved that the Baal was impotent, but by fleeing for his life at this point it seems clear that he is frightened of Jezebel's power to achieve what her gods may not be capable of doing.

Jezebel remains offstage in Episode 2—her words in Episode 3 are conveyed by a messenger—but it is *her* methods that give rise to the confrontation between Elijah and other prophets, and *her* actions that determine Elijah's actions in the series. Just as she had killed YHWH's prophets, Elijah kills *her* prophets. It is due to *her* threat that Elijah flees to the wilderness where he encounters YHWH and his messengers. It is the perceived corruption of the house of Ahab due to *her* influence that brings the determination to anoint a new king over Israel (1 Kgs 19:16). In Episode 3 Jezebel remains powerful but is much more visible and active. *She* is the one giving the commands: to Ahab the king, to her messengers, to the Jezreelite elders, and to the Sons of Beliyya'el. Deceit, murder, and dispossession are carried out at her initiative. In her exhortation of Ahab to "get up, eat bread" (1 Kgs 21:7) she even echoes YHWH's assurance to Elijah via the messenger in the wilderness who had urged Elijah to "get up, eat!" (1 Kgs 19:5, 7). Jezebel, by her presence alone, despite her few actual appearances, surpasses the Baals and comes close to outperforming both Elijah and YHWH!

17. This verse is somewhat ambiguous—although Elijah is addressing Ahab, the narrator breaks in with an additional comment in which YHWH is the subject of the verb "he said," and Jezebel is the object (the construction is "to Jezebel"), but the pronouncement uses third-person verbs, speaking *about* Jezebel's fate.

18. This is not an easy line to translate, but the pent-up fury behind the threat may explain the difficulty in clarity of expression.

Ahab

The character of Ahab in this series is painted quite differently from the portrait that emerges from historical inscriptions of the ninth century BCE. The only suggestion of an influential and decisive ruler comes through Jezebel's reminder that he is "making a kingdom" (1 Kgs 21:7). Otherwise, his actions and spoken lines portray him as sulky, childish, and ineffective. His first significant appearance in Episode 2 shows him giving a command to his overseer Obadiah, yet the work is divided equally between them, emphasized by the narrator's parallel descriptions, such that Ahab positions himself as equal to his employee: "And they divided between themselves the land to cross over her. Ahab went in one way by himself, and Obadiah went in one way by himself" (1 Kgs 18:6). In the presence of Elijah, Ahab is initially defiant, calling him "troubler of Israel" on one occasion and "my enemy" on another (1 Kgs 18:16; 21:20), but he rapidly quails and obeys Elijah's commands (1 Kgs 18:20, 44–45). He is shown up by the prophet physically as well as mentally when Elijah is able to outrun his chariot (1 Kgs 18:46). When Ahab's request of Naboth to purchase his vineyard is rejected, his response is to take himself to bed and refuse to eat, feeling "sore and sullen" (1 Kgs 21:4). The exact phrase is used of him earlier in his story when accused by another prophet of failing to observe the Deuteronomic law (1 Kgs 20:43).

On the other hand, several facts point to Ahab being aware of and respectful towards Israelite covenant traditions. Naboth's refusal to sell his ancestral land is accepted without demur in spite of his resentment. When Elijah confronts him over the death of Naboth and theft of his vineyard and pronounces YHWH's judgment, he removes his royal finery and capitulates to acts of repentance involving sackcloth and fasting. This response could be played out either as genuine repentance and adherence to YHWH, supported by the Yahwistic names of his sons and daughter (Ahaziah, Athaliah, Jehoram), or as a desperate (and successful) attempt to save his own life.

Actions that suggest he had not fully adopted the cult of the Baal do not ameliorate his weak character, shown most obviously in his obedience to Jezebel's commands. He turns a blind eye when she uses his name to arrange Naboth's murder (1 Kgs 21:8), then gets up and possesses Naboth's vineyard when she tells him to (1 Kgs 21:15–16). A gap earlier in the story suggests he is not willing to challenge Jezebel—when Elijah told him to gather "all Israel to Mount Carmel, and prophets of the Baal—four hundred and fifty—and prophets of the Asherah—four hundred—the ones eating at the table of Jezebel" (I Kgs 18:18), the prophets of Asherah are not present in the confrontation at Mount Carmel. Presumably they, "eating at the table of Jezebel," could not be extracted at Ahab's behest. Ahab may have been the symbolic king of the castle and country, but he was easily persuaded to act at the bidding of others.

The Elijah Series

Below is my translation of the four episodes in the Elijah Series, followed by comments under the headings of Creativity, Commentary, and Connections for each episode. A cast list of leading and supporting actors, extras, and any offstage personalities heads the script for each episode. Scene division is determined by changes in location. The setting for each scene has been inferred from the text and is provided prior to the action. The script is written as lines for characters. Where dialogue in the original narrative was connected by brief statements such as "and he said" I have supplied an asterisk (*) so as not to interrupt the flow of the dialogue with superfluous narration. Relevant comments on translation choices are given in footnotes. *Setumahs* and *petuuahs* have been retained in the script as indicators for pauses in the action.

Elijah Episode 1

"A New Prophet"
(1 Kings 17)

Cast:

Leading: Narrator, YHWH, Elijah, the widow-woman

Supporting: the widow-woman's son

Extras: ravens, jar, pitcher

Offstage: Baal

PROLOGUE (17:1)

Setting: The palace, Samaria

Narrator

¹And he said—Elijah the Settler from the Settlers of Gilead—to Ahab:

Elijah

By the life of YHWH the God of Israel who I am standing
before his face

If there will be these years dew or rain

It will be because of my mouth, my word.

ס

SCENE 1 (17:2–7)

Setting: The river cutting

Narrator

²And the word of YHWH happened to him saying:

YHWH

³Go from here and turn yourself eastward, and be hidden
at the river cutting on the face of the Jordan. ⁴And it will be
from the river you will drink, and the ravens I have commanded to sustain you there.

Narrator

⁵And he went and he did according to the Word of YHWH—
he went and he sat at the river cutting that is on the face of
the Jordan. ⁶And the ravens brought him bread and flesh in
the morning and bread and flesh in the evening, and from
the river he was drinking.

⁷And it happened by the end of some days the river dried
up, because there was not a deluge in the land.

ס

SCENE 2 (17:8–15)

Setting: Outside the widow-woman's
house in Zarephath

Narrator

⁸And the word of YHWH happened to him saying:

YHWH

⁹Get up, go to Zarephath which belongs to Sidon and stay there. Behold, I have commanded there a widow-woman to sustain you.

Narrator

¹⁰And he got up, and he went to Zarephath, and he came to the entrance of the city, and behold! There a widow-woman gathering sticks.

And he called to her and he said

Elijah

Take, please, for me a little of the water in a vessel and let me drink.

Narrator

¹¹And she went to take, and he called to her and he said

Elijah

Take, please, for me a scrap of bread in your hand.

Widow-woman

¹²(*) By the life of YHWH your God, if there is to me victuals, if there is fullness of a hand of flour in the jar and a little oil in the pitcher . . . and behold! Here I am gathering two sticks and I will go and make it for me and for my son . . . and we will eat it, and we will die!

Elijah

¹³(*) Do not be afraid. Go in, make as you have said. Only make for me from there a loaf—a small one—first, and bring it to me, and for you and your son make later.

ס

¹⁴For thus says YHWH the God of Israel, the jar of flour will not finish and the pitcher of oil will not empty, until such a day as YHWH puts a deluge on the face of the ground.

Narrator

¹⁵And she went in and she made like the word of Elijah—and she ate: she, and he, and her house, for days! ¹⁶The

jar of flour did not finish and the pitcher of oil did not end according to the word of YHWH which he spoke by the hand of Elijah.

פ

SCENE 3 (17:17–24)

Setting: Inside the widow-woman's
house in Zarephath

Narrator

[17]And it happened after these things he fell sick—the son of the woman—the mistress of the house. And it happened his sickness was very severe until no spark[19] was left in him. [18]And she said to Elijah:

Widow-woman

What is there between me and between you, man of God? You came to me to bring to mind my iniquity and to cause the death of my son!

Elijah

[19](*) Give to me your son.

Narrator

And he took him from her lap and he brought him up to the high room[20] where he was staying there and he laid him on his bed. [20]And he cried out to YHWH and he said:

Elijah

YHWH my God, what moreover on the widow—the one who I am sojourning with her? Are you bringing evil to kill her son?

Narrator

[21]And he stretched himself upon the lad three times and he cried out to YHWH and he said

---

19. נְשָׁמָה, *nᵉšāmāh*, is usually translated "breath" or "life," but my translation ("spark") distinguishes between this word and the synonyms חַי, *ḥay* ("life") and נֶפֶשׁ, *nefeš* ("breath") that all occur in this episode.

20. The "high room" where the widow-woman's son is restored (עֲלִיָּה, *ʿăliyyāh*) is almost a homonym for the name Elijah (אֵלִיָּה, *ʾēliyyāh*).

> **Elijah**
>
> YHWH my God, let it return please, the breath of this lad into him.
>
> **Narrator**
>
> [22]And YHWH heard the voice of Elijah and it returned—the breath of the lad—into him and he lived. [23]And Elijah took the lad and brought him down from the high room of the house and he gave him to his mother, and Elijah said to her:
>
> **Elijah**
>
> See—life in your son!
>
> **Widow-woman**
>
> [24](*) Now this I know—that a man of God you are, and the word of YHWH in your mouth is truth.
>
> פ

Creativity in Episode 1

A rapid change of setting early in the action artfully reminds the audience that the prophet Elijah is a maverick, completely dissociated with the kingdom of Israel and the power and influence of the royal house. Just as suddenly as this new prophet appears, Elijah disappears into the wilderness, and then into enemy territory (the home of the Baal, no less!). Sustenance is provided by YHWH during these periods away from Israelite civilization. The same phrase—"I have commanded ... to sustain you"—shows that YHWH is able to use different agents in the same way, whether they be ravens or widow-women.

This first episode is dominated by contrasting themes, most of which continue into the subsequent episodes. An opening prediction of drought includes three different Hebrew words for precipitation: טַל (*ṭal,* "dew"), מָטָר (*māṭār,* "rain"), and גֶּשֶׁם (*gešem,* "deluge"), underscoring the complete lack of needed moisture for sustenance. The "little of the water" asked for by Elijah (v 10) similarly stresses the scarcity of water. The withholding of rain that comes to an end midway through Episode 2 is contrasted with the excessive water that Elijah pours over his offering, and when *gešem* appears for the rain that subsequently arrives (1 Kgs 18:41, 44–45), it is clearly to be understood as heavy rain, hence my translation "deluge." Thus scarcity and abundance are themes played with across the first two episodes.

Drought is matched by famine, felt both in Israel and beyond its borders. The widow-woman's expectation that she and her son will soon die of starvation contrasts with the unending supply of oil and flour. Famine and fecundity interweave with the theme of death and life, another recurring motif across the series. Once again, three different Hebrew words are used to denote life, as if it cannot be contained with one simple definition: נְשָׁמָה (nᵉšāmāh, "spark"); חַי (ḥāy, "life"), and נֶפֶשׁ (nefeš, "breath").

Scene 3 shows Elijah taking the widow-woman's son up to his high room, and bringing him down again with a new spark of life. The motif of up and down is used again several times. As befits an ancient world-view, "up" is closer to the heavenly realm where YHWH is active, and "down" represents the world of humanity where the prophet is YHWH's envoy. Hence the boy is healed in the upper room; fire falls from heaven to consume Elijah's offering and later his enemies; the rain comes first to the top of Mount Carmel; Elijah is taken up in a chariot of fire to the heavens. By contrast, the boy is brought down to his mother as proof of YHWH's power; the prophets of Baal are taken down to the River Kishon for slaughter; Ahab is told to go down to Samaria ahead of the deluge; and Elijah is instructed to go down to meet both Ahab and Ahaziah to pronounce judgment on them.

A final contrast that continues from this episode into the next is skepticism and faith. The sarcasm of the widow-woman when asked to provide for the prophet (17:12) is followed by a pause (a *setumah* in the script), forcing Elijah to support his request with a promise of miraculous provision. This provision does not seem to fully convince the widow-woman of YHWH's care for *her*. She may well have understood the miracle of flour and oil as a consequence of the prophet's presence rather than for the benefit of her family, as her accusation to Elijah shows: "What is there between me and between you, man of God? You came to me to bring to mind my iniquity and to cause the death of my son!" (17:18). The restoration of her son to life, however, is the key to a new faith in this "man of God" and the truth of the "word of YHWH" (17:24).

Commentary on Episode 1

EPISODE-SPECIFIC CHARACTERS

Widow-Woman

Widows are paradigmatic of the poorest of the poor in both biblical law and narrative, being without male protection in a patriarchal world. The naming of the character in this story stresses her vulnerability, she is both a woman *and* a widow. She could have been forgiven for assuming this male stranger was attempting to take advantage of her except that his tempered language (using the word "please" alongside his imperative verbs) and the audience's knowledge that YHWH has already prepared her to sustain Elijah excludes that possibility. The *setumah* after Elijah's request for a loaf before she makes any victuals for her own family gives us pause to think, and her too. It isn't until Elijah follows it up with the promise of sustained provision that she goes and does as requested. As a non-Israelite woman from the homeland of Jezebel, her acquiescence to Elijah, her growing trust in him shown when she allows her dying son to be taken into his care, and her nascent faith in YHWH, form a significant contrast to the more powerful character. Initially the widow-woman refers to "YHWH *your* God"; then her circumstances "bring to mind" her own iniquity; then the knowledge grows within her of the truth of YHWH and his representative man. It is the crisis of her son's illness and restoration rather than the miraculous provision of the oil and flour that opens her eyes to the power of YHWH through the prophet.

Widow-Woman's Son

The boy is a passive and vulnerable character, always on the edge of existence. When first introduced he is about to starve to death, and in the next scene he has a sickness that leads to death. He is envisaged as quite young—able to be carried up and down stairs. With no voice, and no action, he should be a marginal character, yet in dramatic performance silent characters can have a powerful presence. Elijah's anguish in the face of the boy's apparent death indicates that this is the one character throughout the Elijah Series who has had an emotional connection to the prophet. As the recipient of two life-giving miracles, the widow-woman's son becomes a potent symbol of what is possible when YHWH is invited to become present in the midst of ordinary lives.

Ravens, Jar, Pitcher

The ravens (17:6) and even the inanimate objects jar and pitcher (17:14, 16) are subjects of active verbs and could thus be viewed as characters as well as props in the story. Like the prophet, they are instruments for the provision of YHWH's power.

SETTINGS

The entire Elijah Series begins and ends at the Jordan and therefore on the border of Israelite territory. It is fitting, therefore, that action outside of Israel is as significant as action within Israel. The Prologue is a statement from Elijah to Ahab, and presumably takes place at the palace in Samaria. The rest of Episode 1 is set outside of Israel, but important links are made back to the Israelite worldview. Elijah is directed to the "River Cutting" (17:3), often translated "Wadi Cherith." The Hebrew noun כְּרִית (kᵉrît) is related to the verb כרת (krt) which is the technical term used to describe the making of the covenant ("to cut a covenant"). The setting, therefore, is a reminder of Israel's covenant with YHWH that has been broken by Ahab's behavior. Withdrawing rain is one of the curses for a broken covenant (Deut 28:22–24). Scene 2 is set in Zarephath in Sidon, also in drought. Since this is the homeland of Jezebel and Baal, the fertility god, this setting is a reminder that following after other gods will not bring good things whereas the faithful prophet's presence does guarantee YHWH's abundance in the midst of scarcity.

EMBODIMENT

Two details in this episode highlight the theme of embodiment beyond the presence of YHWH in the faithful performance of his prophet Elijah. First, the miracle of sufficient flour and oil is described this way: "The jar of flour did not finish and the pitcher of oil did not end according to the word of YHWH which he spoke by the hand of Elijah" (17:16). "Speaking by the hand" could imply a written record, or it could reflect a Mediterranean person who is unable to communicate without hand gestures! Either way, the event is an enactment of the spoken promise. The second recorded miracle is the revival of the widow-woman's son, achieved by Elijah stretching out on the lad (17:21). The Septuagint's version is that Elijah "breathed" into the boy three times. The exact nature of this ancient form of CPR is discussed by commentators. Marvin Sweeney describes it as an act of sympathetic magic in which the prophet takes the illness into himself,[21] whereas Simon De Vries believes Elijah is not performing magic but merely a "symbolic act."[22] It is interesting to note that the verb מדד (*mdd*), translated "stretched" can also be translated "measured." In 2 Sam 8:2, King David makes vanquished Moabites lie on the ground and measures them to determine who will be killed and who will be spared. David stretches/measures for death while here Elijah stretches for life!

READY-MADES

"Do not be afraid" (17:13) is a prophetic ready-made, usually classified as a salvation oracle, assuring the listener that YHWH has taken note of their circumstances and will intervene. It comes again in the final episode, but that time addressed *to* the prophet (2 Kgs 1:15). Since it is addressed here to a foreign widow who would probably not understand it as a ready-made, its purpose was undoubtedly to show the original Israelite audience that foreigners are not outside God's care and concern. Likewise, the "day of YHWH" (17:14) is a ready-made expressing judgment or blessing, determined by YHWH. This prophetic ready-made would be well understood by an Israelite audience but perhaps would not be as potent for the Sidonian widow. In both of these instances the audience would see beyond the face value of the phrases and be surprised by their reuse in relation to non-Israelites.

PROPHETIC PERFORMANCE

Elijah's commanding performance in Episode 1 comes through both word and action. The word of YHWH and the word of Elijah are almost indistinguishable (17:1, 14–16, 24), but the prophet's touch is also needed for the miracles (17:16, 21). Elijah's anguished "crying out" and attributing "evil" action to YHWH (17:20) suggests an inner lack of confidence that YHWH will act, but when speaking directly to others Elijah's speech is decisive (17:1, 14, 19a, 23b). The final scene confirms him as a "man of God" who speaks "truth"—establishing Elijah's credentials for the subsequent episodes.

21. Sweeney, *I & II Kings*, 215.
22. De Vries, *I Kings*, 222.

Connections with Episode 1

Several insights may be gained from Episode 1 for an attentive contemporary audience interested in re-enacting prophetic performance in new settings.

The initial episode that introduces this Israelite prophet takes place predominantly in a cross-cultural context. Miracles are enacted on behalf of an impoverished non-Israelite widow and her child. Orphans, widows, and strangers are the quintessential powerless persons in the Hebrew Bible. Recalling that the preclassical prophets were intimately linked to the royal houses, it is significant that Elijah's first acts establishing him as a man of God and connecting him to the life-giving power of YHWH are directed to unimportant, ordinary folk in foreign territory. The particular miracles of abundant food and restored life are a testimony to God's goodness in a world that continues to be marked by economic disparity and child mortality. It was these *acts* of salvation, rather than mere words, which enabled faith to grow for the widow-woman.

An aspect of reenactment is the "abiding astonishment" engendered in audiences who continue to be amazed by miracles that are told over and over, "event[s] retold in the life of the community with an enduring capacity in each rehearing to reopen life to the gifts of God."[23]

One troubling note that emerges in this episode for a contemporary audience is the introduction of Elijah as the "Settler." Israel's modern settlement movement in Palestinian territory purportedly includes an anthem celebrating Elijah.[24] I have chosen to allow this connotation by translating *Tishbi* as "settler," but I believe this performance undermines political support for this settler movement by showing that YHWH's attention is given to non-Israelites.

Elijah Episode 2

"Jezebel Strikes Back"
(1 Kings 18–19)

Cast:

Leading: Narrator, YHWH, Elijah, Obadiah, Ahab

Supporting: Elijah's lad, messenger of Jezebel, messenger of YHWH, Elisha

---

23. Brueggemann, *1 & 2 Kings*, 211.
24. Hazleton, *Jezebel*, 60.

Extras: Prophets of Baal, prophets of Asherah, the people

Offstage: Jezebel, Baal, the other gods

Waiting in the wings: Hazael, Jehu

SCENE 1 (18:1–19)

Setting: On the road—stage right

Narrator

¹And it happened [after] many days the word of YHWH was to Elijah in the third year saying:

YHWH

Go, be seen before Ahab and I will set rain upon the face of the ground.

Narrator

²And he went—Elijah—to be seen before Ahab. And the famine was severe in Samaria.

Setting: On the road—stage left

³And he called—Ahab—to Obadiah who was overseer in the house.

(an aside to the audience)

Now Obadiah was fearing YHWH greatly. ⁴And it happened when Jezebel cut off the prophets of YHWH, he took—Obadiah—a hundred prophets and hid them—fifty men in the cave—and sustained them [with] bread and water.

Ahab

⁵(*) Go in the land to all the springs of the waters and to all the rivers. Perhaps we will find grass and we may keep alive horse and mule and not cut off the livestock.

Narrator

⁶And they divided between themselves the land to cross over her. Ahab went in one way by himself, and Obadiah went in one way by himself.

Setting: On the road—stage right

⁷And it happened Obadiah was on the way and behold! Elijah was calling him. And he recognized him, and he fell on his face, and he said

Obadiah

Is this you—my master Elijah?

Elijah

⁸(*) It is I. Go, tell to your master "Behold! Elijah!"

Obadiah

⁹(*) What? Have I sinned that you would give your servant into the hand of Ahab to kill me? ¹⁰ By the life of YHWH your God, if there is a nation or kingdom where my master has not sent there to seek you, and they say, "not here," he makes the kingdom or the nation swear that he has not found you. ¹¹But now you are saying, "Go, tell to your master, Behold! Elijah!" ¹²And it will happen I will go from you and the spirit of YHWH will lift you to where I don't know and I will come to declare to Ahab and he will not find you and he will slay me! And your servant was fearful of YHWH from my youth! ¹³Has it not been declared to my master what I did in Jezebel's slaughter of the prophets of YHWH? How I hid the prophets of YHWH a hundred men—fifty by fifty men in each cave and I sustained them (with) bread and water? ¹⁴And now you are saying "Go, tell to your master, Behold! Elijah!" But he will slay me!

ס

Elijah

¹⁵(*) By the life of YHWH of hosts, who I am standing before his face, today I will be shown to him.

Narrator

¹⁶And he went—Obadiah—to meet Ahab and he declared to him; and *he* went—Ahab—to meet *Elijah*. ¹⁷And it happened when Ahab was seeing Elijah Ahab said to him:

Ahab

Is this you—the troubler of Israel?

Elijah

18(*) I haven't troubled Israel, but rather you and the house of your fathers, in your forsaking the commandments of YHWH and going after the Baals! 19And now send, gather to me all Israel to Mount Carmel, and prophets of the Baal—four hundred and fifty—and prophets of the Asherah—four hundred—the ones eating at the table of Jezebel.

SCENE 2 (18:20–46)

Setting: Mount Carmel

Narrator

20And he sent—Ahab—for all the sons of Israel; and he gathered the prophets to Mount Carmel. 21And he approached—Elijah—to all the people and he said:

Elijah

Until when will you all be limping between two opinions? If YHWH is the God, go after him and if the Baal, go after him!

Narrator

And the people did not answer him a word. 22And Elijah said to the people

Elijah

I am left a prophet to YHWH alone, but the prophets of the Baal are four hundred and fifty men. 23Let them give to us two bulls and let them choose for themselves one bull and let them cut it in pieces and let them put it on the sticks and let them not put fire. And I will make ready the other bull and I will set it on the sticks and I will not put fire. 24And you will call on the name of your gods, and I will call on the name of YHWH, and let it be the god who answers with fire—he is the God.

Narrator

And all the people answered and they said

People

Good is the word!

Narrator

[25]And Elijah said to the prophets of the Baal

Elijah

Choose for yourselves one bull and prepare it first—surely you are the most. And call on the name of your gods but fire don't put.

Narrator

[26]And they took the bull which he gave to them and they prepared, and they called on the name of the Baal from the morning until the midday saying

Prophets of Baal

The Baal, answer us!

Narrator

But not any voice, and not any answer. And they limped around the altar which he made. [27]And it happened at midday he mocked at them—Elijah—and he said:

Elijah

Call out with surround sound.[25] Surely he is God. Surely a meditation. Or surely doing "his business." Or surely wandering his own way. Perhaps he's asleep. Perhaps he is waking.

Narrator

[28]And they called out with surround sound and they cut themselves like their custom with swords and spears, until blood was pouring out over them. [29]And it happened like passing of the midday they prophesied until the offering of the oblation,[26] but not any voice, and not any answer, and not any response.

[30]And he said—Elijah—to all the people

Elijah

Come near to me

---

25. Attempting to replicate the rhyme in Hebrew: בְקוֹל־גָּדוֹל, *b^eqōl gādōl*.

26. A proper time to give an offering

Narrator

And they came near—all the people—to him. And he healed the altar of YHWH—the one that had been destroyed. [31]And Elijah took twelve stones according to the number of the tribes of the sons of Jacob, to whom had come the word of YHWH saying "Israel will be your name." [32]And he built with the stones an altar in the name of YHWH, and he made a trench like a house of two measures of seed[27] around the altar. [33]And he arranged the sticks, and he cut in pieces the bull which he arranged on the sticks. [34]And he said

Elijah

Fill four jars of water and pour out on the offering and on the sticks. (*) Do it a second time!

Narrator

And they did it a second time.

Elijah

(*) Do it a third time!

Narrator

And they did it a third time. [35]And they went—the waters—around the altar, and also the trench filled with waters. [36]And it happened in offering up the oblation he came near—Elijah the prophet—and said

Elijah

YHWH, God of Abraham, Isaac, and Israel, this day let it be known that you are God in Israel and I your servant. And with your word I have done all these words. [37]Answer me, YHWH, answer me, and they may know—this people— surely you YHWH are the God and you have turned around their hearts backwards.

Narrator

[38]And the fire of YHWH fell and she ate the offering, and the sticks, and the stones, and the dust! And the waters that were in the trench she licked up! [39]And they saw—all the people—and they fell on their faces, and they said

---

27. That is, very large!

All the people

YHWH—he is God! YHWH—he is God!

Elijah

[40](*) Seize the prophets of the Baal—let not a man escape from them!

Narrator

And they seized them, and he brought them down—Elijah—to the River Kishon and he slaughtered them there. [41]Elijah said to Ahab

Elijah

Go up. Eat and drink. Surely the sound of the roar of the deluge.

Narrator

[42]And he went up—Ahab—to eat and to drink. And Elijah went up to the head of the Carmel and he crouched down on the land and he placed his face between his knees. [43]And he said to his lad

Elijah

Go up, please. Observe the way of the sea.

Narrator

And he went up, and he observed, and he said

Lad

Not anything!

Elijah

(*) Return seven times.

Narrator

[44]And it happened on the seventh he said

Lad

Behold! A cloud—tiny—like the hand of a man—coming up from the sea.

Elijah

(*) Go up, say to Ahab, "Hitch up and go down so the deluge won't hold you back."

Narrator

45And it happened by and by that the heavens darkened with clouds and a spirit and there was a great deluge. And he mounted—Ahab—and he went to Jezreel. 46And the hand of YHWH was on Elijah and he girded his loins and he ran before the face of Ahab until you get to Jezreel.

SCENE 3 (19:1–3)

Setting: Samaria

Narrator

1And he declared—Ahab—to Jezebel all that he—Elijah—did, and all whom he slew—all the prophets—with the sword. 2And she sent—Jezebel—a messenger to Elijah to say

Messenger of Jezebel

Thus let the gods do and thus let them add to what they do if by this time tomorrow I [have not] put your breath like the breath of one of them.[28]

Narrator

3And he saw,[29] and he got up, and he went for his breath, and he came to Beer-Sheba which belongs to Judah, and he left his lad there.

SCENE 4 (19:4–8)

Setting: The Wilderness

28. A reference to her own prophets slain by Elijah.

29. Some manuscripts read "and he was afraid" (וַיִּרָא, *wayyirāʾ*) instead of "and he saw" (וַיַּרְא, *wayyareʾ*) here. "Afraid" is appropriate in the context and could have been changed by later transcribers who could not accept a fearful Elijah. Notice, however, that Elijah is described as "afraid" in 2 Kgs 1:15, undermining this proposal of editorial manipulation. So "saw" could also be accepted as the original intention. We know from the Episode II (Series 3) that Jezebel communicated by letter, which is perhaps how the message was delivered in this situation also.

Narrator

⁴And he went into the wilderness, on the way for a day, and he came and he sat under a solitary *rothem*.³⁰ And he asked his breath to die, and he said

Elijah

Too much now YHWH. Take my breath because no better am I than my fathers.

Narrator

⁵And he lay down and fell asleep under a solitary *rothem*. And behold! This messenger touching him and he said to him

Messenger of YHWH

Get up! Eat!

Narrator

⁶And he observed and behold! At his head a loaf of hot coals and a pitcher of water. And he ate and he drank and he turned and he lay down. ⁷And he turned—the messenger of YHWH—a second time and he touched on him and he said

Messenger of YHWH

Get up! Eat! For too much from you is the way.

Narrator

⁸And he got up and he ate and he drank, and he went in the strength of that eating forty days and forty nights until the mountain of God—Horeb.

SCENE 5 (19:9–18)

Setting: Mount Horeb

Narrator

⁹And he came there to the cave and he spent the night there. And behold! The word of YHWH to him and he said to him

---

30. There is much speculation in commentaries as to the identity of this plant. It has been transliterated in the Septuagint, and I have also settled for a transliteration.

YHWH

What are you doing here Elijah?

Elijah

[10](*) Zealously zealous[31] have I been for YHWH the god of hosts while *they* have forsaken your covenant—the sons of Israel: your altars they threw, your prophets they slew[32]—with the sword—and I am left, I alone, and they are seeking my breath to take it.

YHWH

[11](*) Go out and stand on the mountain before the face of YHWH. And behold! YHWH is passing.

Narrator

And a spirit—great and strong—tearing away mountains and breaking cliffs before the face of YHWH. But not in the spirit was YHWH. And after the spirit an earthquake. Not in the earthquake was YHWH. [12]And after the earthquake, fire. Not in the fire was YHWH. And after the fire a sound *demāmāh daqqāh*.[33] [13]And when he heard—Elijah—he wrapped his face in his cloak and he went out and he stood at the entrance of the cave, and behold! To him a sound. And he said

YHWH

What are you doing here Elijah?

Elijah

[14](*) Zealously zealous have I been for YHWH the god of hosts while *they* have forsaken your covenant—the sons of Israel: your altars they threw, your prophets they slew—with the sword—and I am left, I alone, and they are seeking my breath to take it.

ס

31. Two verbs of the same root for emphasis.

32. Attempting to replicate the rhyme in Hebrew: אֶת־מִזְבְּחֹתֶיךָ הָרָסוּ וְאֶת־נְבִיאֶיךָ הָרְגוּ, *ʾet-mizbᵉ ḥōteykā hārāsû weʾet-nebiyʾeykā hāregû*.

33. A rhyming phrase often translated "still, small" or "calm, soft" but arguably could also be translated "roaring and thundering." Translation will determine performance. See discussion below.

YHWH

¹⁵(*) Go. Return to your way to the wilderness of Damascus, and come and anoint Hazael as king over Aram. ¹⁶And Jehu son of Nimshi you shall anoint as king over Israel, and Elisha son of Shaphat from Abel Meholah you shall anoint as prophet under you. ¹⁷And it will be that the escaper from the sword of Hazael—Jehu will kill, and the escaper of the sword of Jehu—Elisha will kill. ¹⁸But I will cause to remain in Israel seven thousand—all the knees that have not bowed down to the Baal and every mouth that has not kissed to him.

SCENE 6 (19:19–21)

Setting: Abel Meholah (Elisha's hometown)

Narrator

¹⁹And he went from there and he found Elisha son of Shaphat and he was ploughing twelve teams before his face and he was with the twelfth, and he passed—Elijah—on him and he threw his cloak on him. ²⁰And he left the cattle and he ran after Elijah and he said

Elisha

Let me kiss, please, to my father and to my mother and let me go after you.

Elijah

(*) Go! Return! For what have I done to you?

Narrator

²¹And he returned from following after him and he took a team of the cattle and he sacrificed them with the trappings of the cattle. He boiled the flesh and he gave to the people and they ate. Then he rose and he went after Elijah and he served him.

פ

Creativity in Episode 2

The composition of Episode 2 is entertaining, with the showdown on Mount Carmel especially being described as presented in a "leisurely, playful way,"[34] "suspenseful" and "comic,"[35] and "redolent with irony."[36] The contrasting themes introduced in Episode 1 continue here, namely, famine and abundance, death and life, up and down, skepticism and faith. With the multiplication of prophets in this episode, both Yahwistic and Canaanite, there is a new and significant theme of prophecy and power. This will be further discussed under "Connections" below.

A number of examples of wordplay can be found in this episode, drawing attention to the playful character of the composition. Elijah mocks the prophets of Baal (18:27) with alliteration ("call out with surround sound") and euphemisms that are not unfamiliar to English speakers even when translated from the Hebrew (with the possible exception of the reference to "meditation," which may mean defecating in a field [cf. Gen 24:63]). Only the last of Elijah's six suggestions uses a verbal form. The very grammar specifies that Baal is a god who can't act.

Wordplay is also found in the more serious latter scenes in the episode. Elijah's protest is that he has been "zealously zealous" even though others had forsaken the covenant: "your altars they threw, your prophets they slew" (19:10, 14). And the passing of YHWH is noted in the "voice of *dᵉmāmāh daqqāh*"—a rhyming phrase difficult to translate. Since this is often considered the high point of the Elijah cycle, it is worth commenting on the possible variations. "Still small voice" (KJV) or "sound of sheer silence" (NRSV) are poetically and theologically popular translations. As J. Lust argues, however, this unusual phrase could justifiably be translated "[a] roaring and thundering voice."[37] In other theophanic texts, the "voice" (קוֹל, *qôl*) of YHWH is understood as thunder.[38] The similarities to Moses and the theophany on Mount Sinai (Exod 19) and the natural expectation that thunder follows lightning (fire) support Lust's conclusion. And yet Scripture supports YHWH's presence in both thunder *and* silence. In the context of a contest between YHWH and the Baals—the storm gods—the "still small voice" may have greater impact, although Elijah's lack of reaction makes even that conclusion uncertain! Translation will determine performance.

---

34. Brueggemann, *1 & 2 Kings*, 219.

35. Matthews, *Social World of the Hebrew Prophets*, 55.

36. Petersen, *The Prophetic Literature*, 231.

37. Lust, "A Gentle Breeze?," 113.

38. Amos 1:2; Pss 18:13; 29:3; 46:6; 68:33; 77:18; 104:7.

Use of Repetition

Irony is highlighted throughout the episode by repetition of words and phrases. Just after the narrator tells the audience that Jezebel has "cut off" the prophets of YHWH (18:4), Ahab is concerned about "cutting off" his livestock (18:5). Obadiah relates how he had hidden a hundred prophets (in groups of fifty!) and sustained them with bread and water, repeating both the narrator's earlier aside to the audience (18:3) and YHWH's earlier sustaining of Elijah (17:13). Both Obadiah and Ahab greet Elijah with the phrase "Is this you?" (18:7, 17), but whereas Obadiah was welcoming, Ahab is accusing. Ahab calls Elijah a "troubler of Israel," only to have the term thrown back in his own face: "I haven't troubled Israel, but rather you . . ." (18:17–18). After "not answering a word" (18:21), the people respond to Elijah's plan in unison: "good is the word" (18:24b). Elijah allows the prophets of the Baal to go first in the contest, highlighting their lengthy lack of success. He challenges them to "call out with surround sound" (18:27), and they do exactly that (18:28) but to no avail. The negative particle אֵין (*'ēyn*, "not any") is used five times in three verses (18:26–29), emphasizing the lack of response from the Baals. By contrast, Elijah's preparations are exaggerated by repetition of his instructions to fill the huge trench with water again and again, resulting in a spectacularly successful conflagration that even consumed the highly symbolic stones. The response of all the people is the repeated exclamation "YHWH, he is God!" The coming of the deluge requires seven observations, and then the tiniest cloud heralds a massive downpour (18:43–45). The repetition of "breath" (נֶפֶשׁ, *nefeš*) in Scenes 3 and 4 raises the question of whether life is truly at the behest of YHWH or subject to Jezebel's power (19:2, 3, 4). YHWH's messenger twice touches Elijah and twice instructs him to "Get up! Eat!" (19:5, 7). The second time, the messenger repeats Elijah's own word of protest: "too much" (רַב, *rab*), underscoring the unwelcome assurance that "too much" is indeed Elijah's calling (19:4, 7). The exchange between YHWH and Elijah on Mount Horeb is repeated exactly (19:9b–10, 13b–14), in ironic reversal of the expectation that a manifestation of YHWH (19:11–12) would change the prophet. His single-minded zeal, emphasized by two verbs of the same root (קַנֹּא קִנֵּאתִי, *qanno' qinnē'tî*), continues into the next scene where Elisha is described following "after" him four times in two verses (19:20–21). The inevitability of YHWH's intervention into the political events of the day is stressed by the repetition "the escaper from the sword of Hazael—Jehu will kill, and the escaper of the sword of Jehu—Elisha will kill" (19:17).

Commentary on Episode 2

EPISODE-SPECIFIC CHARACTERS

The Prophet Obadiah

Obadiah's name means "servant of Yah," and he claims to have been a fol-lower of YHWH from youth (18:12), but the repetition of the terms "master" and "servant" in the dialogue raise the question of whose servant he really is: Ahab's, Elijah's, or YHWH's? Despite being in the employment of Ahab, Obadiah calls Elijah "my master" and refers to himself as "your servant." When Elijah responds, "go tell your master" (meaning Ahab), he is possibly speaking sarcastically. In performance his tone of voice would tell us.

Obadiah's long protest is, in fact, the longest speech in the episode. In it he shows both insecurities and a tendency to overdramatize. Despite his claims, he seems to not really trust either Elijah or YHWH, and his concern that "he [Ahab] would kill me" has become "he will slay me" by the end of the speech. He ensures that Elijah knows his credentials by repeating what the narrator has already told us (18:13; cf. 18:4). The *setumah* that comes after this speech allows Elijah and the audience time for this to sink in, but little reassurance is given to Obadiah other than a repetition of the same oath he used. The resulting events are somewhat of an anticlimax: nothing happens to Obadiah despite his dramatic assertion (twice!) that he would be slain. In fact, he fades away into obscurity, and no more direct mention is made of the prophets he saved.

It is the narrator's approval and Obadiah's actions that add depth to the character revealed by his speech. His hiding and sustaining of one hundred prophets of YHWH (18:4, 13) equates or perhaps even surpasses the action of YHWH, who had sustained the single prophet Elijah (1 Kgs 17:4, 9; 19:5, 7). His quiet, behind-the-scenes action is shown to be just as effective as Elijah's confrontational showdown.[39]

The Prophet Elisha

Elisha is briefly introduced in this episode, but we will learn much more about him in Episode 4 and then his own spin-off series! His name means "my god saves," and his later ministry will show that saving power as well as destructive power available due to the prophetic role of divine

39. There is no historical or literary evidence linking this character to the prophetic book with the same name in the Book of the Twelve. The name is found in several genealogical lists in 1–2 Chr so is not an uncommon name.

intermediary. Unlike Elijah, Elisha is grounded in family, place, and occupation before being swept up in Elijah's movement. We know his father's
name and his home location, we know that ploughing with twelve teams
suggests he was a man of wealth and security, and we know that he felt
some commitment to his family (father *and* mother) since he asks to be
allowed to kiss them before following after Elijah (19:20). He persists in
following despite Elijah's ambiguous response to this request to farewell his
family: "Go! Return! For what have I done to you?" (19:20b). Commentaries vary in their understanding of this as a rebuke or permission—tone of
voice in performance would make it clear. Nonetheless, Elisha knows that
Elijah has done something to him—he has thrown his cloak over the in-
tuitive prophet, who understands his call-without-words and realizes that
nothing less than complete commitment is required.

The Prophets of Baal and Asherah

The use of the term *prophet* for religious functionaries of Baal and Asherah
as well as for Yahwistic adherents puts the characters on an equal footing.
The lack of effectiveness of these prophets, however, suggests that the label is
being used satirically. One could not doubt the enthusiasm of the prophets
of Baal for their role: their limping around the altar, calling out, and cutting
themselves over many hours until blood ran suggests a "zeal" even greater
than that claimed by Elijah (18:26, 28; cf. 19:10, 14).

With no lines in the script, however, this behavior is attributed to them
by the narrator and could be exaggerated for dramatic purpose. The prophets were "seized" and "slaughtered" with no recorded protest and the action
continues on without a break. As characters in this performance they are
not to be taken too seriously.

The Messenger of YHWH

This crowded episode introduces a messenger of YHWH who acts in place
of YHWH himself. Since the same title, מַלְאָךְ (*mal⁾āk*), is given to Jezebel's
messenger sent to deliver her ominous warning to Elijah, this character acts
as a foil to that other messenger. Where Jezebel's messenger, in the name of
her gods, threatens death, YHWH's messenger offers the means for life—
both mental and physical sustenance. Despite the delivery of the message
in imperatives and the repetition of Elijah's own protest "too much," the
messenger of YHWH comes across as caring and concerned, physically
touching Elijah and providing for him.

Elijah's Lad

This is a bit part that does not allow much character development. We never hear from where the lad came or what his fate is after being left behind at the edge of the wilderness by Elijah (19:3). Could he have been the widow-woman's son with whom Elijah had developed a significant relationship? This can only be speculation. But he has a significant role towards the end of Scene 2 of this episode, heralding the end of the long drought. When first instructed to "observe the way of the sea" he responds with that negative particle אַיִן (ʾēyn, "not any"), used so often earlier in the scene. Is there a suggestion that, despite the fire, the adulation of the people, and the victorious slaughter of prophets of Baal, there is still uncertainty as to whether YHWH is capable of bringing the rain? We can picture him running between the view and Elijah seven times before being able to describe "A cloud—tiny—like the hand of a man—coming up from the sea" (18:44). The exclamatory particle הִנֵּה (hinnēh)—"Behold"—expresses the relief that at last there is something to report. The lad seems to be necessary in this scene to allow Elijah's odd crouched stance with hidden face (18:42). The performative nature of this gesture is discussed further below.

Other Characters

The fact that the Baal and Jezebel's other gods remain offstage is highlighted in this episode by the desire that they come *on*stage. The great efforts of the prophets of Baal have no effect, and the audience is titillated by the goading of Elijah, imagining several unflattering postures for the Baal and decreasing any residual awe. Jezebel attempts to reignite the menace that the Baal's power should pose, but her own claim, "*I* will put your breath like the breath of one of them" (19:2) proves that she is the greater power to be feared.

In this episode there are two characters waiting in the wings. YHWH commissions the royal anointing of Hazael of Aram and Jehu of Israel—the latter clearly to be a successor to Ahab although not one from his own family dynasty.

Settings

Episode 2 is the longest in the Elijah Series, comprising six scenes. Scene 1 takes place on the road, but four separate dialogues—between YHWH and Elijah, Obadiah and Ahab, Obadiah and Elijah, and Ahab and Elijah—require localized settings. Following conventional cultural association linking "right" with "good" and "left" with "bad" I have characterized "stage right" as the location for Elijah's encounters, and "stage left" for the introduction of Ahab to the action.

With only two *setumahs* in sixty-seven verses (1 Kgs 18:14; 19:14), the action rushes on from one event to the next. Scene 2 comprises two different events, but both take place on Mount Carmel. Carmel (כַּרְמֶל) in Hebrew is equivalent to *kerem-el*, "vineyard of God," linking it to the setting for Episode 3. The momentum of Elijah's presence builds up through the first two scenes, resulting in both Jezebel's fury and Elijah's self-doubt. A brief scene in Samaria is followed by a long scene set in the wilderness where Elijah has escaped in self-imposed exile. The second *setumah* comes after Elijah's repeated speech defending his presence at Mount Horeb (19:15–18). This speech, presented twice, comes across as defensive and overdramatic. During the speech Elijah's persecutors grow from one queen to "the sons of Israel" who have thrown down YHWH's altars, slain YHWH's prophets, and are now seeking Elijah's own life. In his response to YHWH, Elijah reiterates his claim to be the only prophet who is zealous for YHWH (see 18:22) even though the audience has met the faithful Obadiah and heard of the hundred prophets of YHWH hidden by Obadiah. Since Elijah's speech is exactly the same as his first speech, prior to YHWH's theophanic revelation, the *setumah* implies a pause, perhaps of frustration on the part of YHWH, who may be wondering why nothing has changed for his prophet. YHWH then changes tack and sends him off on new missions, including anointing a new prophet, and mentions the seven thousand faithful YHWH adherents in Israel. The final scene is named for Elisha's hometown—Abel Meholah—but since Elijah passes through with barely a broken step, it could as easily have been characterized as "On the road—stage right"!

Prophetic Performance

In Episode 2, Elijah adds showmanship to his commanding prophetic performance. He moves from being a prophet who lives in solitude or within the household of one humble foreigner to a public persona, on display to "all the sons of Israel" and hundreds of prophets of Baal (18:20). Ahab preempts this new public face of Elijah's in their private meeting on the road by accusing him of being a "troubler"—one who disturbs the peace.

Initially the performance had entertainment value of the nature of "street theater." Elijah's accusation of the people elicited no word, but his suggestion of a prophetic showdown received enthusiasm from the people: "Good is the word" (18:24). The people were up for a show! And like a showman, Elijah exaggerates the contest, drawing out the time allowed for the larger group to achieve their magic, making his own scenario as difficult as possible, but in this case to prove there is no deception or hoax. The public prayer to YHWH shows that what is happening is more than just words. The whole event puts the crowd in a spin, as he prays: "May they know—this people—surely you YHWH are the God and you have turned around their hearts backwards" (19:37). Elijah's success achieves his aim of showing the Israelites which god has most power, but he takes advantage of their enthusiastic affirmation by commanding them to seize and slaughter the unsuccessful prophets. Suddenly the show turns serious—a "winner-take-all" contest where the losers are executed. Is this a troubling or inevitable outcome in a prophetic showdown?

Another form of prophetic performance is seen in this episode also. The quieter style of Obadiah forms a contrast to Elijah's confrontational showmanship. The fact that Obadiah is at the same time an employee in the royal household means that his ministry should be regarded in a different category, as suggested by Walter Brueggemann:

> He is a deeply devoted Yahwist and a loyal follower of Elijah, that is, holding to the 'Yahweh-alone' faith of the prophet. Thus he is for the prophetic movement an insider figure, ostensibly serving Ahab but in fact service precisely the cause that means to subvert and delegitimate the king who practices Baalism. His odd and important position as an undercover agent for Yahwism is never explicitly stated but only given us in the process of the narrative. To be a 'servant of YHWH,' according to this narrative, is to resist the king and his policies.[40]

Embodiment

Elijah's performance on Mount Carmel has earned him the reputation of literally producing the water that comes "because of my mouth, my word" (1 Kgs 17:1). Jewish midrash claims that Elijah commanded his servant to pour water over his fingers as he prepared for the celestial fire to consume the sacrifice, and the water flowed from his fingers to drench the altar and everything on it.[41] But the action that resulted in the deluge from the heavens later in the story is a curled posture with covered eyes—an extremely

---

40. Brueggemann, *1 & 2 Kings*, 221.

41. Hyman, "Elijah: Accuser and Defender," 284. See 2 Kgs 3:11 for a text supporting this interpretation.

embodied form of prayer! Moreover, this posture contrasts with other accounts of Elijah in the presence of YHWH. When he stood before the face of YHWH at the entrance of the cave, albeit with face covered, we are reminded that he introduced himself as the one who stands before YHWH (1 Kgs 17:1), In Episode 2, however, it took some effort to come and stand again. After escaping to the wilderness he sat under a Rothem tree, then lay down on the ground and had to be roused twice before moving on. Then he spent the night in the cave, was told to go and stand at the entrance but not until after the climactic events are we told that he "went out and stood at the entrance of the cave" (1 Kgs 19:13).

When actions take place without words, there is a greater attention to performance. It was the "hand of YHWH" on Elijah that enabled him to run ahead of Ahab's chariot (1 Kgs 18:46). Elijah throws his cloak over Elisha without explanation, so the meaning of this action must have been understood by both potential prophet and audience. There are also a few clues in the script that gesture accompanies words. In the wake of Jezebel's threat via the messenger (1 Kgs 19:3), the narrator tells us "he *saw*, and he got up, and he went for his breath." Perhaps that message had been accompanied by a threatening, throat-slitting gesture to give the message that she wanted his death, not his life.

A final poignant example of embodiment is the touch of YHWH's messenger (1 Kgs 19:5–7). Jezebel wanted to get hold of him and he escaped her clutches, but once alone was prepared to give up the fight. At this point in the drama the touch of the messenger of YHWH is nurturing and protective. Nevertheless, a second touch is needed for Elijah to be convinced he should continue on.

READY-MADES

A number of ready-mades enable the audience to grasp the significance of the prophet's performance in this episode. Elijah's taunting of the prophets of Baal on Mount Carmel probably drew on Ugaritic epic literature portraying the hero on long journeys, or Canaanite rituals associated with ending the summer drought.[42] The challenge to the people—"until when will you all be limping between two opinions?" (1 Kgs 18:21)—may have been deliberately recalling covenant language. The verb for "limping" is פסח—using the same consonants as Pesach (Passover). Is Elijah employing a ready-made in order to discomfort his audience, reminding them of a choice they made long ago to be followers of the Passover God? Likewise, his choice of twelve stones

42. Sweeney, *1 & 2 Kings*, 228.

in the altar clearly evokes the twelve tribes, as does Elisha's twelve teams of oxen. Elijah prays to the God of Abraham, Isaac and Israel, another reference to the Torah tradition. And his slaughter of the prophets of Baal recalled the law relating to treatment of false prophets (Deut 13:1–5).

Numbers act as ready-mades in the Hebrew Bible. The use of the number 7 (seven) and the accompanying "spirit" (רוּחַ, *rûaḥ*, often translated "wind") at the end of Scene 2 evokes the Genesis creation tradition. Elijah's forty days and nights in the wilderness and his encounter on Mount Horeb are ready-mades for the audience, linking him to the great prophet Moses.

In this episode Elijah is instructed to anoint two kings and a prophet. Anointing is a powerful symbolic gesture uniting political and religious realms and would remind the audience of the importance of the prophetic role in Israel's monarchic system. What would be surprising, however, is YHWH's instruction to Elijah to anoint a non-Israelite king! And, even more surprising with this zealous prophet, Elijah is never depicted carrying out the task!

Props that act as ready-mades in this episode include the fire, cloak, loaf, and pitcher. All have appeared or will appear in other episodes. No longer a character now, the pitcher along with the loaf from Episode 1 (1 Kgs 17:13) nonetheless has a role, with both pitcher and loaf functioning as ready-mades for Elijah to remind him that he is not out of God's concern (1 Kgs 19:6). Fire from heaven is the proof of God's true presence (1 Kgs 18:24) and will be important in Episode 4 as a link between Elijah's prophetic identity and YHWH's heavenly presence. It is all the more surprising, then, that the claim is made "not in the fire was YHWH" (1 Kgs 19:12). Does this claim undermine the symbolic role of fire elsewhere? Elijah's cloak is a significant ready-made, reminding the audience that the garments of prophets both identify them and have power to bring about change.

Audience Engagement

Along with the ready-mades already discussed, the audience is especially engaged in the action by the narrator's explanatory asides (1 Kgs 18:3–4, 28–29) and exclamatory comments (1 Kgs 18:7; 19:5, 6, 9, 13). At the end of Scene 2 the grammatical construct is notable: "And the hand of YHWH was on Elijah and he girded his loins and he ran before the face of Ahab until *you get* to Jezreel" (1 Kgs 18:46). The second-person pronominal suffix on the infinitive indicates a turning to the audience directly—their local knowledge of the distance between locations would impress upon them the extent of Elijah's feat.

Connections with Episode 2

The "Battle of the Gods" comes palpably to the fore in Episode 2. The producer's bias is evident, however, since Baalism is not presented even-handedly. The choice offered by Elijah to the people (1 Kgs 18:21) can only be met with silence since tolerance and compromise are not possible in Elijah's world. The contest suggested by Elijah proved that there is no basis to the belief that one can manipulate the gods by ritual, volume, or self-destructive behavior. On the other hand, Elijah's taunting and mocking cannot be a model for interfaith dialogue, and his slaughter of the prophets is an event that, while not unexpected given the precedence of laws relating to false prophets, should raise questions about unbridled power.

The issue of power dominates this episode. YHWH's power is displayed in different ways. The fire falling as a result of Elijah's spoken prayer demonstrates the power of YHWH over the powerlessness of the Baals. YHWH's power is available to Elijah for strength and sustenance (1 Kgs 18:46; 19:8). But the demonstration of YHWH's presence at the cave on Mount Horeb insists that YHWH is *not* present in the destructive spirit, earthquake, or fire. Rather, YHWH is present in a sound of enigmatic quality (1 Kgs 19:11–12). Perhaps this is the significance of the cave encounter immediately after the triumph on Mount Carmel. In response to Elijah's testimony that he has been "zealously zealous" for God, there is a theophany—Elijah is invited to consider what sort of God he is following. Not one who acts destructively, but one who speaks. Elijah's renewed protest in exactly the same words as if nothing had happened suggests he may not have understood the subtle lesson, and his calling down fire for destruction of more enemies in Episode 4 also raises the question of any transformed understanding.[43] Yet when he harnesses the power of YHWH in Episode 1 and Episode 3, it is in order to aid the powerless—a widow-woman and her son and a humble Israelite landholder.

The other sort of power under consideration is power enacted by humans in the name of ideology. Jezebel, although offstage in this episode, has demonstrated destructive power that gives rise to much of the action. Her slaughter of the prophets of YHWH (1 Kgs 18:13) was no doubt in order to establish her own cultic practice in Israel. Elijah initially confronts this power in a very public way, even emulating it, then runs from it. The

43. Indeed later reenactments of this story modify Elijah's response and YHWH's reassurance. In Josephus, for example, Elijah does not repeat his response, and instead God's voice is heard again: "and when all became quiet, a divine voice exhorted him not to be alarmed by what was happening, for none of his enemies should have him in their power" (Josephus, *Antiquities of the Jews*, 8.13.7 §§ 347–54).

character Obadiah illustrates another valid path in defying human power—the practice of "civil disobedience." Despite the terror evident in his speech (1 Kgs 18:9–14), Obadiah has taken risks for his faith and successfully preserves a hundred lives. Elijah wants Obadiah to own his Yahwistic faith more publicly, asking him to announce allegiance to Elijah (1 Kgs 18:8), but the narrated voiceover lets us know that both public opposition and private undermining can be effective in bringing about justice.[44]

Elijah Episode 3

"PREQUEL—The Foreign Menace"

(1 Kings 21)

Characters:

Leading: Narrator, Ahab, Naboth, Jezebel, YHWH, Elijah

Supporting: Elders and Nobles of Jezreel, Sons of Beliyya'el

Extras: The People

Waiting in the wings: Dogs, Carrion birds

SCENE 1 (21:1–3)

Setting: Naboth's Vineyard

Narrator

[1]And it happened after these words a vineyard was to Naboth the Jezreelite which was in Jezreel, beside the palace of Ahab King of Samaria. [2]And he spoke—Ahab—to Naboth saying

Ahab

Give to me your vineyard and let him be for me a garden of greens because he is nearby—beside—my house and I will give to you instead of him a vineyard better than him, or if it is good in your eyes I will give to you silver to the value of this.

Naboth

[3](*) To hell with it![45] To me from YHWH it was given—to me! The inheritance of my fathers to you??

---

44. I am indebted to Dr John Harris for this insight, discussed early in my conception of this project.

45. This particle is usually translated "far be it," but it shares a root with the verb חלל meaning "to profane" or "to defile."

SCENE 2 (21:4–10)

Setting: THE PALACE, SAMARIA

Narrator

⁴And he went in—Ahab—to his house, sore⁴⁶ and sullen over the word which he spoke to him—Naboth the Jezreelite—and he said "I will not give to you the inheritance of my fathers." And he lay down on his bed and he turned around his face and he did not eat bread. ⁵And she came to him—Jezebel his wife—and she spoke to him

Jezebel

What is this? Your spirit sore and you're not eating bread?

Ahab

⁶(*) Because I spoke to Naboth the Jezreelite and I said to him "give to me your vineyard for silver or if it pleases you let me give to you a vineyard other than him." And he said "I will not give to you my vineyard."

Jezebel

⁷(*) You, right now, are making a kingdom over Israel. Get up, eat bread, and let your heart be good. I will give to you the vineyard of Naboth the Jezreelite.

Narrator

⁸And she wrote letters in the name of Ahab and she sealed with his seal, and she sent the letters to the elders and to the nobles who were in his city, sitting with Naboth. ⁹And she wrote in the letter saying

> Call a fast and make him sit—Naboth—at the head
> of the people. ¹⁰And make sit two men, sons of
> Beliyya'el,⁴⁷ in front of him and let them charge him
> saying "you have 'blessed' God and the King.' And
> dethrone him and stone him⁴⁸ and let him die.

---

46. The Hebrew word סַר, *sar*, can be approximated by the English translation "sore."

47. That is, "worthlessness," "wickedness," "uselessness." A "son of Beliyya'el is a known troublemaker and scoundrel (Deut 13:13).

48. Attempting to capture the wordplay of the Hebrew: וְהוֹצִיאֻהוּ וְסִקְלֻהוּ, *wᵉhôṣîʾuhû wᵉsiqᵉluhû.*

SCENE 3 (21:11–13)

Setting: Jezreel

Narrator

[11]And they did—the men of the city—the elders and the nobles—the ones sitting in his city—as she sent to them—Jezebel. As was written in the letters which she sent to them. [12]They called a fast and they made him sit—Naboth—at the head of the people. [13]And they came—two of the men—sons of Beliyya'el—and they sat in front of him and they charged him—the men of Beliyya'el—Naboth—in front of the people—saying

Sons of Beliyya'el

He "blessed"—Naboth—God and the King![49]

Narrator

And they took him out—outside of the city—and they stoned him with rocks[50] and he died.

SCENE 4 (21:14–16)

Setting: The Palace, Samaria

Narrator

[14]And they sent to Jezebel saying

Elders and Nobles of Jezreel

He is stoned—Naboth—and he is dead.

Narrator

[15]And it happened when Jezebel heard that he was stoned—Naboth—and he died, she said—Jezebel—to Ahab

Jezebel

Get up. Possess the vineyard of Naboth the Jezreelite which he refused to give to you for silver because nothing is Naboth's life. Because he died!

49. The euphemistic "bless" that actually means "curse."
50. The verb and the noun have different roots.

Narrator

16And it happened when Ahab heard that he died—Naboth—he got up—Ahab—to go down to the vineyard of Naboth the Jezreelite to possess him.

ס

SCENE 5 (21:17–28)

Setting: Naboth's Vineyard

Narrator

17And it happened the word of YHWH to Elijah the Settler saying

YHWH

18Get up, go down to meet Ahab king of Israel who is in Samaria. Behold! He is in the vineyard of Naboth where he went down there to possess him. 19And you shall speak to him saying "thus says YHWH—have you murdered and also possessed?" And you shall speak to him saying "thus says YHWH—in the place where they licked up—the dogs—the blood of Naboth, and they will lick up—the dogs—your blood, also you!"

Narrator

And he said—Ahab—to Elijah

Ahab

20Have you found me, my enemy?

Elijah

(*) I have found on account of your selling yourself to do evil in the eyes of YHWH. 21Behold me bringing on you evil, and I will sweep away after you. And I will cut off from Ahab each one who pisses against a wall[51] both fettered and free[52] in Israel. 22And I will give your house like the house of Jeroboam son of Nebat and like the house of Baasha son

---

51. An idiom used several times in the Hebrew Bible, not usually translated literally (but see KJV).

52. Attempting to capture the wordplay of the Hebrew: וְעָצוּר וְעָזוּב, *wᵉʿāṣûr wᵉʿāzûb*.

of Ahijah, for the provocation which you have provoked and you have caused Israel to sin.

Narrator

²³And also to Jezebel he spoke—YHWH—saying

YHWH (or Elijah?)

The dogs will eat Jezebel in the ramparts of Jezreel. ²⁴The dead belonging to Ahab in the city the dogs will eat and the dead in the fields the fowl of the heavens will eat.

Narrator (an aside to the audience)

²⁵Indeed there was not (anyone) like Ahab who sold himself to do evil in the eyes of YHWH, [and indeed there was not anyone like] she who incited him—Jezebel his wife. ²⁶And he made abominations great, walking after the turdy idols[53] like all that they did—the Amorites—who YHWH had dispossessed before the faces of the sons of Israel.

ס

Narrator

²⁷And it happened when Ahab heard these words he tore his clothes and he put on sackcloth on his flesh and he fasted. And he lay down in the sackcloth and he went around meekly. ²⁸And it happened the word of YHWH to Elijah the Settler saying

YHWH

Have you seen that he humbled himself—Ahab—before my face? On account of that humbling before my face I will not bring the evil in his days; in the days of his son I will bring the evil on his house.

Creativity in Episode 3

This episode contains ambiguity, irony, and some humor, despite its sobering subject matter. In characterizing this episode as a prequel (see below), I am suggesting that its purpose is to fill in a backstory in order to paint Jezebel's character as "the foreign menace" (the title of this episode). Jezebel

53. See Chapter 5 on Ezekiel for explanation of this translation: page 162.

is the main character, pulling all the strings, working behind the scenes. She is never in direct dialogue with anyone other than her husband. Her other communication is in writing, and even when we are told that YHWH spoke "to Jezebel" (1 Kgs 21:23), the speech that follows speaks of her in the third person and not directly. Though hidden, Jezebel's methods are not subtle. She speaks in imperatives and acts with the power of a queen, and expects Ahab to do the same. The elders of Jezreel are ordered to find men whose very name, sons of Beliyya'el, indicates their willingness to do someone else's dirty work. They are told to accuse Naboth of "blessing" God and King, a euphemism understood to everyone. Following the death of Naboth, Jezebel assumes that Ahab now has the right to possess the vineyard and orders him to get up and do so. Her job is done.

Given the patriarchal nature of biblical literature, this episode equally damns Ahab as deceitful, ineffectual, and weak. He becomes a pathetic character, refusing to interact or eat, "sore and sullen" (1 Kgs 21:4–5). When questioned by Jezebel about the cause of his discontent, he omits important information about Naboth's inheritance, merely claiming that his subject has refused fair payment or exchange for his land. Jezebel reminds him that he is a king, and orders him to cheer up. Later when she tells him of Naboth's death, he seems to not understand her subtle "Nothing is Naboth's life" (1 Kgs 21:15) until she adds "because he is dead"! All seems to be resolved at the end of Scene 4, and a *setumah* creates a pause in the action, perhaps indicating some time has passed before YHWH refuses to let Ahab get away with his possession of Naboth's vineyard. One can sense the frustration in Ahab's greeting of Elijah at the very scene of the crime: "Have you found me, my enemy?" (1 Kgs 21:20). Elijah is an unwelcome, if inevitable, presence for the king of Israel.

There is subtle ambiguity in this episode. In order for the desired vineyard to become available, Naboth is charged with "blessing" God and the king—making use of a euphemism evident to all that "cursing" is the intended charge. Cursing of God and king amounts to a charge of treason. Naboth's response to Ahab ("to hell with it!" 1 Kgs 21:3) and the use of "Elohim" (a generic word for gods) rather than YHWH raises the possibility that the charge is justifiable—Naboth's refusal was in the name of YHWH, but the kingdom at that time, and probably its king, was deferring to the gods venerated by Jezebel. When Elijah brings judgment on Ahab on behalf of YHWH for this event, the indictment is not only for murder and dispossession, but also for leading Israel into apostasy (1 Kgs 21:19, 22). Yet, even if Jezebel is accusing Naboth of flouting laws relating to the Baals and is unaware of Israelite property laws, she cleverly uses the Israelite law to her advantage by ensuring that two witnesses accuse him (see Deut 19:15).

In Scene 5 the word of YHWH comes to Elijah, instructing him to find Ahab and repeat specific oracles (two oracles introduced with "Thus says YHWH"). But rather than repeating these words as would be expected of an envoy, Elijah paraphrases and adds to them, adopting a crude idiom underscored by wordplay to stress the totality of the sentence against Ahab: "And I will cut off from Ahab each one who pisses against a wall both fettered and free in Israel" (1 Kgs 21:21). The crude reference to genitals is no doubt deliberate: the "seed" of Ahab, the Omride dynasty, will be removed from Israel. A judgment against Jezebel is added, even though she had not been mentioned in YHWH's initial instruction. Is this YHWH speaking, then, or Elijah improvising once again?

After this confrontation another humorous note is added as we observe the *setumah* suggesting it took some time for Ahab to work out a strategy that would avert the course of justice that had been dealt him. He adopts the posture and practice of mourning, a fitting reaction to YHWH's judgment on those who have broken his covenant (see Joel 2:12). The narrated voiceover describes Ahab's five actions that needed no words (tore, put on, fasted, lay down, went around meekly; 1 Kgs 21:27–28). He knows the right way to act as an Israelite king, and his performance is effective since it mitigates YHWH's verdict. But even this turn of events is ironic: it is when Ahab is not in Jezebel's presence that he begins acting more like an Israelite!

Commentary on Episode 3

Characters and events in this episode make greater sense if Episode 3 is considered a prequel (in the same way that the Star Wars franchise includes prequels): even though it is the third installment in the series, the events in Episode 3 make more sense if they happened before the events in Episode 2. Nevertheless, given that Elijah is the star of the whole, it is artistically and theologically appropriate to present Episode 3 towards the end of the series, for it is here that Elijah has the last word in the competition for power with Jezebel. Whether speaking on YHWH's behalf or on his own, Elijah adds the contemptuous "the dogs will eat Jezebel" to his condemnation of Ahab. Yet it is hard to imagine him returning from self-imposed exile to speak against Jezebel in her own city after fleeing from her in fear of his life.[54] Furthermore, Jezebel's grisly end is well-known and casts a shadow over

54. Hazleton comments, "The narrative demanded that Elijah not be defeated by Jezebel. It demanded that he have the last word, that he redeem his cowardice and fear, and that he impose the judgment of Yahweh on her. So the vineyard story was dropped in where it was by a later editor because this is where it made emotional sense" (*Jezebel*, 133).

her long and arguably successful reign. There is greater dramatic impact in providing this prophecy early in the chronology of the story.

Ahab's relationship with Elijah also makes more sense if this episode comes earlier than the Mount Carmel scene. The only encounter between them in Episode 1 is the prediction of drought, but for the rest of that episode Elijah is outside of Israel. At the beginning of Episode 2 Ahab is feeling the effects of the drought, but neither Obadiah's claim that Ahab has been searching high and low for Elijah, nor his greeting ("Is this you—the troubler of Israel?") has a basis unless Ahab has already perceived Elijah as an enemy whose presence usually means trouble for him and his household. Elijah's challenge to Ahab to assemble the prophets of Baal at Mount Carmel, the "vineyard of El," is more highly charged if the incident at Naboth's vineyard has already occurred. And Elijah's benign treatment of Ahab at the end of Episode 2 is consistent with the postponement of judgment following his repentance over the Naboth indictment.

Finally, the end of Episode 2 leads more logically to the events in Episode 4. YHWH instructs Elijah to commission Elisha and set the wheels in motion for a change of kingship in Israel and Aram. Elisha leaves all to follow and serve Elijah but then disappears until Episode 4. While the events of the Elijah cycle make sense in the chronological order of the episodes, delaying Episode 2 until later maintains interest by introducing Jezebel as a powerful character in the series while allowing the real star of the show his dramatic exit unsullied by his dark period of self-doubt.

Episode-Specific Characters

Naboth

It has already been noted that the Elijah Series contain many prophets, not just Elijah. The main character introduced in this episode, Naboth (נָבוֹת, *nābôt*) has a name reminiscent of the Hebrew word for "prophet" (נָבִיא, *nābî*). He may have shown poor judgment in his lack of deference to King Ahab, especially obvious in my translation where the root letters of his initial response suggest a profanity. Nonetheless, Naboth prophetically represents Israelite law in insisting that his land was an "inheritance" given by YHWH to his ancestors in perpetuity. Land as inheritance (נַחֲלָה, *naḥălāh*) is a uniquely Israelite concept. Israel's territory was evenly divided among the twelve tribes, and each tribal clan was responsible for passing the land to the next generation. A number of laws in the Torah were designed to maintain this egalitarian system. Confident of his ancestral rights, Naboth had little time for Ahab's proposal that he exchange this land for money or other land (which would presumably have been taken from another clan's inheritance). The tone of voice in Naboth's performance would indicate whether his underlying attitude was respectful or contemptuous.

Little more is known of Naboth—he is not given a chance to defend himself when charged. A reiteration of the judgment on Ahab at a later time states that it was "for the blood of Naboth and for the blood of his sons" (2 Kgs 9:26), indicating either a family that was murdered alongside him or the figurative loss of his potential descendants with his own death.

Elders and Nobles of Jezreel and Sons of Beliyya'el

"Supporting cast" is a good term for these characters, all of whom act exactly as instructed by Jezebel in her correspondence. Despite writing letters "in the name of Ahab" (1 Kgs 21:8), it is likely they knew she was the instigator, since they sent their messages back to Jezebel (1 Kgs 21:14)—although the script does not make it clear whether these characters came into Jezebel's presence themselves or played her game by writing a letter ("they sent to Jezebel saying . . ."). The Sons of Beliyya'el are a euphemism personified. Their name means "worthlessness" or "wickedness" so the audience already expects them to act without honor. Yet it is possible to argue they acted within the letter of the law, as postulated above.

PROPS AND READY-MADES

The etymological link between "vineyard" (כֶּרֶם, *kerem*) and "Carmel" has already been noted. It is a reminder, as Naboth claims, that all *kerem* belongs to God in Israel and cannot be bought and sold. But the vineyard is also a biblical symbol of well-being. The spies brought back a large bunch of grapes from the land of Canaan (Num 13:23), attesting to the goodness of the promised land. Unlike bread and oil, which are daily staples, vineyards represent luxury and abundance. All of these qualities contribute to the ready-made nature of Naboth's vineyard, coveted by Israel's king.

Ready-mades can be found in the oracles of judgment in Scene 5. The covenant verb "cut" is used again (1 Kgs 21:21). YHWH accuses Ahab of "murdering" (1 Kgs 21:19) where before the verbs relating to Naboth's death were "killed" and "stoned." "You shall not murder" is an injunction in the Decalogue (Deut 5:17), so YHWH is insisting it is covenant law that has been breached by Ahab. Dead being eaten by dogs in the city and carrion fowl in the fields are conventional prophetic threats, used already by the prophet Ahijah against the house of Jeroboam (1 Kgs 14:11) and the prophet Jehu against the house of Baasha (1 Kgs 16:4). Audiences familiar with the earlier stories would understand the implication that Ahab's dynasty would end just as the previous dynasties had.

Jezebel's letter and the reply she receives are significant props in this episode. The use of written letters in a largely oral and illiterate context is a way to exert authority and power. It is also possible to deceive because unlike a speaker, the author of the letter is stated but not necessarily proven. Although the letter has Ahab's seal, the multiple references to Jezebel by the narrator make clear to the audience that Jezebel instigated the correspondence.

As in other performances, sackcloth is a costume that carries significant meaning, identifying with mourning for death or remorse. Perhaps Ahab also remembered that fasting and laying on the ground were actions that had been practiced by a penitent king with positive effect (2 Sam 12:16).

PROPHETIC PERFORMANCE

Elijah's performance in this episode has none of the showmanship of Series 2, nor the compassion of Episode 1. Here he is a righteous defender of YHWH, covenant, and Israelite land rights. His very presence before Ahab elicits a confession "have you found me" (1 Kgs 21:20)—where "found" (מָצָא, māṣāʾ) has the double meaning of "discover" and "uncover." Ahab has been found out. And Elijah shows no mercy, condemning Ahab, Jezebel, and their descendants to a fate worse than death. They will not only die, but become carrion, destroyed to the point of remaining unburied (an ancient and horrific curse). No trace of self-doubt is seen in the prophetic performance in this episode, only righteous fanaticism.

The exchange between YHWH and Elijah that closes the scene suggests that Elijah's determination to punish is even greater than YHWH's. YHWH was willing to respond to Ahab's display of contrition, and it is YHWH who brings the change of heart to Elijah's attention, not the other way around. Elijah's defense of the voiceless Naboth is to be applauded, but his unyielding opposition to Ahab and Jezebel that allows no grace means that he is no Nathan, encouraging a repentant sinner to turn back (see 2 Sam 12:13).

Connections with Episode 3

Lesley Hazleton relates how a Palestinian woman from one of the Gaza settlements wrote to then prime minister of Israel Ariel Sharon in 2005 about her community that had been dismantled under his order:

> I want to ask you whether you are able to look me straight in the eye and tell me to leave my home, the same home where my son grew up until the age of eighteen, and give it as a gift to the murderers of my son. *Ha-ratzachta v-gam yarashta*—Have you murdered and also taken possession?[55]

Dispossession of the weak by the strong continues to be a real issue in the Holy Land, and elsewhere around the world. A biblical theology of land undergirds Israel's identity, both ancient and present. Paradoxically, it was when ancient Israel was landless, either as sojourners on the way to the land of promise or exiles in Babylon, that their creativity was greatest and biblical faith most fully expressed.[56] Thus, God's gift of land should always be held lightly, never exploited, considered both gift and task, such that those in possession of land must show genuine compassion and just treatment of those without.

A reenactment of the story of Naboth's vineyard would continue to contrast community-based egalitarianism with tributary politics that insists those with power and resources have a right to purchase and own real estate for their own benefit. The ideology of "a place to belong" would be held up against an ideology that claims payment or exchange is sufficient reason for trading away that place. Perhaps more importantly, however, an audience would be encouraged to condemn unjust use of power to achieve possession. It is the prophetic voice that brings this issue to the foreground, and prophetic voices such as the Palestinian woman quoted above will continue to unsettle and challenge the "rights" of those who possess and amass land at the expense of other lives.

Elijah Episode 4

> ### "Return of the Prophet"
> (2 Kings 1–2)

---

55. Hazleton, *Jezebel*, 119–20.
56. See Mathews, "Deuteronomy 30: Faithfulness in the Refugee Camps."

Cast:

Leading: Narrator, Ahaziah, Elijah

Supporting: Messengers of the king; Messenger of YHWH; First Chief of Fifty, Second Chief of Fifty, Third Chief of Fifty, Sons of the Prophets.

Extras: 3 x Battalions of Fifty

Offstage: YHWH; Baal Zebub, god of Ekron.

Waiting in the wings: Moab

SCENE 1 (1:1–17a)

Setting: The Palace, Samaria—stage left

Narrator

¹And he revolted—Moab—against Israel after the death of Ahab. ²And he fell—Ahaziah—through the lattice in his high room which is in Samaria and he became ill. And he sent messengers, and he said to them

Ahaziah

Go, seek with Baal Zebub, the god of Ekron, if I will live from this illness.

ס

Setting: On top of Mount Carmel—stage right

Narrator

³And the messenger of YHWH spoke to Elijah the Settler—

Messenger of YHWH

Get up, go to meet the messengers of the king of Samaria, and speak to them "is it that there is not any God in Israel all of you are going to seek with Baal Zebub god of Ekron?" ⁴And therefore, thus says YHWH, "the bed where you have gone up there you will not go down from her because to death you will die."

Narrator

And he went—Elijah.

Setting: The Palace, Samaria—stage left

⁵And they returned—the messengers—to him. And he said to them,

Ahaziah

What is this—you have returned?

Messengers of the King

⁶(*) A man came up to meet us and he said to us "Go, return to the king who sent you and speak to him, thus says YHWH: "is it that there is not any God in Israel you (sg) are sending to seek with Baal Zebub, the god of Ekron? Therefore the bed where you have gone up there you will not go down from her because to death you will die."

Ahaziah

⁷(*) What impression of the man who came up to meet you all, and he spoke to you all these words?

Messengers of the King

⁸(*) A man—a Baal of hair and a girdle of a fur girded[57] on his loins.

Ahaziah

(*) Elijah the Settler is he!

Setting: On top of Mount Carmel—stage right

Narrator

⁹And he sent to him a Chief of Fifty and his fifty, and he went up to him and behold! He was sitting on top of the mountain. And he spoke to him

First Chief of Fifty

Man of God, the king has spoken: Come down!

Narrator

¹⁰And he answered—Elijah—and he spoke to the Chief of Fifty

---

57. Note the wordplay in the Hebrew in this phrase עוֹר, better translated "skin" or "leather," but the three words are homonyms in Hebrew, so I've tried to replicate the soundplay.

Elijah

If a man of God am I let fire come down from the heavens!
And let her eat you and your fifty.

Narrator

And fire came down from the heavens and she ate him and
his fifty. [11]And he returned and he sent to him a Chief of
Fifty—a second one—and his fifty. And he answered and
he spoke to him

Second Chief of Fifty

Man of God, thus says the king: Quickly! Come down!

Narrator

[12]And he answered—Elijah—and he spoke to them

Elijah

If a man of God am I let fire come down from the heavens!
And let her eat you and your fifty.

Narrator

And fire came down from the heavens and she ate him and
his fifty. [13]And he returned and he sent a Chief of Fifty—a
third one—and his fifty. And he went up and he came—a
Chief of Fifty—the third one—and he knelt on his knees in
front of Elijah and he implored to him and he spoke to him

Third Chief of Fifty

Man of God, let her be precious, please—my breath—and
the breath of your servants—these fifty—in your eyes. [14]Be-
hold! Fire came down from the heavens and ate two of the
chiefs of the Fifty—the first and their fifty. And now, let her
be precious—my breath—in your eyes.

Narrator

[15]And the messenger of YHWH spoke to Elijah—

Messenger of YHWH

Come down with him, do not be afraid from before his face.

Narrator

And he got up and he came down with him to the king.
[16]And he spoke to him

Elijah

Thus says YHWH, because you sent messengers to seek with Baal Zebub the god of Ekron—is it that there is not any God in Israel to seek with his word? Therefore tие bed where you have gone up there you will not go down from her because to death you will die.

Narrator

¹⁷And he died like the word of YHWH which he spoke—Elijah—and he ruled—Jehoram—in his place

 פ

—In the second year of Jehoram son of Jehoshaphat, king of Judah, for there was not to him a son. ¹⁸And the rest of the words of Ahaziah which he did, are they not written in the book of the words of the days of the kings of Israel?

SCENE 2 (2:1–6a)

Setting: On the road between Gilgal,
Beth-el, and Jericho.

Narrator

¹And it happened when YHWH was to take up Elijah in the whirlwind to the heavens, and he went—Elijah *and* Elisha—from the Gilgal. And he said—Elijah to Elisha—

Elijah

sit please here because YHWH sent me to Beth-el

Elisha

²(*) By the life of YHWH and by the life of your breath if I leave you!

Narrator

And they went down to Beth-el. ³And they came out—the sons of the prophets—who were in Beth-el to Elisha. And they said to him

Sons of the Prophets

Do you know that this day YHWH is taking your lord from over your head?

Elisha

(*) Also I know. Be quiet!

Narrator

[4]And he said to him—Elijah to Elisha—

Elijah

sit please here because YHWH sent me to Jericho.

Elisha

(*) By the life of YHWH and by the life of your breath if I leave you!

Narrator

And they came to Jericho. [5]And they approached—the sons of the prophets—who were in Jericho to Elisha. And they said to him

Sons of the Prophets

Do you know that this day YHWH is taking your lord from over your head?

Elisha

(*) Also I know. Be quiet!

Narrator

[6]And he said to him—Elijah—

Elijah

sit please here because YHWH sent me to the Jordan.

Elisha

(*) By the life of YHWH and by the life of your breath if I leave you!

SCENE 3 (2:6b–18)

Setting: The Jordan River.

Narrator

And they went on, the two of them. [7]And fifty men from the sons of the prophets went and they stood in front of them from a distance. And the two of them stood above the

Jordan. [8]And he took—Elijah—his cloak and wrapped up and struck the waters and they divided here and here. And they crossed over—the two of them—on dry ground. [9]And it happened like their crossing Elijah said to Elisha

Elijah

Ask what I can do for you before I am taken from with you.

Elisha

(*) Let it be please a double opening[58] of your spirit to me.

Elijah

[10](*) You are making difficult this ask. If you see me taken from you, let it be for you thus. And if not anything, it will not be.

Narrator

[11]And it happened they were going—going and speaking—and behold! A chariot of fire and horses of fire and they separated between the two of them.

And he went up—Elijah—in the whirlwind to the heavens. [12]And Elisha was seeing and he was crying out

Elisha

My father! My father! A chariot of Israel and his horsemen.

Narrator

And he did not see them again. And he took hold of his clothes and he parted them into two parts.[59] [13]And he raised the cloak of Elijah which had fallen from over him and he returned and he stood on the lips of the Jordan. [14]And he took the cloak of Elijah which had fallen from over him and he struck the waters and he said

Elisha

Where is YHWH the god of Elijah? Indeed, is it he?

---

58. The literal Hebrew word is "mouth" but a "double mouth" does not really convey the intention whereas a "double opening" does.

59. This translation reflects the use of the same root in the verb and noun (קרע).

Narrator

And he struck the waters and they divided here and here and he crossed over—Elisha. ¹⁵And they saw—the sons of the prophets—who were in Jericho in front, and they said

Sons of the Prophets

She rested—the spirit of Elijah—on Elisha.

Narrator

And they came to meet him and they bowed down to him on the land. ¹⁶And they said to him

Sons of the Prophets

Behold! Please—there are your servants, fifty men, sons of strength. Let them go please and let them seek your lord lest he lifted him—the spirit of YHWH—and threw him on one of the mountains or in one of the valleys.

Elisha

(*) Do not send!

Narrator

¹⁷And they urged him until abashed and he said

Elisha

Send!

Narrator

And they sent fifty men and they sought three days and did not find him. ¹⁸And they returned to him and he was in Jericho. And he said to them

Elisha

Did not I say to you "do not go"?!⁶⁰

---

60. The negating Hebrew particle translated "did not" is הֲלוֹא (hălôʾ), tempting me to translate Elisha's response in very contemporary idiom: "*Hello*, did not I say to you 'do not go'?"

Creativity in Episode 4

Repetition of words and concepts form ironic contrasts in Episode 4. King Ahaziah, the son of Ahab killed in battle (1 Kgs 22:29–40), is introduced for the first time in the Elijah Series. His introduction is ominous—as a result of an accident he seeks the advice of a Baal. On the way to do so, his messengers meet Elijah, and they describe him as a Baal to the king—a Baal of hair (2 Kgs 1:8). The messengers are sent to consult one Baal as to whether the king will be healed or not but are met by another who emphatically claims he will not.

Elijah's question, repeated three times (2 Kgs 1:3, 6, 16), can only be understood as rhetorical due to Ahaziah's Yahwist name and the audience's familiarity with the character of YHWH, even though currently offstage! He speaks through his messenger and his prophet. A reference back to Episode 2 is made with the word אֵין (ʾêyn, "not any"). At Mount Carmel it had been shown that the Baal made "not any" response, whereas YHWH did answer Elijah's prayer. So Ahaziah is clearly incorrect in his implication that there is "not any" god in Israel such that he must consult Baal Zebub.

The three battalions of fifty soldiers bring to mind the two groups of fifty prophets hidden in caves by Obadiah (1 Kgs 18:4, 13) and foreshadow the band of fifty prophets who will observe Elijah disappearing and set off to seek him (2 Kgs 2:7, 16). Repetition of fifty represents forces for and against YHWH, and highlights their different fates: protection and destruction respectively.

Furthermore, the fire from heaven that had destroyed the groups of fifty sent by the apostate Ahaziah (2 Kgs 1:10, 12) contrasts with the fire from heaven transporting the faithful Elijah to the heavens (2:11). Once again, fire and Elijah are united in both retribution and victory.

The motif of up and down reappears in this episode even more strongly. The king goes up to his bed but will not come down to reign again. Elijah is told to go "up" to meet the messengers of the king, but the chiefs of fifty with their fifty all go "up" to meet him. In that scene the verb "come down" (ירד, yrd) is used nine times in seven verses (2 Kgs 1:9–15). Two of the chiefs order Elijah to "come down," and each time Elijah responds by ordering fire to "come down" and consume the chiefs and their fifty. The third chief takes a different approach, resulting in Elijah coming down after all to speak with the king. When Elijah goes up in the whirlwind to the heavens, he doesn't come down again, but nor is his death ever reported. By contrast, Ahaziah goes up to his bed in order to die—a death that is emphatically predicted three times as well as announced in the usual manner (2 Kgs 1:17–18). The death of the Omride dynasty ("there was not to him a son") is reported here also in the concluding regnal resume. Thus death and life, another theme in the Elijah Series, has an impact in this episode. In seeking life from the wrong source, Ahaziah dies. In seeking to control the force of life, Ahaziah's battalions die ("eaten" by fire). Elijah and YHWH have control of the "breath" of life—the breath of the third chief and his fifty is spared (2 Kgs 1:13–14), and the breath of Elijah is the life-force of Elisha's faith and commitment (2 Kgs 2:2, 4, 6).

Commentary on Episode 4

This episode is divided into three scenes with the long first scene taking place in two locations. Once again I have characterized "stage right" as the location for Elijah's encounters and "stage left" for locating the apostate Ahaziah. Ahaziah is in the high room of the palace in Samaria, and Elijah is on the top of a high mountain. Groups of messengers and chiefs with their battalions of fifty go back and forth between the two.

A typical pattern in Hebrew narrative, seen elsewhere in the Elijah Series also, is repetition of similar events with a variation on the last time. This is equally effective in performance with a buildup of audience expectation and inevitable surprise at the turn of events. In this episode we see this pattern in Scenes 1 and 2. The first two chiefs and their battalions make the same demand (note, however, the demand of the second is slightly ramped up from "Come down!" to "Quickly! Come down!"), but the third chief, aware of the fate of the previous groups, appeals to Elijah's pity and is spared along with his fifty. In Scene 2 the same exchange is made between Elijah and Elisha in three locations, and the same rather amusing exchange between Elisha and the sons of the prophets in the first two of the three locations. A change comes at the Jordan River where everyone witnesses the miracle of the parting water, Elijah offers a parting request, and Elisha sees the wonderful departure of Elijah into the heavens.

Clues from Hebrew section markings are not so helpful for scene division in this episode. The first *setumah* following 2 Kgs 1:2 is logical—providing a space between Ahaziah sending messengers, and a messenger of YHWH speaking to Elijah, but where we might expect further such breaks there are none. The scene ends with a narrated voiceover giving relevant information to the audience, but this information is inexplicably broken by a *petuuah*. The Hebrew Bible maintains the momentum of the action by quickly continuing to the next scene, while translators of the Septuagint added material introducing Jehoram's reign at this point.

Episode-specific Characters

Ahaziah

Ahaziah's character is not allowed much development in this Elijah episode, but like all characters in sagas, has a backstory. Information in 1 Kgs 22 informs us he is the son of Ahab, and probably the son of Jezebel since a reference is made to his mother, which is unusual for kings of Israel although standard for kings of Judah. Deuteronomistic editors inform us that he did evil, walked in the ways of his parents, served Baal, and provoked YHWH (1 Kgs 22:51–53). But he had also attempted to introduce maritime trade to Israel, suggesting that he had more ambition than his father. When Ahaziah is introduced in the Elijah Series, an ominous note is sounded in the report that neighboring Moab was spoiling for a fight (2 Kgs 1:1), but events in Scene 1 are dominated by Ahaziah's accident. His decision to consult a Baal seals his apostasy and sets events in motion that fulfill the prior knowledge that his reign only lasted two years (1 Kgs 22:51).

Ahaziah's attempts at command and authority are continually thwarted by a stronger authority at work. His first messengers return with a warning and description of a man that Ahaziah immediately recognizes—perhaps his parents had prepared him for the inevitability of Elijah's involvement in his affairs. His failed attempts to summon the prophet and loss of troops in the process must have left him frustrated, but he has no further lines in Scene 1 so seems to acquiesce to his fate.

Baal Zebub, the god of Ekron

This name is unknown elsewhere in the Hebrew Bible. It is sometimes translated "lord of the flies" but may also be a deliberate mispronunciation of "Zebul" (prince) in order to denigrate the name. Ekron is the northernmost Philistine city. The Philistines were the greatest foes of the Israelite kingdom under Saul and David, but Ahaziah's relations with them, perhaps under the influence of Jezebel, were clearly cordial since he assumed his messengers would receive a welcome. As befits the Baals in this series, Baal Zebub remains offstage and uninvolved.

Messengers

In this episode, messengers of the king contrast with the messenger of YHWH. The king's messengers are purely functionary, reporting what they see and hear. Rather comically, their returning message to Ahaziah is a quote within a quote within a quote (2 Kgs 1:6). They are linguistically distancing themselves from their unwelcome message. The messenger of YHWH truly represents YHWH in this episode, who otherwise makes no appearance. The comforting touch of the messenger in Episode 2 is absent, but this messenger does offer the prophetic ready-made "Do not be afraid" to reassure Elijah, who seems to be withdrawing into self-doubt once again.

Chiefs of Fifty

Each of the three chiefs address Elijah as "Man of God," as did the foreign widow-woman in Episode 1. It is a title that separates him from ordinary men,[61] proven in both Episodes 1 and 4 by his miraculous actions. The third chief stands out as an individual capable of turning from his commanded duty to save the lives of himself and his fifty. The narration stresses the efforts he took to do this: kneeling in front of Elijah, imploring him, speaking to him, using emotive and deferential language. Although we are not told so directly, it appears this strategy was effective.

The Prophet Elisha

The character of Elisha is further developed in this episode. We know from Episode 2 that Elisha had to leave his own father, so it is understandable if Elijah became a father figure for him. It seems that, however half-hearted, Elijah must have accepted that role since he offers a "deathbed" blessing. Elisha audaciously asks for a "double opening" of Elijah's spirit, something even Elijah is not sure is possible (2 Kgs 2:9–10), but reflecting the right of the firstborn son (Deut 21:17). Elisha's exclamation "My father, my father" as Elijah disappears in the whirlwind also suggests this father-son relationship was active in Elisha's mind.

Elisha's faithful persistence despite Elijah's discouragement could be viewed sympathetically or cynically. Knowing that he is the commissioned successor, he has to stick close to be able to receive any expected benefit, and is rewarded with a blessing, a vision, and the miracle-wielding cloak. He seems to inherit Elijah's arrogance also! The final exchange with the sons of the prophets indicates that he is able to be swayed by opinion, but can't resist "I told you so" when his first impulse is vindicated (2 Kgs 2:16–18). The

---

61. Compare this with Ezekiel, whose characteristic title is "Son of Humanity" (see Chapter 5). The contrasting titles support the notion of different prophetic performances.

Elisha Series will reveal a prophet who is comfortable dealing with political systems, working with a servant, and using power to his advantage.

Sons of the Prophets

The sons of the prophets act in unison and together are in turn condescending, curious, deferential, energetic, and persistent. They accept Elisha as the commissioned leader of the prophets, but want to offer their advice and assistance. This group of characters will have a much greater involvement in the Elisha Series than they have been permitted to have here, given Elijah's preference to work alone.

PROPS, COSTUMES, AND GESTURES

Elijah's costume as described by the messengers of Ahaziah is distinctive, enabling the king to identify him immediately. It is a costume that continued to be identified with prophecy (see Zech 13:4). Garments made from hair and fur suggest an untamed personality, who has existed outside of civilization. It is unsurprising that such a person came into conflict with the sophistication of a royal court.

The cloak (אַדֶּרֶת, ᵓaderet) that is used here to part waters draws again on a ready-made known to be an identifying garment and a power-laden object. Fire is again used as a weapon of judgment by Elijah against apostasy and evidence of the heavenly presence of YHWH vindicating Elijah's life and confirming Elisha's succession.

A number of gestures are implied or warranted in the script of this episode. The same phrase describes first Elijah and then Elisha dividing the waters of the Jordan: "he struck the waters and they divided here and here" (2 Kgs 2:8, 14). The demonstrative pronoun suggests a gesture on the part of the performer. Another part of the script that would benefit from gestures is the narrator's aside at the end of Scene 1. Just who is being referenced is not clear in the script. Are there two different Jehorams—one in Israel and one in Judah? Is the "he" who had no son definitely Ahaziah? Visual identification or gestures pointing to relevant characters would be very helpful!

READY-MADES

A number of ready-mades add depth to the audience experience of Episode 4. The first is a ready-made from an earlier episode. The fact that

YHWH's power was seen in a "high room" in Episode 1 (1 Kgs 17:19) would suggest to the audience that YHWH's hand is behind the "accident" of Ahaziah, forming part of the judgment on the house of Ahab. That the word for "high room" (עֲלִיָּה, ʿ ăliyyāh) sounds so similar to the name Elijah (אֵלִיָּה, ʾ ēliyyāh) implies the prophet's active involvement in the downfall of the Omride dynasty.

The message Ahaziah receives from Elijah includes a very familiar phrase for audiences aware of Israelite law. When Ahaziah is told "to death you will die," he is hearing the death penalty formula (cf. Exod 21:12–15; Lev 24:17). There is a surprising element here, however, in that the law codes proscribe the death penalty for murder, whereas Elijah is proscribing it for apostasy.

The locations Gilgal, Jericho, and the Jordan River are all familiar from the Joshua traditions so may be ready-mades signaling that Elisha's succession of Elijah is akin to Joshua's succession of Moses. We know from earlier episodes that Elijah is drawn with Moses in mind, so Elisha is likewise drawn with the successor of Moses in mind. The parting of the Jordan also links Elisha to Joshua (see Josh 3), where Joshua's miraculous action was already making use of Moses's parting of the Reed Sea as a ready-made (see Exod 14).

The word רוּחַ (rûaḥ), translated "spirit" throughout this Elijah Series, has a particular role as a ready-made in this episode. The spirit of YHWH signifies prophetic endowment as seen in the book of Judges and elsewhere. When Elisha requests a double opening of Elijah's spirit, he is wanting to tap into that prophetic power he has seen in his predecessor. When Elisha repeats the miraculous action of Elijah, the sons of the prophets are able to recognize Elijah's spirit in Elisha (2 Kgs 2:15). Subsequent reference to the "spirit of YHWH" who may have "thrown" Elijah on a mountain or in a valley (2 Kgs 2:16) indicates a wariness regarding the power of YHWH's spirit.

The chariot and whirlwind that break into the ordinariness of walking and talking is portrayed in this script as a surprising event (2 Kgs 2:11). Both phenomena, however, are well known-features in theophanic passages of the Hebrew Bible.[62] Whirlwinds portray power but at the same time elusiveness. Wheeled chariots are appropriate conveyances for the "rider on the clouds." Jewish "Merkevah" Mysticism arose from such traditions.[63]

Elisha's first reaction to Elijah's disappearance is the tearing of his clothes (2 Kgs 2:12). This action was also undertaken by Ahab at the end

62. See Deut 33:26; Isa 19:1; Jer 23:19; Ezek 1:8–11; Hab 3:8; Zech 9:14; Ps 68:5, 34; Ps 18:11/2 Sam 22:11.

63. See Chapter 5 of this book where discussion of Ezekiel's contribution to Merkevah Mysticism is continued.

of Episode 3. In both cases the audience would have known the action as a ready-made expressing grief and loss.

PROPHETIC PERFORMANCE

In this episode Elijah's performance begins with characteristic commanding, autocratic presence, representing the word of YHWH to an apostate king of Israel. His treatment of Ahaziah's chiefs and their battalions are reminiscent of his callous execution of the prophets of Baal, as if there is a contest in which he has an unfair advantage by being able to access the powerful fire of the heavens. The lack of response to the third chief does not allow us to view the compassionate side that we saw in Episode 1. Rather, we are glimpsing renewed self-doubt as Elijah needs reassurance from the Messenger of YHWH that he can safely go down into the presence of the king whose fate he has already prophesied.

Scenes 2 and 3 present a prophet who is aging, diminishing, unsure of himself. He doesn't want company, he begrudgingly allows Elisha to follow but isn't sure whether Elisha will be able to see through to the end with him. His response to Elisha's request for a double opening of the spirit indicates his view that a prophet is one who is able to see spiritual visions. We have no words or description of Elijah as he is taken up other than what we hear from Elisha. He disappears as mysteriously as he had come onto the scene, without explanation. He leaves his powerful cloak behind, ready to pass on the mantle that has been so burdensome for him.

Connections with Episode 4

Sometimes words are not enough. When Elisha asks for a double opening of Elijah's spirit he has to *see* something first. The vision that he sees, of Elijah ascending with a fiery chariot and horses, no doubt confirms his sense of call and purpose.

Episode 4 does not offer much that is new in the Elijah Series. Like earlier series, the prophet is required to announce indictment to an apostate Israelite ruler, to show that the god YHWH is more powerful than any Baal, and to pass on his prophetic role to a worthy successor. My discussion here, then, will focus on the contemporary audience's response to the entire Elijah Series.

Several times we have discussed Elijah's prophetic performance. The narrator has not offered any public criticism, but an attentive audience will have noted some problematic aspects in the Elijah Series.

This prophet does not always act in accordance with the Word of YHWH, and occasionally decides himself what that word will be. This prophet is quick to offer judgment but slow to offer mercy. He is reluctant to acknowledge others who are supporting the cause of Yahwism, even though the audience members are well aware of Obadiah, of the hundred prophets of YHWH that Obadiah hid in caves, of the seven thousand mentioned by YHWH himself who did not bow the knee to Baal, of Elisha, and of the bands of fifty sons of the prophets at several locations frequented by Elijah. He even seems reluctant to share his company, knowledge, and power with his own appointed successor. He seems unresponsive to care shown to him, as seen by the need for the messenger in desert to rouse him twice. He seems indifferent to YHWH's revelation on Mount Horeb. He is eager to bring destructive fire down on others.

Yet in this series Elijah has been an instrument of miraculous provision and healing. His life is an example of YHWH's active concern outside of the land of Israel as well as within its borders. He stands up against injustice by the powerful against the vulnerable. His transport to the heavens with heavenly chariot and horsemen seems to be a special blessing and has earned him a revered role in Jewish theological expectation.

Elijah's performance challenges an audience when they are looking for simple answers to complex problems. It reminds us that there is no one easy answer. At times confrontation is necessary, at other times civil disobedience. Zeal *and* mercy both have a role. Trust in God is important, *and* the ability to recognize that God is able to work through others. There is value in care for the needy even if they don't acknowledge God's sovereignty, as illustrated by the widow-woman and her son.

The Elijah Series, with its dramatic up-and-down motif, reminds us that the God of the heavens is willing to reach down to our time and place. But the ways of that God are broader than the experience and the methods of one zealous prophet.

5

Case Study 2: Ezekiel 1–11

Ezekiel in the Context of Israel's Prophetic Tradition

MY SECOND CASE STUDY—THE prophet Ezekiel—comes from the scroll bearing his name—one of the scrolls of the Latter Prophets (which is the second subdivision of the second major section, the Prophets, in the Hebrew Bible). The Latter Prophets comprise four scrolls: Isaiah, Jeremiah, Ezekiel, and the Book of the Twelve. Sometimes called the classical prophets, these characters are distinguished by the body of oracles collected in one book named after an individual prophet. The presentations of the prophets as God's messengers are not ordinarily embedded in a third-person narrative, (as they are in the Former Prophets) but are preserved as first-person records of messages conveyed through a variety of oral and literary genres.

Ezekiel's oracles are frequently framed by specific dates. This enables a degree of certainty in knowing when he lived, where he prophesied, and to which audience. Among biblical scholars there is confidence that the book includes authentic words of the prophet, leading Katheryn Pfisterer Darr to claim: "Today many—though not all—critics agree with Fohrer's decision to take seriously the scroll's witness concerning its author and origins."[1] Ezekiel is notably the first Israelite prophet to see visions of YHWH outside of the land of Israel/Judah. The radical nature of this claim may explain the lengthy and detailed inaugural "prophetic call" vision described in the book such that Ezekiel "felt the need to prove his legitimacy as an 'off-site' prophet."[2]

The literary setting for the book of Ezekiel is the exilic community on the River Chebar in Babylon, but Ezekiel's visions periodically take him to "the valley" (Ezek 3:22–23; 8:4; 37:1–2) and back to Jerusalem (Ezek 8:3;

---

1. Darr, "Ezekiel among the Critics," 251. Cf. Fohrer, *Die Hauptprobleme des Buches Ezechiel.*

2. Brettler, *How to Read the Jewish Bible*, 186.

40:2). Ezekiel is introduced in the opening verses of the book as a member of a priestly family among the Golah[3] by the River Chebar in the "fifth year of the exile." The exile can be confidently dated to 597 BCE which places the first part of the book in the year 593 BCE. Ezekiel would have been among the first group of exiled Judeans, who, according to the biblical witness, were the "elite of the land" (2 Kgs 24:14–16, NRSV). As Darr notes: "Not surprisingly, then, the book of Ezekiel reveals an author of unusual intellect, sophistication, knowledge and literary gifts, and we should assume that his audience, Judah's cognoscenti, was equipped to understand him."[4]

The book of Ezekiel is certainly influenced by the Priestly/Chronicler's school, as evidenced by its priestly vocabulary and concepts. Strong affinity is especially seen between Ezekiel and Lev 17–26, the Holiness Code. In the few verses below, for example, all of the underlined vocabulary is found in Lev 26, a passage that lays out covenant curses:[5]

And it happened—the word of YHWH—to me, saying:

YHWH

Son of humanity, put your face to the mountains of Israel

And prophesy to them.

And you will say 'Mountains of Israel, hear the word of Adonai YHWH,

Thus says Adonai YHWH

To the mountains and to the heights

To the ravines and to the gorges:

Behold me, I am bringing upon you a sword and I will destroy your high places.

And your altars will be deserted and your incense stands will be broken

and I will throw down your slain ones before the face of your turdy idols.[6]

---

3. That is, the exile community. This word, transliterated from the Hebrew, is still used to refer to the Jewish diaspora community.

4. Darr, "Ezekiel among the Critics," 257.

5. All translations in bordered sections are my own, unless otherwise indicated.

6. For "turdy" idols see explanation below, page 162.

And I will put the <u>cadavers</u> of the sons of Israel before their turdy <u>idols</u>

And I will scatter your bones around your <u>altars</u>.

In all your dwelling places the <u>cities</u> will be <u>wasted</u> and the <u>high places</u> will be deserted,

Because your altars will be <u>wasted</u> and pasted, and your turdy <u>idols</u> are damaged and destroyed, and your <u>incense stands</u> cut off and your works wiped off.

And slain will fall in the middle of you

And you will know that <u>I am YHWH</u> (Ezek 6:1–7)

Even more striking, perhaps, is the exact repetition of the phrase "I will break for you a tribe/staff of bread" found in Lev 26:26 and Ezek 5:16. These and other intertextual allusions reveal a work that creatively reshapes Israelite traditions for new historical circumstances, specifically for the crisis of the exile.

The text of Ezekiel includes over 130 *hapax legomena* (words not found elsewhere in the Hebrew Bible). Some have argued that the text of Ezekiel needs "smoothing out" (as Zimmerli has done by comparing the MT to LXX and other versions to determine where scribal error and accretions have slipped in).[7] On the other hand, it has been argued that repetition and redundancy characterizes Ezekiel's literary technique and should be accepted as authentic.[8] Repetition is also characteristic in oral delivery, and could attest to oral foundations for the literary work. My translations of portions of the book are of the MT without recourse to other versions. Deliberate replication of the same English word for the same Hebrew root highlights repetitive elements in the text.

Current scholarship debates the priority of oral proclamation over literary work in this prophetic book. Was Ezekiel *himself* primarily an orator or writer? Does his book represent the beginnings of "scribal prophecy"— words that were written first and spoken later? Darr reminds us of the fluidity between the media when she writes:

> Yet written composition need not rule out public proclamation of texts . . . to the contrary, the presence of certain devices

7. Zimmerli, *Ezekiel*, 1:74–77.

8. Carley, *Ezekiel among the Prophets*; Boadt, "Textual Problems in Ezekiel."

(for example, repetition, striking visual metaphors, formulaic refrains) suggests a mode of delivery both congruent with past proclamation and audience expectations, and innovative enough to respond to the needs of a community in transition.[9]

Indeed, it has been argued that Ezekiel was *the* prophet who straddled the historic shift from oral prophetic proclamation to a permanent written source of authority for ongoing communities. The account of Ezekiel swallowing the scroll (Ezek 2:8–10) functions as a potent metaphor for this transition.[10] The conflation of priest and prophet within the one figure ("A prophet by calling, a priest by birthright")[11] likewise signals a shift in the locus of authority in the exilic and postexilic communities of ancient Israel. Julius Wellhausen's late-nineteenth-century assessment of Ezekiel as the one who "first pointed out the way which was suited for the time . . . the connecting link between the prophets and the law"[12] draws on the concept of "liminality" that is fundamental in Performance Criticism.[13] His prophetic role during the crisis of the exile—the "in-between" place where rules and rituals were open to negotiation—enabled a significant influence on the evolution of Israelite thought and theology.

The importance of the period of exile has amplified in recent decades with the greater knowledge that has been gained about the period via archaeological, sociological, and anthropological studies. In addition, postcolonial studies offer fresh insights into the period of Israel's history when the nation was dominated by more powerful empires. Where once the book of Ezekiel was largely ignored owing to the obvious priestly influence, or poorly understood with its hallucinatory visions, the book is now attracting greater attention due to its transitional importance.

While historical and literary questions can sometimes be viewed as polar opposites, both approaches can shed light on the book of Ezekiel and the prophet at its core. A performance approach to the book reminds us that prophets were actual performers in concrete settings and with live audiences, yet the performances have enough potency to be preserved, edited, and transmitted through reenactment for other settings and audiences.

9. Darr, "Ezekiel among the Critics," 255.

10. See Davis, *Swallowing the Scroll*; Darr, "Write or True?" 245.

11. Levitt Kohn, "Ezekiel at the Turn of the Century," 265.

12. Wellhausen, *Prolegomena*, 421.

13. See Turner, "Liminality and Communitas," 80.

Ezekiel as a Performance

Any discussion of performance in relation to the prophetic literature in the Hebrew Bible should include analysis of Ezekiel. Indeed, Shimon Levy claims that he is "the most theatrical prophet, and the holiest of actors."[14] His performances, especially those described in the first few chapters, have been variously called symbolic acts (Lundbom),[15] symbolic action reports (Sweeney, Nogalski),[16] sign acts (Carvalho and Niskanen),[17] street theater (Lang, Ruiz),[18] and body theater (Levy).[19]

Georg Fohrer's proposal that prophets were representative of an ancient Near East magical worldview including an established repertoire of gestures and actions is generally critiqued by contemporary scholars who see the prophet Ezekiel as a "imaginative and creative performer rather than [a] magician who relies on traditional rituals."[20] Nonetheless, the cultural background of incantation texts could have been used as ready-mades for the prophet as suggested by the performance of Ezek 3:24b–27 (see the note attached to "Miming a Mantra" below).

Unlike Elijah's drama series driven by its cast of colorful characters, Ezekiel's performances were largely individual acts presented before an audience of fellow exiles. As Levy points out, Ezekiel's priestly training would have meant he was experienced in public communication.[21] Nonetheless, his acts were highly unusual, and an alternative theatrical medium is needed to analyze them.

A few studies have used the terms *performance artist* and *performance art* when referring to Ezekiel and his ministry.[22] I find this designation convincing for a number of reasons. First, performance art privileges the body, and in the book of Ezekiel we see the prophet frequently using his body in the transmission of his message. Second, the performances of Ezekiel are episodic rather than connected in a narrative plot. They are a series of acts

14. Levy, *The Bible* as *Theatre*, 10.

15. Lundbom, *The Hebrew Prophets*, 209–16.

16. Sweeney, *The Prophetic Literature*, 35–36; Nogalski, *Interpreting Prophetic Literature*, 68–69.

17. Carvalho and Niskanen, *Ezekiel, Daniel*.

18. Lang, "Street Theater," 298–316; Ruiz, *Reading from the Edges*, 71–82.

19. Levy, *The Bible* as *Theatre*, 199.

20. Lang, quoted in Ruiz, *Readings from the Edges*, 76. Cf. Fohrer, *Die symbolischen Handlungen der Propheten*.

21. Levy, *The Bible* as *Theatre*, 178.

22. Hornsby, "Ezekiel Off-Broadway," 2.1; Sherwood, "Prophetic Scatology;" Ruiz, *Reading from the Edges*, 75.

rather than a drama with connected scenes. Third, performance artists use ordinary objects and actions in extraordinary ways in the public square, as does Ezekiel. Fourth, many of Ezekiel's performances are provocative. YHWH warned that Ezekiel would meet with resistance and stubbornness (Ezek 2:4–9), yet it is clear from the book of Ezekiel that he did not have an especially hostile audience. The elders sought him out (Ezek 8:1; 14:1; 20:1), and he seems to have offered entertainment value for the Golah community (Ezek 33:30–33). Daniel Block comments that "public apathy toward his message seems to have been a more serious problem than malevolence toward his person."[23] If we assume Ezekiel was facing an apathetic audience, there is all the more reason to assume that he intended to shock his fellow exiles with his performances. A final motivation for viewing Ezekiel as a performance artist is that it is a valid way of interpreting the behavior in the book that others have analyzed by way of psychology. The prophet has been labeled a paranoid schizophrenic,[24] has been psychoanalyzed as exhibiting a morbid dread and loathing of female sexuality,[25] and, more sympathetically, has been diagnosed as suffering from post-traumatic stress disorder.[26] But the activity that has prompted these readings could equally be understood as deliberately provocative acts by a highly imaginative artist and/or highly demanding director!

Before discussing Ezekiel as a performance artist, however, I want to focus on other aspects of creativity in the book of Ezekiel. I have largely restricted my comments to the first eleven chapters of the book. The book of Ezekiel can broadly be divided into four sections. It begins with Ezekiel's call and commissioning (chapters 1–3), followed by prophecies of judgment for Judah (chapters 4–24), oracles against the nations (chapters 25–32), and finally prophecies of hope and restoration (chapters 33–48). A natural break comes at the end of chapter 11 where Ezekiel is transported back to the Golah community following his visions of the glory of YHWH leaving the Jerusalem temple.

23. Block, *The Book of Ezekiel, Chapters 1–24*, 155.

24. Broome, "Ezekiel's Abnormal Personality."

25. Halperin, *Seeking Ezekiel*. Ezekiel's use of the daughter/wife metaphor in chapters 16 and 23 especially have been extensively treated and are worth careful contemplation, but this aspect of Ezekiel is beyond the scope of this chapter, which is predominantly focused on performance in Ezekiel 1–11.

26. Smith-Christopher, "Ezekiel on Fanon's Couch."

Creativity in Ezekiel

Language

From the opening chapter of Ezekiel onwards it is clear that the prophet struggles to clearly articulate the vision he wishes to describe. Anyone who has been conversing with members of Generation Z will find the language uncannily up-to-date, sprinkled as it is with that ubiquitous filler "like"! But other synonyms are repeated also: "likeness," "appearance," "semblance," "something like"; these words are used so frequently in the report of the vision that we get the message that all language for God must be hesitant, provisional, and ultimately inadequate. Indeed, the frequency of these words increases towards the end of the vision where YHWH himself appears:

> And from above the firmament that was over their heads, like the semblance of a stone of sapphire, a likeness of a throne. And above the likeness of the throne, a likeness like the semblance of a human above him from above. And I saw like an eye of electrum[27] like the semblance of fire housing it around, from the semblance of his loins upwards. And from the semblance of his loins downwards I saw like a semblance of fire and brightness all around him. Like the semblance of the bow that is in the cloud on the day of rain—thus was the semblance of the brightness all around him—the semblance of the likeness of the glory of YHWH. (Ezek 1:26–28)

It is not only the vocabulary that conveys the difficulty of describing the vision. The living beings with multiple faces, wings, and wheels, though described in great detail, are difficult to imagine as can be seen by the variety of artistic impressions one can find. Interestingly, when the creatures are described a second time with much of the same vocabulary (in chapter 10), they are named "cherubim"—as if the vision had firmed up in Ezekiel's mind in the interim. Yet the singular feminine pronoun is used in parallel with the four cherubim in 10:15 and 10:20 in order to express the idea that one living "Spirit" was animating the creatures (see 10:17).

Ezekiel's language provides both heights and depths that at one moment delight and the next disgust. His descriptions of YHWH's radiant

---

27. The translation is uncertain—it is some sort of shining precious stone or metal. I've chosen "electrum" to convey the "electric" atmosphere of the vision.

glory include several different words for "light," "precious gems," "fire," and "rain." The living creatures, likewise, are majestically portrayed as otherworldly beings that nonetheless have affinities with Ezekiel's world with their familiar creaturely faces and hands. Some beautiful expressions that have made their way into English parlance can be found: "Like the semblance of a bow that is in the cloud on a rainy day" (Ezek 1:28); "Like doves of the valley, all of them are moaning" (Ezek 7:16); "I will remove the heart of stone from their flesh and I will give them a heart of flesh" (Ezek 11:19). The message of YHWH to be conveyed by Ezekiel, however, is predominantly characterized by words such as *unclean, abomination, iniquity, wickedness, evil, sword, famine, pestilence,* and *death.* Whenever idols are mentioned, the word used is גִּלּוּל, (*gillûl*), a word probably derived from round logs but associated with excrement. This association is made explicit in Ezek 4:12 where Ezekiel is instructed to bake his bread over human *gillûl*. In my translation of Ezekiel I have connected the repeated use of this word by translating "turds of human excrement" in 4:12 and "turdy idols" where it occurs elsewhere (Ezek 6:4, 5, 6, 9, 13; 8:10).[28]

Chapter 7 stands out due to its transmission in poetic form in the MT. A portion of it below illustrates the terse phrasing and urgency of judgment it conveys:[29]

> Thus said Adonai YHWH /
>
> Evil after evil! Behold, it comes! //
>
> An end has come, comes the end.
>
> Upended against you,/ behold she comes! //
>
> The fate comes against you,
>
> dweller of the land./
>
> It will come. The time is near—the day of tumult—
>
> and no shout for the mountains.//
>
> Now soon I will pour out my wrath against you

28. "The adoption of this word as a designation for idols may have been prompted by the natural pelletlike shape and size of sheep feces or, less likely, the cylindrical shape of human excrement. Cf. Ezekiel's earlier reference to human excrement as *gelēlê hāādām* in Ezek 4:12, 15" (Block, *The Book of Ezekiel Chapters 1–24,* 226 and n. 44).

29. A single slash marks the *athnach,* the midpoint of the verse, and a double slash marks the end of the verse.

> And I will put an end to my nose upon you
>
> And I will judge you according to your ways /
>
> And I will put against you all your abominations. //
>
> And my eye will not spare and I will not show pity /
>
> For your ways against you I will set.
>
> And your abominations will be in the middle of you
>
> And you will all know that I YHWH can smite! //
>
> Behold the day, Behold it comes, /
>
> The fate has come out:
>
> The tribe blossomed, the insolence sprouted.//
>
> The violence rose up to become a tribe of wickedness /
>
> Not from them, and not from the many
>
> Not from their moaning, not from the mighty of them . . . //
> (Ezek 7:5–11)

Alliteration in the Hebrew text in the final verse may have determined the expression, as the wording is obscure, and one is left with the impression that perhaps even YHWH was lost for words! Later in the poem is the expression "all the hands will grow slack/and all the knees go to water//" (Ezek 7:17). The translation in the LXX is "knees will run with urine"—the unpleasant image of losing bladder control in the face of peril is clearly the intended meaning here.

The MT preserves only a few of Ezekiel's oracles in poetic form. But much of the material is characterized by parallelism and metaphor as illustrated in the verses translated below. The oracles must therefore be considered to fall somewhere in the middle of the continuum between prose and poetry.

> And he said to me,
>
> **YHWH**
>
> Son of humanity, I am sending you to the sons of Israel,

to nations of rebellious ones who rebelled against me,

They and their fathers transgressed against me until this self-same day.

And the sons are stubborn of face

and hard of heart.

I am sending you to them.

And you will say to them, 'Thus says YHWH'!

And whether they hear

or whether they forbear

—that house of bitter rebellion—

They shall know that a prophet was among them.

פ

And you, Son of humanity, do not be fearful of them and their words

Do not be fearful though thistles and thorns surround you

and among scorpions you are sitting

Of their words do not be fearful

and of their faces do not be afraid

—for a house of bitter rebellion are they—

And you will speak my word to them

whether they hear

or whether they forbear

—for bitter rebellion are they—.

פ

(Ezek 2:3–7)

"Resumptive Exposition"

Borrowing a term from Daniel Block, it is worth noting in this "Creativity" section that the book of Ezekiel reuses earlier traditions which are interpreted in the light of a later situation, not only from other biblical sources but from within the book itself. In Performance Critical terms this could be characterized as reenactment—the reuse in later contexts of material that is introduced in earlier sections. Within the first eleven chapters the most obvious example is the vision of the glory of YHWH and the living beings/cherubim (Ezek 1:1–28; 8:1—11:25), but other motifs that occur more than once include coals of fire (Ezek 1:13; 10:6–8), the unsheathed sword (Ezek 5:2, 12, 17; 11:8), abominations in the sanctuary (Ezek 5:11; 8:1–18), the hand of YHWH (Ezek 1:3; 2:9), and mountains of Israel (Ezek 6:2–3, 13; 7:7, 16). Furthermore, a number of motifs introduced in these early chapters are revisited later in the book of Ezekiel, such as words of hope to a remnant of Israel (Ezek 5:3; 6:8–10; 11:17–20), Ezekiel as a watchman (Ezek 3:16–21; 33:1–9), a vision in the valley (Ezek 3:22–23; 37:1–2), Jerusalem as a pot of meat (Ezek 11:1–12; 24:1–14), and prophecy to the mountains of Israel reversed from judgment to hope (Ezek 6:1–14; 36:1–15).

Ezekiel as a Performance Artist

Performance art resists simple definition as it is a general term that covers a range of experiences. Connections to early-twentieth-century art can be seen, such as Marcel Duchamp's "ready-mades" in which ordinary objects were re-positioned to become artworks. In a similar manner, performance artists turned real-life activities into art or created an artwork from their own bodies. Performance art is identified as primarily developing in the 1970s and 1980s as part of the postmodernist movement. Bernhard Giesen begins a chapter discussing performance art by listing examples from the visual arts, dance, theater, circus, music, and pop culture as activities and movements that can be described as performance art. The crossing and fusing of boundaries is a feature of performance art, according to Giesen.[30] In addition, a focus on the artist's body is a crucial component, as stated by Marvin Carlson, who defines the performance artist's "interest in developing the expressive qualities of the *body*, especially in opposition to logical and discursive thought and speech, and in seeking the celebration of *form and process* over content and product."[31]

30. Giesen, "Performance Art," 315.

31. Carlson, *Performance*, 110 (italics added).

A few examples of performance art installments illustrate the range of activities and emphases: "body art," using the body as brush on a canvas, often involving nudity and blood; "life art," heightening ordinary activities such as sitting in a chair or lying in a bed via the frame of performance; the removal of pretense from activities, most infamously seen in Chris Burden's *Shoot* (1971), in which the artist was shot in the arm with live ammunition;[32] use of the artist's body parts as material for the artwork, exemplified in the ongoing series of artworks titled *Self* (1991–present) by Marc Quinn, created from the artist's own blood filling casts of his head;[33] involvement of the audience, sometimes unwittingly, in the performance, illustrated by Vito Acconci's *Seedbed* (1971), in which individuals visiting the installation were not aware that the artist was masturbating under the floorboards until they had reached the raised section and read an inscription of the artwork; *persona* performances in which the individual embodies a type for a social or satirical purpose.

Perhaps most simply put, performance art is art where the artist him- or herself is the artwork. But even this definition has been pushed to the boundaries, such as when Acconci removed himself altogether in his *Command Performance* (1974), which consisted of an empty space with an empty chair and a video monitor with a soundtrack inviting viewers to create their own performance. Defining performance art in relation to the artist alone also prevents us from recognizing the important role the audience plays within the performance.

Bernhard Giesen highlights three common features that aid us in defining performance art:[34]

1. The focus is shifted from a completed work to a volatile and corporeal performance.

2. The performances are often deliberately provocative, surprising, even shocking; reflecting the postmodern disdain for tradition.

3. The boundaries between art and reality, actor and audience are blurred.

A focus on these features provides obvious links to prophetic performance, and, in particular, to the performances of Ezekiel.

When considering Ezekiel as a performance artist, the acts that suggest performance art to me include several performances that involve the body, that are ongoing over a significant time period, and that also set out to both

32. See Kutner, *Shot in the Name of Art.*

33. See the artist's website for pictures in this series: http://marcquinn.com/artworks/self/.

34. Giesen, "Performance Art," 315–16.

shock and implicate his audience. I think this is true for both Ezekiel's audience in antiquity and subsequent generations of audiences of biblical traditions. I therefore propose the following catalogue of Ezekiel's installations:[35]

Ezekiel as a Performance Artist
(593–585 BCE — the Catalogue of Major Works)

The Scroll Swallower: A Taste of Honey (Ezek 3:1–3)

The first of numerous street performances involving danger and a risk of injury: the artist demonstrates a scroll inscribed on both sides with laments and sighing and woe, then rolls it up and swallows it. This is a once-only performance because the scroll becomes food for the artist who claims it tastes much sweeter than wine.

Miming a Mantra: Torso-Tied and Tongue-Tied (Ezek 3:24b–27)

The artist wordlessly reenacts a ready-made — a well-known Babylonian incantation relating to demon-possession — by allowing himself to be taken to his home and immobilized with cords by fellow artists. A long period of silence is only occasionally interrupted with the words "Thus says YHWH" in order to convey to his Israelite audience that YHWH is the power that needs to be respected, not demons.[36]

Diorama of a Siege (Ezek 4:1–3)

A white clay brick inscribed with a map of Jerusalem, to which miniature battering rams and a plate of iron have been attached. The artist stares at the plate of iron then presses his outstretched arm toward the brick until the brick begins to crumble. This Diorama is reused in several other performances.

A Lying Prophet (Ezek 4:4–8)

A classic example of body art: the artist lies on his left side for 390 days. The high point of the performance comes at day 391 when he turns to his right side where he lies for a further forty days. This work incorporates *The Diorama of a Siege*, with the artist facing the earlier work from his lying position.

---

35. Note that this catalogue includes material from later parts of the book, illustrating the performative nature of Ezekiel's prophecy throughout his ministry.

36. For discussion of Akkadian incantations that describe experiences similar to those of Ezekiel see Block, *The Book of Ezekiel Chapters 1–24*, 159–60.

Holy Crap (or, *My Kitchen Rules*) (Ezek 4:9–17)

In a parody of *My Kitchen Rules*, the artist prepares, bakes, and eats bread that has been cooked over a stove fueled with dried cowpats. The observant audience may enjoy the witticism inherent in the artist's insistence that in *his* kitchen the fuel will be animal dung, not human excrement as suggested by the offstage director. The audience should be prepared for unpleasant odors.

Ezeki-Odd: The Sabre Barber of Chebar (Ezek 5:1–4)

A performance in which the artist cuts his own beard and hair with a sword, weighs it, and divides it into three equal parts. One-third is burned within the Diorama of the city; one-third is distributed around the Diorama by the sword; one third is scattered to the wind. Finally, a few of the scattered hairs are gathered and deposited into the hem of his robe.

Digging through a Wall of Sh*t (Ezek 8:8–11)

Viewers follow the artist through a hole that has been dug out of a wall. Once inside, viewers see light shone on petroglyphs of lowlife—animals that live in the dung of other animals. A sweet smell of incense that rises from censers conveys an incongruous dissonance.

More Honorable to Breach Than to Observe (Ezek 12:1–7)

Viewers are again invited to observe the artist digging a hole in the wall, but this time lighting is shone on the outside of the wall to enable observation of the silent and blindfolded artist moving through the hole dressed as an exile with a backpack of belongings. Lights are dimmed towards the end of the performance, and audience members are left to speculate on its meaning.

Bloody Bridegroom (Ezek 16)

A series of performances over several decades. Controversial use of child performers, nudity, blood, and sex.

A Sign of the Times (Ezek 21:19–23 [MT:21:24–28])

The artist draws a map of roads that meet at a junction, then fashions hands that point in different directions: one to Rabbah of Ammon and the other to Jerusalem of Judah. With a sword in his hand and a crown on his head, the artist then creates a caricature of ancient divination by drawing straws (belomancy), casting stones (consulting the teraphim), and inspecting the liver (hepatoscopy). In each test the omen falls on Jerusalem. No accolades or donations expected.

Cutthroat Kitchen (Ezek 24:3–13)

Employing the meat pot used for sacrifice and an all too rare feast of meat as a ready-made, the artwork whets viewers' appetites by the odor of cooking meat but finds within the pot a bloody mirror reflecting their own faces. Instead of being potential eaters, the onlookers turn out to be the eaten.

Requiem Miss (Ezek 24:15–24)

The artist stands beside a coffin containing a female corpse, a woman dead in the prime of life. The artist, dressed in party clothes, is deadpan throughout the performance.

Message Sticks (Ezek 37:15–28)[37]

A conjurer's trick in which the artist joins two separate sticks into one. Random members of the audience are invited to try to examine the stick and are surprised to find their own name inscribed upon it.

I have characterized these passages from the book of Ezekiel as a catalogue of performance art events. My interpretations attempt to replicate the Hebrew text faithfully. What I have named "petroglyphs of low life" in 8:8–11 reflects the use of the underlying Hebrew word גִּלּוּל (gillûl), usually translated "idols." As noted earlier, I translate גִּלּוּל (gillûl) as "turdy idols," hence the title of the event (Digging through a Wall of Sh*t). Chapter 24 (Cutthroat Kitchen) is introduced as a מָשָׁל (māšāl), often translated "proverb" or "parable," but the poem is so visually evocative that it should have been performed. After all, Ezekiel the priest was unable to fulfill the normal priestly functions in exile but would have expected a reaction if acting out those functions.

From the earliest history of interpretation until now there is resistance to viewing these performances as anything other than visions.

---

37. This title resonates with a traditional Indigenous Australian form of communication in which handheld pieces of wood etched with lines and dots were passed between different clans and language groups to establish information and transmit messages.

Jean-Pierre Ruiz quotes Maimonides: "God forbid that God would make his prophets appear an object of ridicule and sport in the eyes of the ignorant, and order them to perform foolish acts."[38] Nonetheless, the biblical script focuses our attention on the body of the prophet as a vehicle for transmitting the message he is asked to present to his audience. Live performance has a greater impact than words alone, and the strangeness of Ezekiel's performances would have piqued his audience's interest. If the original prophetic message was intended to shake them from their complacency, the shock value of using ordinary objects in extraordinary ways or employing out-of-place behaviors would have had a much greater impact if experienced as actual performances.

In the book of Ezekiel and in other prophetic books the performances are frequently followed by explanations of their meanings. According to Marvin Carlson, there has been a trend in performance art back to using language: "the initial emphasis on body and movement, with a general rejection of discursive language, has given way gradually to image-centered performance and a return to language."[39]

With the aid of the text to guide our interpretation of Ezekiel's performances, viewing them as performance art enables us to gain an appreciation of their shock value, helps us focus on the importance of the audience, and encourages the preservation of the script for future audiences.

Commentary on Ezekiel as a Performance

The Nature of Prophecy

Attending to the performances of Ezekiel gives insight into the nature of prophecy. The prophet is the instrument of YHWH, who is commanded by his god (as seen by the frequency of imperative verbs in YHWH's address) with instructions for what to do and what to say. The verb *prophesy* itself in Hebrew (הִנָּבֵא, *hinnāvēʾ*) is found only in *nifal* and *hitpael* stems, both of which can have a reflexive meaning. The grammar therefore conveys the idea that the prophet himself is not the primary agent of the message. Like an actor, the prophet performs the words prepared by the scriptwriter. Furthermore, a reflexive meaning suggests that the message is directed to the prophet as much as to the audience.

In his autobiographical performances, Ezekiel also makes clear that being a prophet is a bitter-sweet experience. Swallowing the scroll (Ezek

38. Maimonides (c. 1190), quoted in Ruiz, *Readings from the Edges*, 74.

39. Carlson, *Performance*, 128.

2:8–10) is reported as a delightful experience, in spite of the bitter inscriptions ("laments, and sighings, and woes"). But the prophet is immediately told he will have an unreceptive audience, whose lack of response will be embodied in their posture (see below under "Embodiment": pages 175–78). We sense the difficulty Ezekiel has in transmitting his messages not only in the hesitant speech with which the book opens, but also in the substance of his commissioning where he is not given an actual message, but is merely told to say, "Thus says YHWH" (Ezek 2:4; 3:11, 27). As a "watchman" Ezekiel must deliver his message and ensure that it is heard, because otherwise he carries the responsibility of the fate of the people whose blood will be upon his hands (Ezek 3:17–21). And all this is to be done "whether they hear or whether they forebear" (Ezek 2:5, 7; 3:11). The experience, he is told, will be akin to sitting among thistles and thorns and scorpions (Ezek 2:6), yet YHWH's reassuring exhortation "do not be afraid" is underscored by repetition (Ezek 2:9; 3:6). Prophecy is no comfortable calling: Ezekiel is bound and tongue-tied (Ezek 3:25–26) and compelled to repetitive and restricted action by lying in one place for vast lengths of time and by eating the same diet (Ezek 4:4–11). Nonetheless, the awed descriptions of his visions of the glory of YHWH (Ezek 1:4–28; 10:4, 18–19; 11:22–23) give a glimpse into a sense of privilege felt by the visionary prophet. Furthermore, this prophet (like others in the Hebrew Bible) is not totally subservient to God. When he describes himself falling on his face in YHWH's presence, Ezekiel was twice encouraged to "stand on your feet" (Ezek 2:1–2; 3:24), a posture that suggests dignity and equality. The prophet is also confident enough to protest on occasion against what he is told or shown. Ezekiel's protest in the matter of cooking his food over human excrement seems to contribute to a change of mind in YHWH:

YHWH

And you, take for yourself wheat and barley and broadbeans and lentils and millet and spelt and set them into one vessel and make them for yourself into bread.

For the number of the days when you are lying on your side: three hundred and ninety days you will eat it.

And your eats which you are eating it in weight will be twenty shekel for the day

From time until time you are eating it.

And waters in measure you will drink one-sixth of the hin

From time until time you will drink.

And a loaf of barley you will eat her

And she on turds of excrement of the human you will bake her before their eyes.

ס

Ezekiel

And YHWH said

YHWH

Thus they will eat—the sons of Israel—their bread unclean

Among the nations where I have banished them there.

Ezekiel

And I said Ahah Adonai YHWH behold my flesh was never unclean and neither corpse nor animal carcass have I eaten from my youth until now and never came into my mouth flesh of carrion!

ס

And he said to me,

YHWH

See, I have given to you the dung of cattle instead of the turds of humans.

So make your bread over them!

Ezekiel

And he said to me

YHWH

Son of humanity, behold me breaking the tribe of bread in Jerusalem. And they will eat bread in weight and with anxiety

And waters in measure and horror they will drink.

Because they lack bread and waters

They will be dismayed—a man and his brother—and they will be wasted in their iniquity.

פ

(Ezek 4:9–17)

The two *setumahs* in this text could be interpreted as stage instructions indicating pauses in the performance. The first pause comes immediately after the shocking instruction "on turds of human excrement you will bake her *before their eyes*" (Ezek 4:12). Although the explanation for this action is given by YHWH, Ezekiel, who has been struggling with the implications of this instruction, bursts out with a cry of anguish (אֲהָהּ, *'ăhāh*), protesting that he has never eaten unclean food. The second *setumah* gives another pause, during which YHWH thinks over the prophet's protest, then gives in and changes the instruction to something a little less confronting for both Ezekiel and any audience expected to observe his actions as indicated by the phrase "before their eyes" (Ezek 4:12). But the change prompts a further explanation on YHWH's part, linking the eating of bread and drinking of water with the covenant curses of Lev 26. This whole episode concludes with the *petuuah*, allowing a period of time before the next major performance.

Ezekiel continues to use אֲהָהּ (*'ăhāh*) as an expression of protest. When he is shown a vision of the destroyers of Jerusalem, we hear: "And I fell on my face and I cried out and I said 'Ahah Adonai YHWH, are you destroying all those left in Israel when you pour out your wrath on Jerusalem?'" (Ezek 9:8). YHWH responds by justifying the destruction on the basis of the iniquity of the land: "The iniquity of the house of Israel and Judah is great—very—exceedingly—and the land was filled with blood and the city was full of perversion." (Ezek 9:9). Upon seeing a vision of the death of one of the officials in Jerusalem, we again hear Ezekiel's protest, but this time amplified: "And I fell on my face and I cried out—a great sound—and I said Ahah Adonai YHWH will you make an end of the remnant of Israel? ס" (Ezek 11:13). The *petuuah*—long pause—that follows this protest results in the first of YHWH's oracles of promise and hope (Ezek 11:16–20) and suggests that once again that the prophet's response to God has contributed to a change of mind.

Names

As in much of the Hebrew Bible, names in the book of Ezekiel have significance. The name of the prophet himself could be translated "God strengthens" or "May God strengthen." Use of the same root in a phrase in 7:13 is perhaps a play on this name:

> For the seller to the sold will not return
>
> Though their lives be living;
>
> For a vision to all the multitude will not return
>
> And <u>a man in his iniquity will not strengthen his life</u>.
>
> (Ezek 7:13)

Could we translate the underlined phrase as "a man in his iniquity will no Ezekiel be"?!

The characteristic way that Ezekiel addresses the deity is "Adonai YHWH," using both the title "the Lord" and God's proper name "YHWH." The repeated use of this title stresses the contrast between the community of Israel who do not recognize the lordship of their God and the prophet who does. Rather than addressing Ezekiel by name, however, YHWH most frequently uses the title "son of humanity" (בֶּן־אָדָם, *ben-ʾādām*) when speaking with him. This title indicates that although Ezekiel is a conversation partner with God, his primary role is to identify with the Golah community in their state of exile and punishment.

The names of the Jerusalem officials in chapters 8 and 11 are usually transliterated in English translations, but their derivations are easily determined and, in my view, contribute irony to the performance if allowed to be translated literally. Ezekiel has been taken in a vision back to the Jerusalem temple where he sees first seventy men in an inner sanctuary—among them "YHWH Hears" son of Shaphan (Ezek 8:11), and then, later, twenty-five men at the eastern gate worshipping the sun, disregarding temple and provoking YHWH (Ezek 8:16–17). He sees the same group at the eastern gate again later (Ezek 11:1), naming the "officials of the people" that he sees among them as "YHWH Hears," son of "He Helps" (the patronym indicating a different individual from Ezek 8:11) and "YHWH Has Delivered" son of "YHWH has Built Up." But the word that comes from YHWH is that he will *not* hear (Ezek 8:18), as it is *these* men who have plotted vice and planned plans of evil (Ezek 11:2); who have multiplied slayings in the city (Ezek 11:6). At any rate, these men have acted in such dissonance with their Yahwistic names that they deserve judgment rather than protection. Yet when Ezekiel protests upon hearing of the death of "YHWH Has Built Up" in Ezek 11:13, his question to YHWH ("Will you make an end of the remnant of Israel?") is implicitly a reminder that YHWH was ultimately responsible for the existence of Israel and would need to ensure that its end was never irrevocable. It is this reminder thaι prompts words of promise and hope (Ezek 11:16–20).

The other individual who has a significant role in these first eleven chapters is the "Man Clothed in Linens" (Ezek 9:2–3, 11; 10:2, 6–7). Holding the writing kit of a scribe, his task is to mark the foreheads of all those who share YHWH's distress over the abominations being committed in the city so that they will be preserved at the time of destruction. In the final mention of this individual, the title "Clothed in Linens" alone is given (Ezek 10:7) such that it seems to have migrated from a description to a nickname.

Embodiment

From the very beginning of the book of Ezekiel we are conscious of the prophet as an embodied entity. Unusually for a prophetic book, it opens with a first-person narrative, and the pronoun "I" is mentioned before any reference to God or the דְּבַר־יְהוָה (*dᵉvar-yhwh*, "word of YHWH"). An elaborate vision of "the semblance of the likeness of the glory of YHWH" causes the prophet to fall on his face (Ezek 1:28) before being instructed to stand up on his feet to be addressed by the subject of the vision. Two phrases that recur in the book emphasize an embodied presence of God for Ezekiel: "the hand of YHWH upon me" (Ezek 1:3; 3:14, 22; 8:1; 33:22; 37:1; 40:1); "a spirit entered/lifted me" (Ezek 2:2; 3:12, 14, 24; 8:3; 11:1, 24; 43:5). While "spirit" does not have a definite article, the context makes clear that both "hand" and "spirit" are metonyms for God's power.

Ezekiel's embodied actions are critical to his prophetic ministry. The first commissioning speech culminates in an instruction to eat the scroll—the first profound concrete embodiment of God's message for the exiles. Despite the sweet taste of the scroll, the instructions that followed were unpalatable, even if expected for a prophet. Although he was to present God's words to his community, they would bounce back virtually unheard. Indeed, the words of commission are riddled with body parts as highlighted below:

YHWH

Son of humanity, go! Come to the house of Israel and you will speak my word to them.

For not to a people incomprehensible of <u>lip</u> and heavy of <u>tongue</u> are you being sent,

But to the house of Israel!

Not to many peoples incomprehensible of lip and heavy of tongue where you cannot listen to their words

Surely to them if I sent you, they would listen to you!

But the house of Israel are not willing to listen to you because neither are they willing to listen to me,

Because the whole house of Israel are hard of head and stubborn of heart. They are!

Behold! I have given your face hardness corresponding to their faces,

And your head hardness corresponding to their head.

Like adamant[40] stronger than flint I have given your head,

So you will not be afraid of them and not be dismayed by their faces

Because a house of bitter rebellion are they!"

Ezekiel

And he said to me,

YHWH

Son of humanity, all my words which I am speaking to you take in your heart and with your ears, hear!

And go! Come to the Golah, to the sons of your people, and speak to them,

and say to them 'Thus says YHWH of hosts'

—Whether they hear or whether they forbear!

(Ezek 3:4b–11)

Ezekiel embodies this lack of response in his own being by sitting among the exiles for seven days, stunned, immobile, and silent. After further words of commission he is taken in another vision to a valley—the same valley where the vision of dry bones will be recorded later in the book (Ezek 3:22; cf. 37:1–14). Once again the prophet falls on his face in the presence of God, and once again he is lifted to his feet to face his instructions head-on (Ezek 3:23–24). More actions are described, although it is not always clear who is doing the actions. He is to be shut in his house, bound with cords,

---

40. A type of hard stone, but a particularly apt translation in this context!

and his tongue will cleave to his palate. Paralyzed and tongue-tied, it is evident that Ezekiel will only be able to speak at the behest of Adonai YHWH. A demanding director indeed!

Ezekiel's embodied involvement in his prophetic ministry is evident in the text. Throughout the book he is instructed to look, and see (Ezek 3:8; 4:8, 15; 7:5–6, 10; 8:6, 9, 15, 17; etc.). This prophet is not only hearing the words of God, but is asked to use his eyes and senses to *experience* them. His orientation and posture is important. Directions—particularly the east—are often noted (Ezek 8:16; 10:19; 11:1). He is by the river, but sets his face to the mountains of Israel (Ezek 6:2). He stamps and claps to accompany oracles (Ezek 6:11)—described as "verbal exclamation marks" by Daniel Block, which doesn't quite capture the impact of the actual bodily movements.[41] His head comes into focus—first by being shaved with a sword (Ezek 5:1–4) and later when he is lifted by the lock of his hair (presumably after it had grown back) by a spirit (Ezek 8:3). We hear often of him eating and drinking, sometimes distastefully, but always with an exaggerated performance: "Mortal, eat your bread with quaking, and drink your water with trembling and with fearfulness" (Ezek 12:18, NRSV). As can be seen in the catalogue of performance artworks above, Ezekiel uses parts of his own body in his performances: lying on his side for protracted periods, stretching out his arm, eating and drinking unclean bread, shaving his head, digging through and crawling through a wall, carrying luggage on his shoulder. Many of these actions involve him bearing in his own body the iniquity that is due to Israel:

YHWH

And you, lie on your side—the left side—and put the iniquity of the house of Israel upon her.

The number of days that you will lie upon her <u>you will bear their iniquity</u>.

And I will set for you years of their iniquity for a number of days: three hundred and ninety days,

And <u>you will bear the iniquity</u> of the house of Israel.

And you will make an end of these and you will lie on your side—the right side—secondly, and <u>you will bear the iniquity</u> of the house of Judah,

Forty days, a day for a year, a day for a year, I have set for you.

---

41. Block, *The Book of Ezekiel Chapters 1–24*, 234.

> And towards the siege of Jerusalem make firm your face
> and your arm will be bared
>
> And you will prophesy upon her.
>
> And behold, I have set against you cords
>
> And you will not be turned from your side to your side
>
> until you have made an end of the days of your siege.
>
> (Ezek 4:4–8)

As with several other Hebrew prophets, embodiment is taken to such a degree that Ezekiel was prepared to surrender his own pride, dignity, and comfort for the sake of transmitting God's message.

The hand of YHWH as a metonym for power has been noted, but other body parts of YHWH are mentioned in Ezekiel. Reference to YHWH's nose is an idiom for anger or long-suffering (Ezek 5:13, 15; 7:3, 8), and YHWH's eyes determine judgment (Ezek 5:11; 8:18). These anthropomorphic references are a reminder that YHWH is an actor within prophetic performance scripts (see below).

Props and Ready-Mades

Performances are memorable because Ezekiel uses his own body as his canvas, and several performances are enhanced by specific props. These are often introduced in the text with the words "take for yourself":

- And you, Son of humanity, *take for yourself* a white brick and set her before your face (Ezek 4:1);

- And you, *take for yourself* a griddle of iron and set her as a wall of iron between you and between the city (Ezek 4:3);

- And you, *take for yourself* wheat and barley and broadbeans and lentils and millet and spelt and set them into one vessel (Ezek 4:9);

- And you, Son of humanity, *take for yourself* a sharp sword—a razor of the barbers—and take her to yourself and pass over your head and over your beard (Ezek 5:1a);

- And *take for yourself* balances of weight (Ezek 5:1b).

The Hebrew word that I have translated "a white brick" is לְבֵנָה (lᵉbēnāh), a word evoking the snowy caps of Lebanon and ensuring that what was inscribed on it could be clearly seen. Tablets of clay with maps of the city of Nippur of Babylon inscribed upon them have been found verifying that this sort of artifact could well have been used as a prop in a prophetic performance.[42]

The corporeality of the sweet scroll is emphasized by it being seen, pointed out, and tasted:

פ

YHWH

And you, Son of humanity, hear whatever I am speaking to you—do not be bitter like the house of bitter rebellion.

Open your mouth and eat what I am giving to you.

Ezekiel

And I looked, and behold—a hand stretched out to me.

And behold, in it, a scroll of a book.

And he spread her out before me and she was written (on), front and back,

And written on her were laments and sighing and woe.

ס

And he said to me,

YHWH

Son of humanity, what you find, eat!

Eat this scroll and go! Speak to the house of Israel!

Ezekiel

And I opened my mouth

And I ate this scroll.

And he said to me,

YHWH

Son of humanity, in your belly it will be food, and let your stomach fill—this scroll that I am giving to you.

---

42. See Pritchard, *The Ancient Near East in Pictures*, 80.

> **Ezekiel**
>
> And I ate, and it was in my mouth like sweet honey.
>
> פ
>
> (Ezek 2:8—3:3)

This section is bracketed by *petuuahs*, suggesting that it is one complete scene and raising the question of whether "my word" that follows (Ezek 3:4) has any relationship with the scroll of laments and sighing and woe. The *setumah* in the middle of the scene suggests a pause for Ezekiel to digest the contents of the scroll mentally before doing so physically.

Other props used by Ezekiel include cords with which he was bound (Ezek 3:25), his food and drink rations: eats weighing twenty shekels and waters measuring one-sixth of a hin (Ezek 4:10–11), fuel for cooking bread (Ezek 4:12, 15), and fire for burning his hair (Ezek 5:2, 4). Among the props mentioned in judgment oracles are altars, incense stands, and idols (Ezek 6:4–6); cadavers and slain ones (Ezek 6:4–5, 13; 9:7; 11:6–7); a trumpet (Ezek 7:14), sackcloths (Ezek 7:18); silver and gold (Ezek 7:19); the chain (Ezek 7:23); censers for incense (Ezek 8:11); tools for annihilation and destruction (Ezek 9:1–2); the writing kit of the scribe (Ezek 9:2–3, 11); and a sword of judgment (Ezek 11:8, 10).

An unusual prop used by apostate worshipers in the temple links their actions directly to YHWH's anger:

> And he said to me
>
> **YHWH**
>
> Do you see, Son of humanity, with what little regard the house of Judah makes abominations that they have made here? For they have filled the land with violence and have come back to provoke me. Behold them, <u>sending the zemorah to their nose</u>!
>
> (Ezek 8:17)

The *zemorah* is an artifact: a branch of vine or cluster of twigs used in Persian sun worship. Block describes the action here as "sticking the branch up YHWH's nose."[43] We might also say that the sun-worshippers are rubbing YHWH's nose in their worship of other gods.

At the beginning of this chapter I pointed out similar vocabulary found in Ezek 6 and Lev 26. It seems obvious that the covenant curses listed in the Holiness Code serve as ready-mades for Ezekiel's prophetic warnings. Consequences for disobedience to the law that were part of the Torah tradition were now unfolding. The celebration of Passover could also have functioned as a ready-made, with YHWH through the prophet subverting the tradition by speaking of blood passing *through* in judgment rather than *over* in salvation:

> And I will send upon you famine and evil beasts and miscarriage and pestilence and the blood and it will pass through you
>
> And a sword I will bring upon you. I—YHWH—have spoken.
>
> פ
>
> (Ezek 5:17)

The mark on the forehead of the righteous (Ezek 9:4) has become a ready-made that *originated* with Ezekiel and has been used often since its original performance:

> **Ezekiel**
>
> And he called in my ear with a great sound saying
>
> **YHWH**
>
> The visitations of the city will draw near,
>
> And each a tool of his annihilation in his hand.
>
> **Ezekiel**
>
> And behold! Six men coming from the way of the gate—the upper one—that were turning northward, and each a tool of destruction in his hand, and one man in the middle of them Clothed in Linens, and the writing kit of the scribe in his loins.
>
> And they came and they stood beside the altar of bronze.

---

43. Block, *The Book of Ezekiel Chapters 1–24*, 299.

And the glory of the God of Israel had gone up from over the cherub that was over him to the threshold of the house

And he called to the man, the one Clothed in Linens, who had the writing kit of the scribe in his loins.

ס

And YHWH said to him

YHWH

Pass over in the middle of the city in the middle of Jerusalem

And <u>mark a mark on the foreheads of the men</u>—the ones groaning and the ones moaning[44] over all the abominations being made within her.

Ezekiel

And to these he said in my ear

YHWH

Pass over the city after him and smite.

Do not spare your eyes and do not show pity.[45]

Old, a young man and a maid and a little one and women you shall slay for destruction, but <u>on every man who has on him the mark you shall not touch</u>. And from my holy place you shall begin.

(Ezek 9:1–6)

The scene is described in great detail, including costumes and props. The reference to the "north" (Ezek 9:2) could also be understood as a ready-made since judgment in the form of foreign armies usually came from the north in Israel's experience rather than crossing the desert directly from the east. The *setumah* after verse 3 suggests an ominous pause prior to the onslaught of the slaughter.

My translation "mark a mark" (Ezek 9:4) reflects the Hebrew where the same root letters form the verb and the noun. But the noun in Hebrew is literally "*taw*"—the name of the last letter of the Hebrew alphabet (ת),

44. Following Block, I have translated הַנֶּאֱנָחִים (*hanne'ĕnāḥîm*) as "the ones moaning" and הַנֶּאֱנָקִים (*hanne'ĕnāqîm*) as "the ones groaning" in order to replicate the rhyme and assonance of the Hebrew (Block, *The Book of Ezekiel Chapters 1–24*, 307).

45. This phrase repeats pronouncements of YHWH in Ezek 5:11 and Ezek 8:18, indicating that the annihilators are to emulate YHWH's own resolve.

usually transliterated with the letter *t* (and pronounced "tav"). In old Hebrew script this letter looked more like an *x* The mark was to be placed where it could be easily seen, on the foreheads.

The Damascus document from the Qumran community records the same ritual. Those bearing a *taw* on their forehead will be saved at the time of the final judgment. The Church Father Origen also referred to the tradition, recording explanations given to him by Jewish commentators. One noted that *taw* is the first letter of the word Torah, so the one with the *taw* is the one who has followed the law from aleph (א) to Taw (ת)—the equivalent of from *A* to *Z*. Another Christian Jew suggested that it represented the cross, the *T* of the Christian faith. In Rev 7:2–3 an angel marks the 144,000 servants of God with a "seal" on their foreheads, destining them for eternal salvation.

Each of these references to the forehead mark could be understood as a reenactment of Ezekiel's script. Yet another reenactment makes a notable improvisation by referring to the mark on the forehead as the sign of those who are marked out for *punishment*, rather than preservation (Rev 13:16–17; 14:9–11). It is this forehead mark that has survived most strongly in popular culture, known by the name "the mark of the beast."

Settings and Stage Directions

In Ezekiel's performances the use of space is prominent. The book opens in a definite location, in the land of the Chaldeans on the River Chebar, but the vision that unfolds takes Ezekiel out of that location and into another world—one that is full of light and noise. Coming back down to earth at Tel Aviv is described as a bitter experience (Ezek 3:14–15) and is followed by seven days of inaction. The next direction from YHWH takes Ezekiel to the valley (Ezek 3:22), undoubtedly the same one that features later in the book with the vision of dry bones (Ezek 37:1–14). The initial valley scene is short, however, because he is immediately directed to be shut in his house, isolated from his community.

The house is presumably the location for the series of performances found in chapters 4 and 5, but it is clear that Ezekiel, contrary to being isolated, has an audience for these acts (see Ezek 4:12). Jerusalem and the mountains of Israel are the addressees for the next few oracles, but Ezekiel's location does not change until he is transported by a spirit to Jerusalem (Ezek 8:3). so it is likely he was addressing the diorama he had created, and posturing himself to face in the direction of Israel. Once Ezekiel appears in Jerusalem, the locations are again specific: the gates and courtyards of the temple. The instruction to dig through the wall (Ezek 8:8) moves the scene from the outer public areas of the temple into a secret hidden chamber in which illicit worship was taking place. The mention of censers and clouds of incense suggest a dim scene that forms a striking contrast between the light of YHWH's presence in Ezekiel's throne room visions and the darkness of the activity of people still located in the Jerusalem temple. After further excursions around the temple and city of Jerusalem, Ezekiel is finally transported back to the Golah community at the River Chebar.

Actors

Ezekiel is central to this performance and often is the focus of attention, especially when engaged in performance art. At other times, however, he steps off center stage and observes the activity of others. The heavenly visions are full of unusual beings performing choreographed movements. Ezekiel's hesitant descriptions and the shift between descriptions of plural "cherubim," a singular "cherub," and a "spirit" contributes to a lack of clarity in the appearance and role of these beings, yet their human hands and their interactions with the "Man Clothed in Linens"—an actor who has only one line in the previous scene (Ezek 9:11b) but important actions nonetheless— show that they are actors integrated in the performance:

Ezekiel

And I looked and behold! Towards the dome that is over the heads of the cherubim like a stone of sapphire, like the appearance of the likeness of a throne

It appeared over them.

And he said to the Man Clothed in Linens and he said

YHWH

Come in to between the willy-willy[46] to under the cherub and fill your palms with coals of fire from between the cherubim and throw on the city.

---

46. The Hebrew word is גַּלְגַּל (gal°gal)—could be translated wheel, rolling thing, or whirlwind. *Willy-willy* is a term for a mini whirlwind in outback Australia—and captures the reduplication of sounds as in the Hebrew word.

Ezekiel

And he came before my eyes.

And the cherubim were standing to the right of the house when the man came in

And the cloud filled the court—the inner one.

And it rose up—the glory of YHWH—from over the cherub to the threshold of the house

And the house was filled with the cloud and the court was full with the brightness of the glory of YHWH.

And a sound like the wings of the cherubim was heard as far as the court—the outer one—

Like the sound of El Shaddai in his speaking.

And it happened in his commanding of the Man Clothed in Linens he was saying

YHWH

Take fire from between the willy-willy from between the cherubim.

Ezekiel

And he came in and he stood beside the wheel.

And the cherub sent his hand from between the cherubim to the fire that was between the cherubim

And he lifted up and set towards the palms of "Clothed in Linens" and he took and he went out.

And it appeared for the cherubim something like a hand of a human under their wings.

And I looked and behold! Four wheels beside the cherubim: one wheel beside one cherub, and one wheel beside one cherub,

And the appearance of the wheels was like the eye of the stone of Tarshish.

And their appearance was a likeness—each one of the four of them—

Which was like being the wheel in the middle of the wheel.

In their going to four of their sides they went, not being turned in their going,

Because the place where the head turned, after him they went, not being turned in their going.

And their whole body, and their rims, and their hands, and their wings

And the wheels were full of eyes all around the four of them—their wheels.

For the wheels

They were called the "willy-willy" in my ears.

And four faces to each one:

The face of the first was the face of a cherub,

and the face of the second was the face of a man,

and the face of the third was the face of a lion,

and the face of the fourth was the face of an eagle.

And they rose up—the cherubim.

She is the living creature that I saw at the River Chebar.

(Ezek 10:1–15)

In an earlier scene Ezekiel observed the actions of seventy men in the dark inner room (Ezek 8:11), worshiping amidst the cloud of incense; two women weeping the Tammuz (Ezek 8:14), and twenty-five men worshiping the sun (Ezek 8:16). As noted above, three of the men are identified by name. Their lines in the script are significant contributions to the drama, and, like their names, provide dramatic irony. The group of seventy with their censers in the darkened inner room claim "YHWH does not see us; YHWH has forsaken the land" (Ezek 8:12b). There is irony in that YHWH is showing this vision to Ezekiel, so clearly *does* see, and at that point is still present in the temple, so has not yet forsaken the land. But the words are prophetic also: YHWH will choose to *not* spare his eye (that is, to *not* see—Ezek 5:11; 8:18), and YHWH's glory *will* leave the temple within a short time of this statement (Ezek 10:18). The group of twenty-five men by the eastern gate claim, "It is not necessary to build houses . . . She is the pot, and we are the flesh" (Ezek 11:3). For them, the city of Jerusalem is a vessel of protection. But this imagery is taken over by YHWH and his prophet. First a response comes in a decisive rebuttal:

Thus says YHWH Adonai, "your slain ones that you have placed in the middle of her—*they* are the flesh, and *she* is the pot, and *all of you* will be taken out from the middle of her."[47]

(Ezek 11:7)

Later in the book the pot is again employed in an elaborate piece of performance art (24:1–14). Meat is boiled in a rusty pot, removed, then the pot is boiled dry in order to remove any remaining impurities. The fate of Jerusalem is represented by the fierce heat exerting a fiery judgment on the city as its inhabitants are carried away to exile. YHWH first instructs Ezekiel to "allegorize an allegory" (מְשֹׁל מָשָׁל, *mᵉšōl māšāl*) and the performance is presented in poetic form, perhaps even as a protest song. The words of the men at the gate have thus become an important leitmotif in the overall performance.

YHWH, clearly, is a major actor in this performance, fulfilling the role of both director and actor. A refrain from later chapters sums up the divine self-introduction of this actor-director:

I, YHWH, have spoken, and I will act

(Ezek 17:24; 22:14; 24:14; 36:36; 37:14).

This actor-director has a heightened sense of drama. The buildup towards his first appearance is impressive (Ezek 1:4–28), his voice is commanding, and his on-stage directions decisive. The drama has one major plotline—Israel has rejected his covenant and must be punished, but a new future is possible. This actor-director will do whatever it takes to convey that message. Along with embodied performance art, the script includes visions, fables, songs, proverbs, soliloquies, and pornography. This is a director who is willing to shock his audience and even to risk alienating them.[48]

YHWH often allows the actor-prophet to speak, but frequently takes center stage to address the audience directly in second-person pronouns

47. The pronouns are emphasized here because they are, somewhat unusually, present in the Hebrew text.

48. Likening the Israelites to an innocent child bride turned rampant whore (chapter 16) would have been as reprehensible to an ancient male Israelite audience as it is to a contemporary feminist reader.

and verbs (e.g., Ezek 5:8–17; 11:9–12). These speeches are usually marked with the formula "utterance of YHWH Adonai" to underscore their rhetorical significance.

A secondary plotline in this performance is that Israel's God is not confined to the Jerusalem temple, and nor are God's people confined to Israel. A series of visions and statements articulate this ground-breaking truth for Ezekiel's audience including the description of the winged creatures that accompany the glory of YHWH from the temple (Ezek 10:4–5) and the revision of the pot metaphor from a place of protection to a place of judgment (11:3, 7). The end of this first main act in the book of Ezekiel ends with words of hope:

> Therefore say 'Thus says Adonai YHWH, Indeed I have removed them into the nations and indeed I have scattered them into the lands
>
> But I was for them a sanctuary while in the lands when they came there.'
>
> Therefore say 'Thus says Adonai YHWH, And I will gather all of you from the peoples and I will assemble all of you from the lands where you were dispersed in them
>
> And I will give to all of you the territory of Israel.
>
> And they will come there
>
> And will remove every detestable thing and every abomination from her.
>
> And I will give to them one heart, and a new spirit I will set in their midst
>
> And I will remove the heart of stone form their flesh and I will give to them a heart of flesh.
>
> So that in my statutes they will go and my judgments they will keep and make them.
>
> They will be for me a people, and I will be for them a God.
>
> But if to a heart of detestable things and their abominations their hearts are going,
>
> Their ways on their heads I will set. Utterance of Adonai YHWH.
>
> (Ezek 11:16–21)

Notice the concluding formula and the shift from third-person address to second-person address partway through this oracle. The plural pronouns show that it is not just Ezekiel who is being addressed here. The audience members are drawn in to hear the promises directed at each of them. Yet the promise is still tempered by a warning. Despite YHWH's willingness to change their hearts, ultimately they will determine their own ways by choosing obedience to or rejection of the covenant.

Connections with Ezekiel

Earlier I discussed how Ezekiel's performance gives insights into the nature of prophecy. Likewise, this performance models prophetic action in the world that can be emulated in our own time. Whilst inspired by heavenly visions, Ezekiel was called to identify with and minister to his own grounded community. He represented truth and justice even in the face of resistance to his performance. Finally, he gained attention through embodied, imaginative, and provocative action.

The book of Ezekiel opens with a concrete record of the time and place in which the prophet was active. The precision of dating when compared with extant Babylonian calendars enables scholars to confidently place the prophet in June or July in the year 593 BCE.[49] It quickly moves to a heavenly vision full of light, sound, and wonder, with some of the language of storm theophanies found elsewhere in the Hebrew Bible (Ezek 1:4–28; cf. Exod 15; Judg 5; Pss 18; 68; Nah 1; Hab 3). Ezekiel claims to see "semblances of God," using the word מַרְאוֹת (*mārʾôt*) that is also used in the passage that claims Moses saw God "face-to-face" (Num 12:6–7). The claim to have a direct encounter with YHWH is audacious and may explain the cautious language, but it was clearly an inspirational experience. The prophet describes further similar encounters in chapters 8–11 and 43. The first great movement of Jewish mysticism known as Merkevah Mysticism traces its roots to this passage.[50] Indeed, if mysticism is defined as "knowledge of God from experience,"[51] a prophet like Ezekiel should be understood as a mystic. Yet Jewish mysticism rarely allows itself to remain in an "otherworldly" state:

> It can not be over-emphasized that to the Jew mysticism did not mean eschewing this world in the selfish concern with personal

49. Greenberg, *Ezekiel, 1–20*, 40; Block, *The Book of Ezekiel Chapters 1–24*, 83; Sweeney, *The Prophetic Literature*, 128; Odell, *Ezekiel*, 15. Block and Odell are even more specific, asserting the date of Ezekiel's vision was July 31.

50. Segal, "Mysticism," 983.

51. Segal, "Mysticism," 982.

salvation. Jewish mysticism, like all other phases of Jewish tradition, is primarily oriented toward a more just world.[52]

It is consistent with this assertion that Ezekiel was sent back to the Golah community at the River Chebar to deliver YHWH's words. One who has the privilege of inspiration and calling to ministry should not remain in the "other world" but must carry out their tasks *where they are*. The title "son of humanity" reminds us that the visionary should nonetheless be able to identify with the perspective of his or her audience.

For Ezekiel, however, returning to the real world did not initially hold much promise. He was warned that he would be met with implacable resistance, a "house of bitter rebellion" (Ezek 2:5, 6, 7, 8; 3:9, 26, 27). He was to speak "whether they hear or whether they forbear" (Ezek 2:5, 7; 3:11). As has been noted above, the message that Ezekiel was to bring initially had no real content—he was to say merely "Thus says YHWH" (Ezek 2:4; 3:11, 27). His primary role, therefore, was to be the presence of God to his community, reminding them of the claim their God had on them. His series of performance art installations depicted the consequences of the judgment coming to Jerusalem, without an explanation of what the judgment was for. So he acted out the besieging of the city, paucity of food and water, existence amongst unclean nations, the manner of destruction of Jerusalem, and the preservation of a remnant. Not until after the Sabre Barber of Chebar vignette did any words of justification come:

> For my judgments they rejected and my statutes they did not follow . . . my sanctuary you have made unclean with all your vile things and with all your abominations"
>
> (Ezek 5:6, 11)

The technical covenant terminology and the word *covenant* itself that is used frequently in the later parts of the book indicate that rejection of the covenant was the main reason for judgment. Words of indictment that come in the subsequent chapters are mostly focused on illegitimate worship, but a few references to blood and violence indicate that social justice was also a cause for concern:

---

52. Wolk, "Mysticism," 76.

> Make the chain!
>
> For the land is filled with judgments of blood
>
> And the city is filled with violence.
>
> (Ezek 7:23)
>
> For they have filled the land with violence.
>
> (Ezek 8:17)
>
> The iniquity of the house of Israel and Judah is great—very—exceedingly—and the land was filled with blood and the city was full of perversion.
>
> (Ezek 9:9)
>
> All of you have multiplied your slayings in the city—this one—
>
> And you have filled the streets with the slain.
>
> (Ezek 11:6)

Prophets of any era who speak for truth and justice are required to continue speaking even in the face of resistance. But in such an environment, prophets in the public sphere may need to risk the provocation of performance in order to ensure that attention is drawn to a truth the public prefer to ignore. Shocking and confrontational acts might risk censure but will at least confront apathy.

Many examples of contemporary prophetic performance in the public square can be identified that stand in the tradition of the biblical prophets, using unusual acts or installments to gain the attention of the public. An Australian coalition of churches and Christian organizations known as "The Micah Network" advocates for justice and a world free from poverty. At an annual gathering at the Australian Parliament House the participants regularly supplement their pre-arranged political lobbying with colorful events that are open to the public. One year a giant toilet was erected on the lawns in front of Parliament House to draw attention to lack of sanitation in developing countries, an activity that resonates with Ezekiel's "prophetic scatology" (Ezek 4:12–15).[53] In 1997 a new casino was opened in Melbourne, Australia, despite widespread public concern over the social effects of legalized gambling. At the official opening of the casino, actress Rachel Griffiths, dressed in a scanty loincloth and wearing a crown of thorns, disrupted the crowds milling at the entrance by scattering gold coins on the ground before being removed by police. Her appearance and actions evoked the biblical memories of temple-clearing and crucifixion, drawing attention to those who profit at the expense of the vulnerable. The account of Isaiah's stint of naked preaching comes to mind as a similar performance of a person willing to risk their dignity to provoke their audience (see Isa 20). In the wake of the 2018 Marjory Stoneman Douglas High School shootings in Parkland, Florida, Emma Gonzalez effectively used six minutes and twenty seconds of silence in the middle of her speech launching a student movement encouraging lawmakers to address gun violence. The silence represented the time during which the shooter claimed his seventeen victims, and enabled the audience to empathize with the fear, uncertainty, and bewilderment of the school community that day. God's silence experienced by readers of the book of Lamentations, or Jonah's silence when confronted by God's questions (Jonah 4:4, 11) are biblical instances that similarly highlight the dramatic impact of wordlessness.

Some of the most creative interpretations of Ezekiel among contemporary scholars have been those that interface the biblical book with the experiences of refugees and other trauma victims. Ezekiel embodies trauma, engages in truth-telling,[54] and yet is able to begin to imagine a new future for survivors. Because the prophet himself was an innocent man bearing the iniquity of the house of Israel (Ezek 4:4–8), any suggestion that suffering is always deserved must be mitigated. Ezekiel shares his community's fate, interacts with their God in ways that lead to new outcomes, and is able to articulate new realities. Ezekiel shows us that the performer who is willing to put their body on the line in the service of God's word may make significant contribution to the reshaping of theology and community.

53. See Sherwood, "Prophetic Scatology."

54. One thinks of South Africa's Truth and Reconciliation Commission as an example of the necessity of truth-telling to enable a new future for a broken nation.

6

Case Study 3: Jonah

Jonah in the Context of Israel's Prophetic Tradition

The Book of the Twelve

STUDIES OF THE BOOK of the Twelve have been dominated in recent decades by the assumption that the books were compiled to be read together with a deliberate literary structure. Both chronologically and theologically, according to Christopher Seitz, the Book of the Twelve is arranged to show the character of God as just and patient but not without limit, and the individual prophets as models of faithful obedience to this message.[1] The book of Jonah sits uneasily within this framework. Unlike the other books that make up the Twelve, it is primarily a narrative *about* a prophet rather than the words *of* a prophet on behalf of God. Jonah contains only one surprisingly brief oracle that does not include any of the expected prophetic formulae. The prophet Jonah could hardly be held up as a model of obedience and faithfulness; indeed James Nogalski wryly notes "Jonah serves as a paradigmatic character after whom Israel should *not* pattern itself."[2] But it is these differences that make the book of Jonah so interesting and worthy of contemplation.

Even though it was probably written much later, the book is appropriately located in the Twelve by being set in the time of the Assyrian Empire (911–612 BCE). Superscriptions in several of the books of the Twelve suggest an intentional chronological ordering presenting material that begins in the eighth century BCE in the Assyrian era, moves through the Neo-Babylonian era and ends in the fifth century BCE during the Persian period. Jonah comes in the first half of the Twelve, amongst books that are set against the

---

1. Seitz, *Prophecy and Hermeneutics*, 214–16.
2. Nogalski, *The Book of the Twelve* 1:406 (italics added).

background of Assyrian domination.[3] But whereas other Assyrian era books contain oracles related to divine judgment of Assyria, the story of Jonah describes the wholehearted repentance of Assyria's capital Nineveh led by its king, the reversal of God's decision to punish the nation, and the subsequent resentment of the Israelite prophet when God's mercy is extended beyond Israel. The open-ended question with which the book finishes invites both Jonah and readers to contemplate this mercy, and is at odds with the overarching plotline that Seitz proposes for the Book of the Twelve.

And yet there are some affinities between Jonah and other books in the Twelve. Like Zechariah and Malachi, Jonah speaks of non-Jewish peoples worshiping YHWH (Zech 8:22; Mal 1:11). Like Joel, Jonah knows that YHWH-God is merciful and gracious (Joel 2:18). Like Micah, the book of Jonah portrays the delight of God in showing loving-kindness, and God's willingness to deal with sin in the depths of the sea (Mic 7:1–19). Like Nahum, Jonah knows that the city of Nineveh deserves judgment (Nah 1:1–3a). Like Habakkuk, the book includes protest about God's failure to act (Hab 1:2–4) and a prayer in the style of the psalms (Hab 3).

As with any good performance, the audience is therefore presented with material in the book of Jonah that is at once familiar *and* challenging. This will be explored further below.

The Genre of the Book of Jonah

The only time a prophet named Jonah is mentioned outside of the book of Jonah is in 2 Kgs 14:25 where a prophet by the name of Jonah ben-Amittai, described as a servant of YHWH the God of Israel, speaks God's word that was fulfilled during the reign of Jeroboam II of Israel. The negative evaluation of Jeroboam by the Deuteronomistic redactors of the book of Kings notwithstanding, the prophet Jonah is recorded as giving prophetic support for the expansionist policies of Jeroboam during his long reign in the Northern Kingdom. None of the colorful elements of the story in the book of Jonah are corroborated in 2 Kgs or elsewhere: the prophet's flight to Joppa; the swallowing of Jonah by the great fish; the central event of the narrative describing the full-scale conversion of the Ninevites to the God of the Israelites; the use of the term "King of Nineveh" (unknown in antiquity); or the subsequent object lessons involving the plant, worm, wind, and sun.

---

3. Jonah is distinguished by being the only book that is placed in three different places in the extant witnesses: it is fifth in the MT, sixth in the LXX and last in the manuscript fragment 4QXIIa, indicating a late composition date for Jonah. See Nogalski, *The Book of the Twelve* 1:405.

These fantastic elements, together with the use of parody, exaggeration, and humor, lead most scholars to regard the book of Jonah as theological fiction. Perhaps the choice of the prophet mentioned in 2 Kgs 14 for the protagonist of the story in the Twelve is integral to the humor: a prophet supporting the expansion of Israel into neighboring territory unwittingly becomes the vehicle for the conversion of foreigners in order to challenge Israel to widen her theological borders. Furthermore, Jonah's patronym, Amittai, shares its etymology with the word for "truth" (אֱמֶת, *'emet*) and could be translated "my truth"—another ironic touch.

Even if considered theological fiction, the book of Jonah has been included within the category of prophetic literature due to its placement in the Book of the Twelve and its introductory superscription identifying Jonah as a prophet who received the word of YHWH.

Scholars have debated the integrity of the text of Jonah as a whole. The style, perspective, and vocabulary of the prayer-psalm that constitutes chapter 2 differ markedly from the rest of the narrative, leading many to suggest that it was a later addition to the story. I think this is likely, and it is intriguing to speculate which circumstances and editors felt it necessary to inject a pious prayer into an otherwise humorous narrative. Yet the symmetrical nature of the book as a whole suggests that the psalm addressed to YHWH is an important counterbalance to the conversation between YHWH and Jonah in the final chapter. The same verb is used at the beginning of each section: וַיִּתְפַּלֵּל (*wayyitpallēl*, "and he prayed"; Jonah 2:2; 4:2). The first prayer expresses faith and gratitude for the saving grace of YHWH, while the second prayer castigates YHWH for extending saving grace to others. The repetition of the word חֶסֶד (*ḥesed*, "kindness") emphasizes the contrast (2:9, 4:2).

Another way of understanding the psalm as part of the original composition is to take it at face value, in the light of the claim Jonah makes when confronted by the sailors. Even though fleeing from YHWH's presence by taking to the seas, Jonah claims to be a Hebrew who fears the God who made that sea. The prayer of chapter 2, therefore, might "simply be another example of Jonah's tendency to make pious pronouncements of orthodox faith whether sincere or not."[4]

Jonah as a Performance

The book of Jonah stands on its own and can be viewed as a complete performance in two acts. Note that my translation follows the verse division

4. Biddle, *A Time to Laugh*, 63.

found in the Masoretic Text so that chapter 1 ends with the sailors' vows in verse 16 and chapter 2 commences with the appointment of the great fish. Although versification in most English translations includes the appointment of the fish as verse 17 of chapter 1, almost all commentaries divide with the MT by including the appointment of the fish at the beginning of the second scene. As with my other translations, I have retained and interpreted *setumahs* and *petuuahs* in the script, and supplied an asterisk where the superfluous phrase "and he said" breaks the dialogue.

This two-Act play has a cast of characters that suggests the potential for an ensemble performance, bearing in mind that a number of characters are non-human entities. It reads well as a script that assumes an audience, as will become evident in the discussion below. It is possible that it was presented in dramatic form in antiquity and it has held its capacity to both entertain and challenge new audiences across the ages.

JONAH

ACT I

Actors:

Leading: YHWH, Jonah, Sailors

Supporting: Chief of the Riggers

Extras: The Ship, The Sea

Offstage: Nineveh

Setting: The Mediterranean (Israel ↔ Tarshish)

PROLOGUE (1.1–2)

Narrator

¹And the word of YHWH happened to Jonah son of Amittai saying:

YHWH

²"Get up, journey to Nineveh the great city and call out against her because their [masc] badness has come up in my face!"

Scene 1: Jonah on the Sea (1.3–16)

Narrator

³But Jonah got up to flee to Tarshish from the face of YHWH

---

and he went down [to] Joppa and he found a ship

going [to] Tarshish

and he gave her fare and went down in her

to go with them to Tarshish from the face of YHWH.

[4]And **YHWH**[5] hurled a great wind on the sea and there was a great whirlwind in the sea and the ship thought herself to be bashed to bits. [5]And the sailors feared, and they cried out, each man to his gods, and they hurled the wares which were in the ship into the sea to make lighter for them. But Jonah went down to the remotest part of the vessel and he lay down and he fell into a deep sleep. [6]And the chief of the riggers approached him and said to him:

Chief of the Riggers

"What's with you sleeping? Get up, call out to your god. Perhaps the God will consider us and we will not perish."

Narrator

[7]And they said each one to his buddy,

Sailors

"Let us cast lots so we will know on whose account this bad thing is against us."

Narrator

So they cast lots and the lot was cast upon Jonah. [8]And they said to him,

Sailors

"Tell us please on whose account this bad thing is against us?

What is your occupation and from where do you come?

What is your country and from which people are you?"

Jonah

[9][*] "**Hebrew** I am and **YHWH the God of the heavens I** fear who made the sea and the dry land."

---

5. Words in bold in this script reflect unusual word order in the original Hebrew. See page 208 for discussion.

Narrator

¹⁰And the men feared [with] a great fear and they said to him,

Sailors

"What is this you have done?"

Narrator

Because the men knew that because of **the face of YHWH** he was fleeing because he had told them. ¹¹And they said to him,

Sailors

"What should we do to you so the sea will quiet down from over us?"

Narrator

Because the sea was stomping and storming.

Jonah

¹²[*]"Lift me up and hurl me into the sea and the sea will quiet down from over you. Because I know that on account of me this great whirlwind is upon you."

Narrator

¹³But the men rowed to return to the dry land but they were not able to because the sea was stomping and storming upon them. ¹⁴And they called out to YHWH and they said,

Sailors

"Please YHWH

please do not let us perish on account of the breath of this man

and do not give us the blood of the innocent one

because you, YHWH, as you like, you do."

Narrator

¹⁵And they lifted Jonah and hurled him into the sea and the sea stood still from its raging. ¹⁶And the men feared [with] a great fear of YHWH and they sacrificed a sacrifice to YHWH and they vowed vows.

Scene 2: Jonah in the Sea (2:1, 11)

Narrator

¹And YHWH appointed a great fish to swallow Jonah, and Jonah was in the insides of the fish for three days and three nights.

Interlude (2:2–10)

²And Jonah prayed to YHWH his god from the insides of the lady-fish.

Jonah

³[*]

I called out from my distress to YHWH/ and he answered me//

From the belly of Sheol I cried out/ you heard my voice.

⁴And you threw me deep in the heart of the waters/ and a current surrounded me//

All your breakers and your waves/ over me they passed.

⁵And I said to myself, I am cast out/ from before your eyes//

Yet will I again look/ upon your holy temple.

⁶Waters overwhelm me up to my breath/ Deep surrounded me//

A reed is wrapped around my head.

⁷To the roots of the mountains I went down; the underworld with its bars is around me forever//

But you brought up from the pit my life / YHWH my god.

⁸As my breath was weakening over me / **YHWH** I remembered

And my prayer came to you / to your holy temple.

⁹The ones paying regard to idols of worthlessness//

Their kindness they will forsake.

¹⁰But I myself with a voice of praise / I wish to sacrifice to you//

That which I vowed I wish to fulfill / Deliverance to YHWH!

ס (A short silence)

Narrator

¹¹And YHWH spoke to the fish, and he vomited up Jonah onto the dry land.

פ (Intermission)

ACT II

Actors:

Leading: YHWH-God,[6] Jonah, the City of Nineveh, the King of Nineveh

Supporting: The People of Nineveh

Extras: The Livestock of Nineveh, *Qiyqayon* Plant, Worm, East Wind, Sun

Setting: Nineveh and its Eastern Environs

Prologue (3:1–2)

Narrator

¹And the word of YHWH happened to Jonah a second time, saying:

YHWH

²"Get up, journey to Nineveh the great city and call out to her the warning call which I am speaking to you."

Scene 1: Jonah in Nineveh (3.3–10)

Narrator

³And Jonah got up and he journeyed to Nineveh according to the word of YHWH. And **Nineveh** was a great city to God, a journey of three days. ⁴And Jonah began to go into the city, a journey of one day, and he called out and said

Jonah

"Yet forty days and Nineveh is overturned."

6. See discussion in the Actors section, below (pages 211–12), in relation to different names for the deity.

Narrator

⁵And the people of Nineveh believed in God

and they called for a fast

and they put on sackcloths, from the greatest of them to the smallest of them.

⁶And the word reached the King of Nineveh

and he got up from his throne and he removed his cloak from over him,

and he covered himself with a sackcloth and he sat on the ash-heap.

⁷And he proclaimed and said in Nineveh by order of the King and his great ones saying:

The King

"The human and the livestock, the herd and the flock,

let them not taste anything,

let them not graze,

and water let them not drink.

⁸Let them cover themselves with sackcloths—the human and the livestock—and let them call out to God with strength. And let them turn back, each one from his bad way, and from the violence that is in their hands. ⁹Who knows? The God may turn and relent, and he may turn from his burning nose and we will not perish."

Narrator

¹⁰And the God saw their deeds,

because they turned from their bad way;

and the God relented from the bad that he had said he would do to them,

and he did not do it.

Scene 2: Jonah outside Nineveh (4.1–11)

Narrator

¹And it was bad to Jonah, very bad, and he was burning within himself. ²And he prayed to YHWH and said,

Jonah

"Ah YHWH, is not this my word I spoke when I was in my country? Therefore I acted to flee to Tarshish because I know that you are a God of grace and mercy, long of nose and of much kindness, and relenting over badness. ³And now, YHWH, please take my breath from me because better is my death than my life."

ס (A short silence)

Narrator

⁴And YHWH said,

YHWH

"Is it good for you to burn?"

Narrator (as Jonah moves to stage right)

⁵And Jonah went out from the city

and he sat east of the city

and he made for himself there a booth (*Sukkāh*)

and he sat under it in the shade

until he could see what would become of the city.

⁶And YHWH-God appointed a *qiyqayon* plant⁷ and it went up over Jonah to be shade over his head to save him from his badness. And Jonah rejoiced over the plant with great rejoicing. ⁷And the God appointed a worm at the going up of the dawn on the following day and it attacked the plant and it dried up. ⁸And it happened at the rising of the sun God appointed a scorching east wind and the sun smited the head of Jonah and he became faint and wished for his breath to die and he said,

Jonah

"Better is my death than my life."

7. The name of this plant in my translation is a transliteration of the Hebrew. The name does not occur outside of the book of Jonah, and though it is often translated as a castor bean plant due to its rapid growth (commentaries), or gourd (LXX, Syr), or ivy (Vulgate), it seems preferable to allow the plant to retain its own name in this performance.

Narrator

⁹And God said to Jonah,

YHWH

"Is it good for you to burn over the *qiyqayon* plant?"

Jonah

[*] "It is good for me to burn, until death!"

YHWH

¹⁰[*] "You were concerned over the *qiyqayon* plant which you did not toil over nor make it great (which is a son of the morning to become and a son of the night to perish). ¹¹So should I not be concerned over Nineveh the great city where there is in it more than 120 thousand humans who do not know between their right hand to their left, and a lot of livestock?"

Epilogue

Creativity in Jonah

The translation of Jonah is presented as a script that attempts to replicate the artistry of the Hebrew text while maintaining a readable style for an English-speaking audience. Here I want to point out aspects of my performance-oriented translation that can be seen in the script.

Repetition

I have translated the same Hebrew root words with the same English words in order to highlight repetition within the performance. Using the same words in speeches of different characters can link the characters with each other (or contrast them from each other) and form connections between different scenes.

- Jonah's initial commission (1:2) is delivered in three imperative verbs: "Get up" (ירד, *yrd*), "journey" (הלך, *hlk*), and "call out" (קרא, *qr'*)"— replicated in Jonah 3:2 as YHWH commissions Jonah for a second time. Each of these verbs is repeated elsewhere in the story. The chief of the riggers challenges Jonah to "get up and call out" when he finds Jonah asleep at the bottom of the boat (1:6). The chief of the riggers is therefore subtly aligned with God. YHWH's second commission adds a cognate accusative by instructing Jonah to "call out the warning call" (3:2), transforming the root into a feminine noun with a definite article. Jonah "calls out" his brief oracle (3:4). The people of Nineveh respond by "calling out" for a fast (3:5), followed up by the King of Nineveh, who instructs his people (and livestock) to "call out with strength" to God (3:8). The psalm of Jonah begins with the same verb: "I called out from my distress" (2:3). Aside from the sailors, who use a different verb to "cry out" (זעק, z^cq), all of the main and supporting characters who have speaking lines use this verb, and for each there is a response. Jonah is instructed to "get up" three times. The first time (1:2), his response is to "get up" and go in a different direction. The second time (1:6) there is no response, but the third time (3:2) Jonah does "get up" and journeys to Nineveh in obedience to YHWH's command. The root הלך (hlk) is used in verbal and nominative forms and has been translated "journey" three times (1:2; 3:2, 3). It is also the root underlying the sea's action in Jonah 1:11 and 1:13. There it has been translated "stomping" to replicate the parasomania of the Hebrew phrase הוֹלֵךְ וְסֹעֵר (hôlēk w⁽e⁾sōʿēr, see below).

- The verb "[he] went down" (ירד, yrd) is used three times within three verses (1:3, 5). Repetition in translation underscores the deliberate movement of Jonah towards the depths in order to flee from the "God of the heavens" (1:9). In the psalm the word is used again, describing the furthest reaches of the prophet's experience of being cast into the depths until he is "brought up" again.

- The verb "fear" (ירא, yrʾ) is attributed to both Jonah and the sailors in Scene 1. Several Bible translations translate "worship" when Jonah is asked for his identity: "I am a Hebrew . . . I worship the Lord, the God of heaven" (1:9, NRSV) but "fear" when the verb is used with reference to the sailors: "the mariners were afraid . . . the men were even more afraid . . . the men feared the Lord even more" (1:5, 10, 16, NRSV). Use of the same word conveys an important point of the performance: the prophet of YHWH who should "fear" YHWH does not, running away from his commissioned task; whereas pagan sailors who have no prior relationship with YHWH do, in fact, fear him. The phrase "And the men feared [with] a great fear" in Jonah 1:10 is repeated verbatim in 1:16—except in 1:16 the object of their fear is identified as YHWH. A sense of progressive revelation is driven home when the word is translated consistently. That the sailors and the prophet are relating to the same god is underscored by repetition of "sacrifices and vows" made by the sailors in Jonah 1:16 and by Jonah as the appropriate liturgical response to deliverance from danger.

- The verb "hurl" (טול, *ṭûl*) is used four times in Scene 1. It is an unusual Hebrew verb, used only fourteen times in the Hebrew Bible in total. Here it is used for comic effect as several characters imitate each other: YHWH hurls a great wind on the sea (1:4), sailors hurl cargo overboard (1:5), Jonah instructs the sailors to hurl him overboard (1:12), and finally, reluctantly, they do so (1:15). Translating the root with the same English word aligns the sailors with YHWH on the one hand, and Jonah with the cargo on the other. Both YHWH and the sailors have a problem with Jonah, and both deal with the problem in the same way! Notably, in the prayer of Jonah a different verb, "throw" (שלך, *šlk*, Jon 2:4), is used to describe his entry into the sea. The piety of the poetry is deliberately dissociated from the comedy of the narrative.

- The verb "appoint" (מנה, *mnh*) is used four times with YHWH as the subject (2:1; 4:6, 7, 8). YHWH sequentially appoints a fish, plant, worm, and wind to deal with the reluctant prophet. Consistency of translation reminds us that the same God has a variety of techniques available, and the whole of the natural world in the cast of extras from which to draw.

- The root רעע (*rʿʿ*) is used in adjectival, nominal, and verbal forms and has been translated "bad" or "badness" in this performance. Consistency of translation makes it obvious that both the Ninevites (1:2; 3:8, 10) and Jonah (4:1, 6) are bad, and that God contemplates sending bad things to Nineveh (3:8). Furthermore, through the casting of lots, the sailors discover that Jonah is also the cause of the bad things happening to them (1:7, 8). Both God and the Ninevites repent from their badness, but it is unclear whether Jonah is ever delivered from *his* badness.

- The noun נֶפֶשׁ (*nefeš*) is common in the Hebrew Bible, occurring 754 times with a variety of meanings and usages. The most common translations are "breath," "throat," "soul," "life," "person," and "corpse." In this performance it was difficult to find a consistent word to translate the five times it is used (1:14; 2:6, 8; 4:3, 8), and I settled on "breath" as was translated in the Elijah Series. Here also I have used the word "life" to translate another commonly used Hebrew word (חַי, *ḥay*) as I wanted my translation to distinguish between the two different words.

- The root שׁוּב (šûb, "turn") is commonly found in prophetic literature, as it can underlie expressions of repentance. It is used three times in the king's speech (Jonah 3:8–9): first in jussive form in relation to his people ("let them turn back, each one from his bad way") and then twice expressing hope that God will turn back from his intention to punish. In the next verse we are told that God observed this turning of the Ninevites and indeed did relent from punishment (3:10). The root is used earlier in the performance when the sailors row to "return" to the dry land. This action is accompanied by a prayer to YHWH so could be understood to "anticipate its theological use" later in the performance.[8]

- "Sea" (יָם, yām) and "Dry land" (הַיַּבָּשָׁה, yabāšāh) are repeated in the performance. "Sea" dominates Act 1 (Jonah 1:4, 5, 9, 11, 12, 13, 15), justifying it as the setting for the first part of the performance. Scene 2, however, though it takes place in the fish *in* the sea, avoids the word and so once again dissociates the pious prayerful prophet from the recalcitrant actor of the rest of the performance. The repetition of "dry land," however, unites the scenes. Jonah claims to fear the God who made the sea and dry land (1:9), the sailors were unable to return to dry land until they had hurled Jonah from the ship (1:13–15), and the fish vomits him onto dry land at the end of his three-day sojourn (2:11). Finally, the plant, part of the object lesson for Jonah, "dries up" (4:7, from the same Hebrew root). Repetition of these words prompts the paradoxical thought that salvation for Jonah is a greater reality in the sea setting than the dry land setting.

- Another word used just twice is nonetheless worth remarking on because of its theological potency. "Kindness" (חֶסֶד, ḥesed) is found twice on Jonah's lips: in the psalm of Jonah (2:9) and the petulant prayer outside Nineveh (4:2). It is used most often in the Hebrew Bible as a characteristic of God, but also as a quality of human relationships. Jonah subverts the word in both of his speeches. In the psalm, although the meaning is not crystal clear, the line is parallel to "the ones paying regard to idols of worthlessness" (2:8) and so is intended to be a derogatory statement about idol worshipers, against whom the pious psalmist contrasts himself. In the prayer outside Nineveh Jonah quotes a conventional affirmation of the characteristics of God—graciousness and mercy, patience and kindness—but is making it clear that those characteristics are not the ones he wants to see in God. Once again,

---

8. Trible, *Rhetorical Criticism*, 146.

consistency of translation underscores the way in which Jonah is twisting a celebrated quality of relationship.

- Use of the adjective "great" (גָּדֹל, *gādōl*) contributes to the comedic tone of the performance by suggesting hyperbole. YHWH hurls a *great* wind and a *great* whirlwind (1:4, 12). Both the whirlwind and YHWH provoke *great* fear on the part of the sailors (1:10, 16). YHWH then appoints a *great* fish to swallow Jonah, although once Jonah is vomited up the fish is no longer defined as "great." Nineveh is four times characterized as a *great* city by God (1:2; 3:2, 3; 4:11), reiterated by its declared description as "a journey of three days" (3:3),[9] and the "*great* ones" in the city respond to the prophecy as well as the small ones (3:5, 7). The appointment of the plant leads to *great* rejoicing on Jonah's part, even though YHWH reminds him that its greatness was the work of YHWH, not Jonah. Although not the same root, the whole performance ends on another Hebrew word that could be translated "great"—רבב. Within all this hyperbole Jonah's character ends up looking very small!

- There are several instances of repetition of roots in cognate accusatives in this performance. Although English translations often try to avoid repetition for stylistic reasons, a literal translation is simple and effective and underlines the original intention of emphasis: "And the men feared [with] a great fear of YHWH and they sacrificed a sacrifice to YHWH and they vowed vows" (1:16); "call out to her the warning call" (3:2); "And Jonah rejoiced over the plant with great rejoicing" (4:6).

- I have faithfully translated two Hebrew idioms in order to bring out a greater sense of embodiment in this script. The phrase פְּנֵי יְהוָה (*pᵉnēy YHWH*) if often translated "presence of the LORD" but could be literally translated "face of YHWH" as I have done (1:2, 3, 10). There is a pleasing contemporariness of the translation "their badness has come up in my face"! When English translations use the word "anger," the underlying Hebrew word is usually associated with אַף (*'ap*) translated most simply as "nose" or "nostril." The expressions are euphemistic, so that "hot of nose" or a "burning nose" means anger, and "long of nose" means long-suffering or patient. In my translation I have used the word "nose" where אַף occurs, but the other terms for anger have the root חרה (*ḥrh*) underlying them, which I have translated as "burn" or

---

9. Archaeological evidence is that the walled city of Nineveh in the seventh century BCE was approximately twelve kilometers in circumference and three kilometers across! In other words, it was in reality a journey of less than an hour to cross it.

"burning." While God turns from his burning nose (3:9), Jonah begins to burn (4:1) and continues to burn (4:4, 9).

Wordplay

I have made a few attempts to replicate wordplay at the morphological level of the Hebrew script. I have mentioned above the Hebrew phrase הוֹלֵךְ וְסֹעֵר (hôlēk weso'ēr), which I translated "stomping and storming" to capture the similar sounds underlying the phrase. This phrase is used twice (1:11, 13), underscoring the intensity of the whirlwind. The Hebrew phrase חִשְּׁבָה לְהִשָּׁבֵר (hiššebāh lehiššābēr) has been translated "bashed to bits," to replicate at least a little of the alliteration and sibilance. I chose "bad" to translate רַע (ra') in part because the sailors each speak to their "buddy" (רֵעַ, rē') in Jonah 1:7. The piled-up questions of the sailors in 1:8 all begin with the same sound (מ) in the Hebrew script: מִי, מַה, מֵאַיִן, מָה, מִזֶּה (mî-mah-mē'ayin-māh-mizeh); enabling a similar effect in translation since question words in English also begin with the same sound (whose, what, where, what, which). There is interplay between "shade" (צֵל, ṣēl) and "save" (נָצַל, nāṣal) in Jonah 4:6. The latter is often translated "deliver" but the wordplay is more effective in the phrase "to be shade over his head to save him from his badness." Similarly, the aforementioned quality of "kindness" (חֶסֶד, ḥesed) could be translated in a number of ways, as could חוּס (ḥûs) in Jonah 4:10–11. I have chosen to translate "kindness" and "concerned" to pick up the guttural sounds of the beginning of each Hebrew word.

Significance of Word Order

When word order in the original Hebrew is different from the usual there should be some way of conveying this in translation. I contemplated translating the usual Hebrew order of verb-subject-object so that it was obvious when the order is subverted to subject-verb, but the resulting English translation would have been too clunky and distracting. Instead I have placed the words in bold that are in an unusual place. This has the effect of stressing the words, which I think is the intention of the unusual placement in the Hebrew. Thus YHWH is fronted in Jonah 1:4, 9, 10, emphasizing divine activity even as Jonah believes he is fleeing from God's direction. The fronting of Jonah in 1:5 emphasizes his activity of withdrawing to the lowest part of the boat. Phyllis Trible suggests this grammatically accentuates the power struggle between Jonah and YHWH.[10]

Jonah's self-confession in 1:9 is usually translated "I am a Hebrew" (NRSV), but by following the word order in the Hebrew script, the ethnic identification of the prophet is placed at the forefront, reminding the original audience that Jonah is one of them, and reminding subsequent audiences that Jonah is not of the same ethnicity as the sailors. In the same sentence the object of Jonah's fear (YHWH the God of the heavens) is placed before the verb, adding emphasis and humorously contrasting with his attempts to remove himself from YHWH. The fronting of YHWH in the confessional psalm (2:8) again forefronts YHWH over the prophet's actions.

Gendered Translation

Hebrew's lack of a neuter gender aids in performance-sensitive translation as it expands the cast of actors and notes unusual qualities. In the performance of Jonah, Nineveh is a feminine entity against which Jonah is instructed to call out (1:2). The rather ambiguous description "a great city to God" (3:3) entrenches the personification. The city and its citizens are joined in Act 1 by the defining masculine adjective ("their badness," 1:2), but in Act 2 "the city of Nineveh" (3:3–4; 4:5, 11) is separated from the people, the king, and the livestock.

The use of feminine pronouns for the feminine noun אֳנִיָּה (ʾāniyyāh, "ship") highlights the fact that the ship is an actor in its own right and not just a prop. In response to the whirlwind it is the ship herself who thinks she will be bashed to bits (1:4). Although the vocabulary is different, the image of Jonah resting in the "remotest part of the vessel" (1:5) is very similar to his presence in the "insides of the lady-fish" (2:2), giving the idea that both ship and fish are important extras in the performance.

The fish is mentioned three times in Scene 2 of Act 1. When it is the object of YHWH's action a masculine word is used (2:1, 11), but when Jonah prays from inside the fish, the Hebrew uses the feminine form (hence my translation "lady-fish" in Jonah 2:2). This tiny detail is rarely shown in translations but is pregnant with possibility for interpretation![11]

10. Trible, *Rhetorical Criticism*, 135.

11. Rabbinic tradition *does* note such detail and attempts to reconcile it. Grateful that Jonah's presence inside it means the fish won't be eaten by Leviathan, the fish takes delight in showing Jonah the marvels under the sea. God has to send a second fish, a pregnant female, to take Jonah and make him so uncomfortable that he is forced to pray for deliverance. See further detail on this tradition in Nogalski, *The Book of the Twelve*, 1:402.

Commentary on Jonah as a Performance ·

Structure of the Performance

The performance of Jonah is presented in two acts with a natural division of the text occurring where there is a change of geographical location from sea to dry land, supported by the almost exact repetition of the opening line at the beginning of chapter 3 (1:1; 3:1). The addition of "a second time" divides the book into two parts. In both acts there is a commission by YHWH, a response by Jonah, major groups of characters who also respond to YHWH (the sailors with their chief rigger; the Ninevites with their king), Jonah's reaction to events, Jonah's prayers, and natural phenomena appointed by YHWH to interact with Jonah. This division into two symmetrical parts functions to distinguish the book as a performance rather than a narrative with a single plotline.

I have characterized YHWH's instruction to Jonah as a prologue at the beginning of each act, setting the context for the action that follows. The disparate character of the psalm of Jonah warrants its identification as an interlude during Act 1. Important information is conveyed about the character of Jonah, but the action is not advanced. The *narrative* could easily exist without the psalm, but as an interlude it adds dramatic irony to the performance and balances the dialogue between Jonah and YHWH in the second act. The first scene in each act of the performance relies on movement: the journeying of Jonah, the buffeting of the boat, the rowing of the sailors, the tossing of cargo and Jonah into the sea, the journeying of Jonah into Nineveh, the proclamation through the city, the acts of fasting and sackcloth. The second scene in each act places the actors in one location: Jonah inside the fish and Jonah and YHWH-God outside the city. Act 1 ends with decisive action but there is no proper closure to Act 2, indicated in this script as a blank Epilogue.

Pausal markers in the Hebrew script support the division into two acts by the placement of a *petuuah* after Jonah 2:11, indicating the end of a large unit. Two *setumahs* suggest short pauses are warranted in two other places in the script. The first comes immediately after the psalm (2:10), reminding the audience that Jonah was in the insides of the fish for three days and three nights. A short period of silence in the performance at that point, prior to the narrator's description, invites the audience along with Jonah to reflect on events. It also provides space to reflect on the change in *persona* presented by the prophet between Scene 1 and Scene 2 and perhaps prepares the audience for the surprising description of the fish "vomiting" Jonah out. The self-centered piety of the psalmist is no more appetizing than the runaway rebel. The second *setumah* (after Jonah 4:3) again gives the audience the chance to consider the words and attitude of Jonah. His knowledge of YHWH's character is the reason for his initial flight to Tarshish and his subsequent death wish. It also precedes the most interesting portrayal of the YHWH-God actor in the performance, who finally converses with Jonah rather than relating to him in a demanding and controlling manner. The pause here gives YHWH the opportunity to consider a new approach.[12]

Lines of dialogue that include obvious parallelism are set out to make that evident in the script. This reminds us that prophetic material, even when framed in ostensibly narrative form as in this book, nonetheless is highly influenced by poetic genres.

The open-ended epilogue is a clear invitation for audience response. See further discussion below under "Connections."

Actors

In each act I have identified leading actors, supporting cast, and extras. Leading actors have the main speaking roles, supporting actors have one or two lines, and the extras are responsible for action but do not have speaking parts. Some of the extras double as props!

Although not listed in the cast of characters, the Narrator has a significant role in this performance. As well as setting the scenes and moving the plot forward, the narrator makes use of rhetorical devices of repetition (1:1–2/3:1–2; 1:7; 1:10; 1:11/1:13; 1:16; 3:10/4:1; 4:6), parallelism (3:5–6; 4:6/4:8), and chiasms (1:3; 3:10; 4:5). The script has been written to emphasize these aspects.

Two actors vie for the leading role: Jonah and YHWH-God. Both are in each scene. The performance is named *Jonah*, but it is YHWH who has the first and last words. Neither is a simple character.

YHWH

YHWH has more than one name during the performance, perhaps signifying different levels of relationship with other characters. In Act 1 Jonah refers to YHWH by name but also with the nickname "the God of the heavens" (1:9). For the chief of the riggers he is "the God," but the sailors learn his proper name YHWH from Jonah and use it when addressing

---

12. A similar stage instruction was seen in Ezekiel 4:14 where a *setumah* allowed time for YHWH to change instructions. See page 173.

him. The Ninevites, on the other hand, refer to "God" or "the God," and the narrator continues to use "the God" in describing his reaction to the deeds of the Ninevites. Since Jonah did not make any reference to YHWH or God in his brief warning call in Nineveh, there is a logical consistency in the performance. I have already hinted at the development of the character of God in this performance, seen most clearly in the way he relates to Jonah. Relenting of his intentions towards the Ninevites also indicates character development. Phyllis Trible speaks of the change from overwhelming power to persuasion: "a god of distance to a god of dialogue."[13] I agree with Trible to an extent, but wonder at the underlying malice in the object lesson sent in response to the unanswered question "is it good for you to burn?" (4:4). God ensures that Jonah really does burn by providing a scorching wind and smiting sun. Interestingly, the name alternates between YHWH, God, and YHWH-God in the final conversation between Jonah and the deity, signifying a distancing of Jonah from his God even as YHWH is attempting to draw nearer.

Jonah

Jonah's character (and name) remain more constant during the performance. Despite his "obedience" to God's commission in Act 2, his actions continue to try to thwart God's message to Nineveh. In Act 1 he ran away, and in Act 2 he reduced God's message to its bare minimum, offering no hint that the repentance God hoped for from the Ninevites. Both "prayers" of Jonah contain conventionally correct ways of speaking of God's character. Even so, there is ambiguity woven into Jonah's speeches throughout the performance. Initially his actions belie his words. Although claiming to "fear" the God of the heavens who made the sea and the dry land (1:9), Jonah seens to think he could escape the face of God by taking to the seas. When instructing the sailors to "hurl" him into the sea, Jonah aligns himself with God who had "hurled" the wind and whirlwind. Again his words belie his actions and his character. He knew that the whirlwind has been sent "on account of me" (1:12) yet he had taken himself into the recesses of the ship while the sailors desperately prayed for their lives and jettisoned their livelihood. Three times Jonah expresses a death wish (1:12; 4:8, 9) yet the psalm is a prayer of thanksgiving for being saved from death.

Links can be made between the sailors and Jonah, who all "fear" YHWH, and who all "sacrifice" and "vow" when delivered. Yet a grammatical difference can be seen when Jonah's speech and the sailors' speech

---

13. Trible, *Rhetorical Criticism*, 116.

in Scene 1 are carefully translated. The final verse of Scene 1 reads, "and the men feared with a great fear of YHWH and they sacrificed a sacrifice to YHWH and they vowed vows" (1:16). The *wayyiqtol* verbs indicate completed action and the cognate accusatives emphasize the intensity with which they feared, sacrificed, and vowed. In contrast, Jonah uses the verbs as cohortatives: "with a voice of praise I wish to sacrifice to you// That which I vowed I wish to fulfill" (2:10). Jonah's speech signals a potential action—an incomplete action, or even an action that may never start. There is a stark contrast then, between the sailors' fervent acts of worship and Jonah's tentative volatives.[14]

The ambiguity of Jonah's prophetic message to Nineveh also requires analysis. It is famously brief: merely five words in the original Hebrew (literally, "Yet forty day and-Nineveh overturned"). There is no messenger formula introducing the message as God's words. There is no call to repentance. The verb at the end of the sentence (הפך, *hpk*) does, however, hold some ambiguity. It is used in several other places in the Hebrew Bible. In Gen 19:21, 23, 29 the verb denotes the action of destruction of Sodom and Gomorrah, but Deut 23:5 recollects that YHWH "turned" Balaam's curse on Israel into a blessing. A closer intertextual reference is Hos 11:8 where it refers to the heart of YHWH being turned, indicating repentance of his plan to punish. As the scene unfolds, we see that Nineveh is indeed "overturned"—not in destruction but in extravagant repentance so that even the king reverses his position of power into that of abject penitence, sitting on an ash heap instead of a throne. Despite his worst intentions, it seems Jonah spoke a true prophecy!

Performance analysis alerts us to nonverbal aspects of communication. With only the verb "called out" (קרא, *qrʾ*) to describe Jonah's action, we have few clues about his posture, tone, volume, and appearance. But the exaggerated and immediate response of the people of Nineveh must at least cause us to wonder if nonverbal cues in the prophet's delivery contributed to their reaction. In the following scene we are given more explicit stage directions for Jonah to follow—"burning within himself," wishing for death, building a booth, rejoicing (with great rejoicing) over the plant's shade, wishing for death again after its demise. And Jonah's silence (twice) in response to YHWH's direct questions, along with his frustrated quotation of God's own question: "it *is* good for me to burn, until death!" (4:9) allows us to envisage Jonah's nonverbal stance. In my family we would refer to "tripping over your bottom lip"!

---

14. I am indebted to Marie-Louise Craig for pointing out this contrast.

The lack of response by Jonah to YHWH's final question leaves us wondering whether his character *did* or *could* develop in response to the events of the performance. Shimon Levy concludes his chapter on the book of Jonah with this observation:

> It may be said that inasmuch as Jonah flees God, God is in pursuit of Man. From a Kabbalistic point of view, God needs man's willing participation. For the spectator/reader, this crucial issue remains unanswered at the end of Jonah's drama.[15]

God's "pursuit" of Jonah is more successful when initiated through questions rather than imperatives. Only once in the performance does the use of imperative verbs result in action, and even then the action is half-hearted (3:3–4). God's first command is ignored by Jonah (1:2), as is the command of the Chief of Riggers (1:6). But Jonah responds to the politer questions of the sailors (1:8, 11) and to God's question when it is repeated with the plant as a referent (4:9).

Other Leading Actors

I have included the sailors as leading actors in Act 1 on two counts: they have a significant number of lines in the first scene, and they become a foil for the lead actor Jonah in their exemplary response to YHWH. While Jonah stows himself away, the sailors, despite their fear, act to save others: they pray; they determine the cause of the whirlwind; they strive to return to land through sheer effort rather than complying with Jonah's suggestion that they hurl him overboard; and they petition for the grace of YHWH. Unlike Jonah's pious words, their acts of worship are genuine and fervent. Though they disappear from the performance at the end of Scene 1, their prayer to YHWH "as you like, you do" (1:14) is echoed in Act 2 when the narrator tells us about the God who "relented from the bad that he said he would do . . . and did not do it" (3:10).

Leading actors in Act 2 include the city of Nineveh herself and the King of Nineveh. Although the city has no words, she is presented as significant in both size and importance to God. The warning call is that *Nineveh* will be overturned. Furthermore, her presence is necessary to both acts, even though she is an offstage presence in Act 1.

The people of Nineveh respond first, but do not have direct speech. By contrast, the king's words and actions are conveyed in some detail. Notably, the king's proclamation is phrased in volative verbs, which also allow for

15. Levy, *The Bible* as *Theatre*, 172.

the possibility of his called-for actions not happening (i.e., all Ninevites and their animals wearing sackcloth and fasting). This underscores the completely voluntary response from all of the people (greatest to smallest), and presumably from their livestock also. The king's speculation, "Who knows? The God may turn and relent . . . and we will not perish" (3:9) identifies his theology as more profound than that of the Israelite prophet who *does* know that YHWH is gracious and merciful but who acts in opposition to that knowledge. It is the king of Nineveh, therefore, who articulates a key theme in this performance: the freedom of God.

Supporting Actors

One would think the Chief of the Riggers in Act 1 would have equal billing to the King of Nineveh, but his presence on stage is brief and he only has one line (1:6). It is a significant line, however, since it echoes the command of YHWH to Jonah and preempts the theological insight of the king regarding God's freedom (3:9). The people of Nineveh have no lines in the script but are the first to respond to the prophetic call by calling for a fast and covering themselves with sackcloth.

Extras

In both acts nonhuman entities are subjects of active verbs or emotional responses, even though they do not speak: the ship "thought itself to be bashed to bits" (1:4); the sea "stomps and storms" (1:11, 13); the fish "swallows" Jonah (2:1), bizarrely changes gender when housing him (2:2), and "vomits" him up (2:11); the livestock of Nineveh fast and are covered with sackcloth (3:7–8); the *qiyqayon* plant "[goes] up over Jonah . . . to save him from his badness" (4:6); the worm "attack[s] the *qiyqayon* plant" (4:7); the wind and sun "attack . . . the head of Jonah" (4:8). Jonah's exaggerated emotional response to the *qiyqayon* plant gives further agency to it.

Props and Ready-mades

When speaking of the props used in Jonah's "Quest play," Shimon Levy claims they are "both 'real' things on stage and heavily charged items."[16] The cargo hurled overboard by the sailors, for example, are symbolic of Jonah. When they initially hurl the cargo they are seeking a solution to their

16. Levy, *The Bible as Theatre*, 172.

predicament. The casting of lots and the rowing of oars have the same purpose. But they find the solution when they treat Jonah in the same fashion as the cargo, "hurling" *him* into the sea. The sacrifices and vows of the sailors are not only significant because they represent Israelite modes of worship carried out by pagans, but they also function to form a contrast to the half-hearted worship of the Israelite prophet (see discussion above of Jonah as actor). Fasting and the use of sackcloth also recall traditional Israelite worship practices that are being carried out by foreigners, even foreign animals! In fact, there is sackcloth for all: people and king, small and great, livestock, herd, and flock. These symbols of repentance and mourning have been laid on thick, along with the king's ash heap.

The fish is at the same time an actor, a prop, and part of the stage set in which most of Scene 2 is carried out. A double reference to "your holy temple" (2:5, 8) is a ready-made signaling prayer and worship, but curiously is mentioned only within the insides of the fish. The time span of "three days and three nights" (2:1) is another ready-made: a motif frequently used in relation to noteworthy journeys such as Abraham's journey to Moriah (Gen 22:4), Moses's request for time to sacrifice in the wilderness (Exod 3:18; 5:3; 8:27; 15:22), the Israelites' journey from Sinai (Num 10:33).[17] Significantly, the journey across Nineveh is also recorded as three days. This ready-made would signal to the audience that Jonah's experiences ought to be life-changing.

Jonah's booth (*sukkāh*) recalls the joyful harvest festival of Sukkoth when Israelites were commanded to build *sukkoth* (the plural form of the word) to recall YHWH's provision in the wilderness following the exodus (Lev 23:33–34). That festival also makes use of leafy branches. Jonah's extreme rejoicing as the *qiyqayon* plant grows is not out of place, therefore, except that it is sandwiched between burning anger and petulance.

As props and stage directions contributing to the performance, the wind (1:4; 4:8) and sun (4:8) serve more than one function. Wind (רוּחַ, *ruaḥ*) is a potent symbol of God's presence, equally often translated "spirit" or "breath" when used in the Hebrew Bible. It can be both creative and destructive, but in this performance its purpose is as a means of judgment of the prophet. Wind and sun also contribute to the lighting effects, as does the interior of the fish. The wind blows in a whirlwind in Act 1, the absence of sun in the insides of the fish cuts out light altogether, but the performance concludes in the extreme light of a scorching sun. The spotlight is truly on the prophet as he contemplates YHWH's final question.

---

17. See Landes, "The 'Three Days and Three Nights' Motif in Jonah."

A few words and phrases act as ready-mades and are noticeable when they become twists in the plot. The prologue is a typical introduction in prophetic literature, beginning with "the word of YHWH to . . ." and followed by "get up, journey to . . ." These two imperatives are used frequently—we have already seen them as instructions to Elijah (1 Kgs 17:9; 21:18; 2 Kgs 1:3) and Ezekiel (Ezek 3:22). Phyllis Trible notes how the words form a "hurried rhythm that elicits a prompt response."[18] Usually the prophet's response is immediate and obedient, signaled by repetition of the same verbs in a finite form (for example, 1 Kgs 17:10; Ezek 3:23). The fact that Jonah "got up to flee to Tarshish *from* the face of YHWH" (Jonah 1:3) signals that this is no ordinary prophetic account. An audience might expect a verbal protest to the prophetic call (a typical element in the prophetic call narrative form) but never outright disobedience.

Twice in the script Jonah's words are introduced as a "prayer to YHWH" (2:2; 4:2). The root פלל (*pll*) is used eighty-four times in the Hebrew Bible, with its *piel* form usually translated as "judge" and its far more common *hitpael* form translated as "prayed" or "interceded." The two forms in Jonah are *hitpael*, but Jonah's prayers both include surprising features.

Jonah's first prayer takes place from the insides of a fish. It begins with typical words of a lament psalm, and it has the typical *qinah* "limping" rhythm of the lament genre. The opening words "I called out" echo the call of the sailors and the chief of the riggers, who were mortally afraid in a life-threatening whirlwind. Yet as the psalm unfolds, it is best classified as a psalm of thanksgiving! For what is the prophet giving thanks? The psalm climaxes with the phrase "Deliverance to YHWH" (Jonah 2:10). This phrase is used in Ps 3:9 (MT). In the psalm the name YHWH is fronted, while in Jonah the usual Hebrew word order has the verb preceding the subject. The effect is striking, however, since the name of God concludes the psalm. Nonetheless, in the context of the performance this climax to the psalm has a hollow ring to it. Jonah is still in the "insides of the ladyfish," and he has not yet been delivered of either his dangerous situation or his closed attitude.

The second prayer of Jonah (4:2) could be considered "an ancient confession of divine attributes" as it or something like it occurs many times elsewhere.[19] The script of Jonah quotes almost verbatim from Joel 2:13, following Joel's modification of the exodus formula by adding "relenting over badness" to the four attributes of grace, mercy, slowness to anger, and

---

18. Trible, *Rhetorical Criticism*, 125.

19. Trible, *Rhetorical Criticism*, 200. Cf. Exod 34:6–7; Joel 2:13; Pss 86:15; 103:8; 145:8; Neh 9:17. The word pair "grace and mercy" is found even more commonly.

kindness. Jonah twists this ancient confession by making it an accusation against God's character rather than a celebration of it.

The biggest surprise in this script is that the Israelite prophet rarely acts or speaks as one might expect an Israelite prophet to act or speak while the words and actions of non-Israelite actors are faithful to Israelite expectations and nonhuman actors carry out the will of YHWH.

Humor in the Script

Humor is an important aspect in performance. The most tragic of plays can still include the light relief of caricature roles or comic lines. We should be alert to these even when the script is found in Scripture.

In Jonah, along with the prophet acting against expectations, the contrast between the prophet and the pagan actors in the story provides a humorous angle. The seasoned seamen are so fearful in the whirlwind on the sea that they are willing to cast their livelihood over the edge of the ship. In the meantime, landlubber Jonah is relaxed enough to fall into a deep sleep—the LXX translates with a word meaning "snoring"! Once it is clear that Jonah is the cause of the whirlwind, the sailors do all they can to save his life rather than hurl him into the sea, even when he tells them to do so. The sailors act heroically; Jonah acts disgracefully. Yet because of Jonah's disobedience, the sailors become YHWH fearers. The contrast doesn't end there. The fearful sailors sacrifice and vow with all their might, while Jonah's prayer, boastful in its piety, ends on a half-hearted promise to *possibly* sacrifice and vow.

Humor is also integral to the account of the Ninevites. Jonah's message is brief and ambiguous. Yet their response is extravagantly wholehearted. The exaggerated response, in fact, is part of the humor. The "great" city follow a proclamation from the king and the "great ones" that all should fast and be covered with sackcloth, from the "greatest" to the least, and including livestock! Despite the serious conversation that takes place between Jonah and God in the ensuing verses, the script ends with another reference to "a lot of livestock" (4:11). Even if highlighting YHWH's compassion for the least in the Ninevite community, the words form a comical conclusion to the book. Arguably, the lingering impact of this performance is the whimsical wildlife: a bilious fish, a willful worm, and contrite cows.

Prophetic Performance

Against Nineveh's greatness, Jonah seems small, even petty. His badness, which does not seem to abate, stands out against the fulsome repentance of the city from her bad ways. The emotional rollercoaster he exhibits leaves him looking absurd. He goes from defiance to surliness, claiming fear (1:9) and piety (2:9–10), experiencing burning anger (4:1) and excessive joy (4:6), expressing both gratitude for rescue from danger (2:7) and suicidal thoughts (4:8). As an Israelite prophet he is a woeful example. The "prophetic" words he speaks are few and far between, and not even reliably the words of God. His other words are dominated by first-person speech. (The first person as subject, object, or possessive occurs twenty-six times in the psalm.) Through props and embodied actors YHWH-God tries to draw attention to the other, but to little avail. Jonah remains the center of his own attention. As Levy succinctly states: "[Jonah] behaves like a typical Yiddish 'nebech' (simpleton)."[20]

Dynamism

A sense of movement is conveyed in several ways in the script of Jonah. Like many biblical narratives, it makes prodigious use of the *wayyiqtol* verbal form, keeping the action moving. Literal translation of the conjunction highlights this paratactic style. Person shifts also give a dynamic feel to the script. Prophetic literature typically includes shifts from nonthreatening third person forms to second person forms that prompt audience involvement. As we have noted, there is also a liberal use of first person forms in this script. The script moves between third-person narration and dialogue involving first and second-person address. Significantly, it ends with a direct question from YHWH to Jonah that effectively draws the audience into the drama, leaving us to answer the question that is posed.

This drama demands performance. The sailors *act* to save themselves and their passenger (hurl cargo, cast lots, pray, ask questions, row, hurl Jonah), then perform acts of worship in response to their safety (sacrifice, vows). The Ninevites *act* in the hope they will be saved (fasting, wearing sackcloth, praying, turning away from badness). Their actions are underscored by the comment "God saw their *deeds* . . ." (3:10) and the decision by God *not to act* in judgment. He does, however, *act* to teach Jonah his lessons (by hurling a whirlwind; by appointing first a fish, then a plant, then a worm, then wind). Each of these nonhuman actors performs as

20. Levy, *The Bible* as *Theatre*, 163.

appointed: the fish swallows and vomits, the plant grows and shades, the worm attacks, the wind scorches and discomforts. Jonah, on the other hand, rarely acts in response to others, but instead performs self-serving or ambiguous actions (finds a ship heading in the opposite direction from Nineveh, hides away and sleeps in the midst of the whirlwind, walks only partway into Nineveh, preaches a half-hearted sermon, goes out of Nineveh, makes a booth for himself). The *words* of Jonah—his response to the sailors and his psalm in the fish—are on the surface devout but, as noted above, are ambiguous and self-centered. One is left questioning the validity of this prophetic performance.

Connections with Jonah

The prophetic literature in general invites audience involvement, since the prophets communicate the words of God directly to their audiences. Evidence of redaction and interpolation show how these books have already been re-enacted for new audiences in new settings. Jonah's brief and ambiguous oracle does not speak as directly as prophetic words found in other biblical scripts, despite its impact on the Ninevite audience of the narrative world. Yet questions raised in the script are just as compelling for later audiences of this performance.

The implied question when the Chief of the Riggers says "Perhaps the god will consider us" is answered positively by the end of Act 1 when the whirlwind abates and the sailors are brought into relationship with that God. Yet the King of Nineveh displays the same uncertainty in his question "Who knows? The God *may* turn and relent, and he *may* turn from his burning nose." A new crisis brings new questions about God's character and God's actions.

Theological contemplation arising from the story is no less important than questions of justice. The two main justice issues found in this script are concern for the environment and concern for the "other."

YHWH's ultimate question "should I not be concerned?"—a question that remains unanswered in the script—is left hanging for the audience's contemplation. That fact that the script ends with Ninevite livestock as the object of this concern invites new questions for audiences in our time as we struggle to determine the relationship between Judeo-Christian faith and our world's ecological crisis. Jonah cared about the *qiyqayon* plant that grew, but only because it was of service to him. When YHWH challenges this attitude of Jonah, is it really a question for a contemporary audience?

Many commentaries emphasize the graciousness and compassion YHWH shows for the outsider, concluding that this is a challenge for those who claim an exclusive relationship with the god of their faith. But other conclusions can be drawn from this performance if the context is different. An individual or community in crisis might relate positively to the psalm's message of salvation from calamity, but if that crisis results from the cruel hand of an enemy, the justice of YHWH's acceptance of that enemy or failure to act against it might well be questioned. As Chesung Ryu's postcolonial reading of Jonah argues, the prophet's silent resistance to God's questions in the final chapter may be the only possible protest to make on behalf of powerless Judahites in the context of an all-powerful Assyrian Empire.[21] Other biblical prophetic traditions preserve protest against God's inaction and make it clear that such questioning and complaint are integral to a life of faith.

In an anti-Semitic context we would need to hear Jonah's silence as expressing the pain of a covenant people feeling abandoned by the God of the covenant while others prosper. In modern-day Palestine, we would need to hear God questioning Jonah's anger at compassion being shown to those outside of the covenant. In the current context of Islamophobia dominating Western politics, we need to be reminded that when we try to prevent God's compassion from being shown, we who are followers of God might be hurt by our own actions.

Audiences reenacting the story of Jonah in their own contexts will thus find different aspects of its performance persuasive. Reading and interpreting Scripture as performance gives equal authority to the script and the context in which it is read. What *can* be said about the performance of Jonah is that God hears the voices of all who call on him for mercy—whether pagan sailors (1:14), violent Ninevites (3:8), or recalcitrant prophets (2:3).

---

21. Ryu, "Silence as Resistance."

Concluding Reflections

CRITICAL PERFORMANCE ANALYSIS OF the quintessential performative nature of the prophets as embodied spokespersons for YHWH has been presented here in order to understand and clarify YHWH's message to audiences, situations, and communities of the past. Further, this study has offered criticism that engages contemporary audiences through performance analysis. The three case studies chosen in conjunction with my previous study of the book of Habakkuk have shown that Biblical Performance Criticism and Israel's prophets can be brought together in critical and effective dialogue.

Prophets as Performers

In presenting the "word of YHWH" prophets as often *performed* the word as *spoke* the word. Performances were frequently backed up by verbal explanation, but the power of the visual, sometimes strange, thought-provoking, attention-grabbing acts was in the *doing* of them. More often than not, these performances were intimately connected to the prophet's own life experience, frequently in acts that were life-changing. Prophets could not be impartial observers and indifferent messengers of YHWH. Their vocation was to *be* the message—whether it brought them comfort and pleasure (such as Ezekiel's sweet-tasting scroll) or, more often, ignominy and physical or emotional pain (illustrated by the death wish expressed by both Elijah and Jonah in the midst of their prophetic ministry). The biblical prophets were fully engaged as creative performers who connected with their audiences as they carried out their calling from YHWH.

The Creativity of Prophetic Performance

Focusing on the *creativity* of the prophets via performance-sensitive translations allows appreciation for the rhetorical impact of the original performance event, clues of which have been captured in the written script. These include repeated words and themes, wordplay, irony and humor, verbal subjects, Hebrew diacritics, implied gestures and movement, vocal quality, props, and ready-mades. Many biblical translations aim for sound grammar and a pleasing quality of expression even if the underlying Hebrew is obscure and repetitive. The unfamiliarity of a highly iconic translation is thus arresting to the eye and ear, and highlights more effectively the features discussed here. Occasionally the obscurity of the Hebrew can be retained in transliterated form as a reminder that the original performance is ambiguous, and interpretive decisions could result in quite different performances.

Viewing prophetic literature as creative performance opens up new and inventive ways to envisage the material. In the case of *Elijah*, I have reimagined the Elijah Cycle as a miniseries comprising four episodes. Careful attention to character development suggests that one of these episodes could be considered a prequel, even though its position in the series need not change given the dramatic impact of its current placement. My presentation of this biblical material has clearly been influenced by the prominent Star Wars franchise, as shown by the episode titles and the inclusion of a prequel in the structure. The strength of the characters and the backstory of a cosmic battle of the gods made the allusion irresistible for me.

Ezekiel is presented as a practitioner of performance art. Many parallels can be found between performance art and Ezekiel's prophetic performance. Installments using ordinary actions and objects, involvement of the artist's body, provocative spectacle designed to shock the audience, and the series of interconnected yet independent actions all align with material we might find in a catalogue of performance art. This prophet's language also gives us reason to understand why he resorted to performance: at times he was almost inarticulate in trying to describe his visions, his script was far more repetitive than we see with other prophets, and his language is at times crude and uncompromising.

I am not the first to suggest that the book of *Jonah* lends itself to being imagined as a stage play, but performance-sensitive translation particularly highlights settings, scenes, script, actors, and props. Attention to the verbal forms allows us to envisage nonhuman entities as cast members, challenging any default anthropocentric biblical interpretation. Observation of the diacritics in the original script suggests effective pauses in the performance to draw attention to the attitude of the prophet: biliously pious at the end of

Act 1 and pathetically petulant at the end of Act 2. Careful translation high-lights the humor in the script: the contrast between the Israelite prophet and the pagan sailors, underscored by the same verbs applied to each; a fish that turns female while the prophet is inside; the exaggerated response of the city of Nineveh and all its inhabitants to Jonah's famously brief and uninviting sermon; and the lingering image of contrite cows.

Commentary on Prophetic Performance

A focus on creativity in the biblical prophets has brought out the uniqueness of each prophetic performance that deserves further careful commentary. Within each performance the same prophet could represent a model for faithful reenactment at one moment and a poor ambassador for the love and justice of the God of the Israelites at another. The contemporary audience has an important role in discerning how to respond to each performance.

Elijah's performance is varied throughout his Series. On the one hand, he shows concern for a foreign widow-woman and her son, bring-ing a miraculous presence of Israel's God into a situation of suffering and deprivation, and interceding on behalf of them when crisis has struck. He is bold and resolute, confronting political and religious power when the YHWH-Israelite covenant ideals are flouted. At times he is able to speak truth fearlessly. On the other hand, his performance vacillates between arrogance and self-doubt. He makes enemies and stoops to their tactics in the battle for ideology. His prophetic call needs renewed assurances, but even so it is hard to know whether he is changed by the admittedly enig-matic manifestation of YHWH. The ambiguity of the phrase *demāmāh daqqāh* (1 Kgs 19:12) epitomizes the need for audience discernment. Does the power of YHWH or the vulnerability of YHWH hold greater influence for prophetic action in the world?

The Elijah Series includes a second prophetic performance that is worth contemplation. As much as Elijah's confrontational style brings trust in YHWH to the forefront, the quiet but risky path of civil disobedience practiced by Obadiah is shown to be an equally effective means of uphold-ing Yahwistic faith.

Ezekiel's performance gives us further insights into the nature of bibli-cal prophecy. His openness to YHWH brings about wondrous and inspiring visions, but also leads to Ezekiel's strenuous and uncomfortable activity that YHWH demands in order for his message to be transmitted. Several times the prophet protests against YHWH's instruction, and it appears that these protests have the effect of bringing about a change of mind for YHWH.

Ezekiel is also told to stand on his feet in the presence of YHWH. This performance shows us that prophets are not mere puppets, acting and speaking at the whim of the director pulling the strings, but conversation partners with inherent dignity and agency. While many of us would not have the nerve or stamina to perform the provocative acts of Ezekiel, we can be encouraged that the biblical witness suggests that the faithful community is in partnership with God in our world.

Jonah is a prophet who is more useful as a counterillustration than a model to be emulated. If anything, it is a performance that shows us that God's grace and action in the world is *not* dependent upon the obedience of those called to prophetic ministry. Yet Jonah's performance also reminds us that prophecy is never solely blind obedience, but an invitation to engage with God in matters of faith and salvation. At the end of Jonah's drama, the audience is invited onto the stage to continue that conversation of God's justice and concern for the created world. The performance itself, however, has shown that it is a mistake to expect easy answers when contemplating God's action in the world.

All of the prophets in my case studies were loners, whether by nature or enforced by their prophetic calling. Yet the preservation and transmission of their performances indicate they were recognized as authoritative within their communities. In-depth studies of other prophetic performers in the Hebrew Bible, such as Deborah, Nathan, or Jeremiah, would illustrate the validity of collaborative ministry as a model for prophetic action in the world.

Connections with Prophetic Performance

Biblical Performance Criticism with its emphasis on embodied experience rejects a dichotomy between theory and practice. The third aspect of this study has therefore highlighted *connections*, the place where prophetic traditions invite reenactment in our own contexts. Prophets spoke and acted in liminal settings, often during times of crisis, where challenge or encouragement were required and new ways of responding in the world could be invited.

The three case studies I have undertaken have brought out several areas where prophetic performance "hits the ground in practice": welcoming and ministering to "the other"; attending to injustice and exploitation, especially of those living in poverty; attending to the need for healthy and respectful interfaith dialogue; exercising civil disobedience in the context of power misuse by the ruling forces; attending to land rights; and concern for the preservation of the created world in the context of the environmental crisis.

An overarching impression from the study of these three prophets as performers is that God is willing to use each, with their own troubled personalities, in their own concrete circumstances, representing God's presence and covenantal justice whether or not their audience are receptive and responsive. Openness to God's calling within our own particular time, place, and context enables us to make connections with biblical prophetic performance.

Viewing Ourselves as Audiences of Prophetic Performance

Biblical Performance Criticism places a greater emphasis on the role of the audience than other critical methods. Audience response and even transformation is a key goal in performance. In this study, attention has been given to the original audiences of the biblical prophets, noting where repetition with innovation kept audiences engaged, wordplay added interest, the use of ready-mades as elements of surprise or disquiet in scripts added depth of understanding or new insights to the prophetic performance, and second-person verbal forms drew the audience into the action.

For us, a contemporary audience, the traditions themselves are often ready-mades, due to familiarity with their content through long use in church and academy. I am hopeful that through careful performance-sensitive translation many of these aspects of engagement with ancient audiences have been replicated so that contemporary audiences can be similarly surprised and challenged by the prophetic performances presented here. The open-endedness of the performances invites contemporary audience participation, including discernment of the best performance for a specific occasion. Viewing the biblical prophets through the lens of performance, then, makes explicit the need for improvisation in order to allow these ancient traditions to continue to have relevance today. Although we continue to respect these original scripts, ever-changing settings, actors, and audiences will require us to adapt so that these traditions can continue to inspire new performances of this ancient material as we undertake prophetic action in our world today.

Bibliography

Abma, Richtsje. "Travelling from Babylon to Zion: Location and Function in Isaiah 49–55." *Journal for the Study of the Old Testament* 74 (1997) 3–28.

Adams, Jim W. *The Performative Nature and Function of Isaiah 40–55*. Library of Hebrew Bible/Old Testament Studies 448. New York: T. & T. Clark, 2006.

Allegue, Ludivine, et al., eds. *Practice-as-Research in Performance and Screen*. New York: Palgrave Macmillan, 2009.

Amit, Yairah. *Reading Biblical Narratives: Literary Criticism and the Hebrew Bible*. Minneapolis: Fortress, 2001.

Athas, George, and Ian M. Young. *Elementary Biblical Hebrew: An Introductory Grammar*. 4th rev. ed. Croydon Park, NSW: Ancient Vessel, 2013.

Baltzer, Klaus. *Deutero-Isaiah: A Commentary on Isaiah 40–55*. Translated by Margaret Kohl. Hermeneia. Minneapolis: Fortress, 2001.

Bartholomew, Craig G., and David J. H. Beldman, eds. *Hearing the Old Testament: Listening for God's Address*. Grand Rapids: Eerdmans, 2012.

Barton, John. "Reading the Prophets from an Environmental Perspective." In *Ecological Hermeneutics: Biblical, Theological, and Historical Perspectives*, edited by David G. Horrell et al., 46–55. London: T. & T. Clark, 2010.

Bauman, Richard. "Folklore." In *Folklore, Cultural Performances, and Popular Entertainments: A Communications-Centered Handbook*, edited by Richard Bauman, 29–40. New York: Oxford University Press, 1992.

———. *Story, Performance, and Event: Contextual Studies of Oral Narrative*. Cambridge Studies in Oral and Literate Culture 10. Cambridge: Cambridge University Press, 1986.

Ben Zvi, Ehud, and Michael H. Floyd, eds. *Writings and Speech in Israelite and Ancient Near Eastern Prophecy*. Symposium Series 10. Atlanta: Society of Biblical Literature, 2000.

Ben Zvi, Ehud, and James D. Nogalski. *Two Sides of a Coin: Juxtaposing Views on Interpreting the Book of the Twelve / the Twelve Prophetic Books*. Analecta Gorgiana 201. Piscataway, NJ: Gorgias, 2009.

Berrin, Shani. "Qumran Pesharim." In *Biblical Interpretation at Qumran*, edited by Matthias Henze, 110–33. Studies in the Dead Sea Scrolls and Related Literature. Grand Rapids: Eerdmans, 2005.

Biddle, Mark E. *Reading Judges: A Literary and Theological Commentary*. Reading the Old Testament. Macon, GA: Smyth & Helwys, 2012.

———. *A Time to Laugh: Humor in the Bible*. Macon, GA: Smyth & Helwys, 2013.

Block, Daniel. *The Book of Ezekiel, Chapters 1–24*. New International Commentary on the Old Testament. Grand Rapids: Eerdmans, 1997.

Boadt, Lawrence. "Textual Problems in Ezekiel and Poetic Analysis of Paired Words." *Journal of Biblical Literature* 97 (1978) 489–99.

Boda, Mark J., and J. Gordon McConville, eds. *Dictionary of the Old Testament: Prophets*. Downers Grove, IL: IVP Academic, 2012.

Boda, Mark J., et al., eds. *The Prophets Speak on Forced Migration*. Ancient Israel and Its Literature 21. Atlanta: Society of Biblical Literature Press, 2015.

Brettler, Marc Zvi. *How to Read the Jewish Bible*. Oxford: Oxford University Press, 2005.

Briggs, Richard. "The Use of Speech-Act Theory in Biblical Interpretation." *Currents in Research* 9 (2001) 229–76.

Broome, Edwin. "Ezekiel's Abnormal Personality." *Journal of Biblical Literature* 65 (1946) 277–92.

Bruch, Debra. "The Prejudice against Theatre." *Journal of Religion and Theatre* 3/1 (2004) 1–18.

Brueggemann, Walter. *1 & 2 Kings*. Smyth & Helwys Bible Commentary. Macon, GA: Smyth & Helwys, 2000.

———. *Theology of the Old Testament: Testimony, Dispute, Advocacy*. Minneapolis: Fortress, 1997.

Brummitt, Mark. "Of Broken Pots and Dirty Laundry: The Jeremiah *Lehrstücke*." *The Bible and Critical Theory* 2 (2006) 3.1–3.10.

Carley, Keith W. *Ezekiel among the Prophets: A Study of Ezekiel's Place in the Prophetic Tradition*. Studies in Biblical Theology 2/31. London: SCM, 1975.

Carlson, Marvin. *Performance: A Critical Introduction*. 2nd ed. New York: Routledge, 2004.

Carr, David M. *Writing on the Tablet of the Heart: Origins of Scripture and Literature*. Oxford: Oxford University Press, 2005.

Carroll, Robert P. *When Prophecy Failed: Reactions and Responses to Failure in the Old Testament Prophetic Traditions*. London: SCM, 1979.

Carvalho, Corrine L., and Paul V. Niskanen, *Ezekiel, Daniel*. New Collegeville Bible Commentary. Collegeville, MN: Liturgical, 2016.

Childs, Brevard S. "The Canonical Shape of the Prophetic Literature." *Interpretation* 32 (1978) 46–55.

———. *Introduction to the Old Testament as Scripture*. Philadelphia: Fortress, 1979.

Clines, David J. A. *The Concise Dictionary of Classical Hebrew*. Sheffield: Sheffield Phoenix, 2009.

Conquergood, Dwight. "Of Caravans and Carnivals: Performance Studies in Motion." *The Drama Review* 39 (1995) 137–41.

———. "Performance Studies: Interventions and Radical Research." *The Drama Review* 46 (2002) 145–56.

Cousins, Melinda. "Pilgrim Theology: Worldmaking through Enactment of the Psalms of Ascents (Psalms 120–134)." PhD diss., Charles Sturt University, 2016.

Craigo-Snell, Shannon. "Command Performance: Rethinking Performance Interpretation in the Context of *Divine Discourse*." *Modern Theology* 16 (2000) 475–94.

Crane, Ashley S. *Israel's Restoration: A Textual-Comparative Exploration of Ezekiel 36–39*. Supplements to Vetus Testamentum 122. Leiden: Brill, 2008.

Crystal, Leon. "Theatre." In *The Universal Jewish Encyclopaedia*, edited by Isaac Landman, 10:208–39. New York: Universal Jewish Encyclopaedia, 1943.

Darr, Katheryn Pfisterer. "Ezekiel among the Critics." In *Recent Research on the Major Prophets*, edited by Alan H. Hauser, 249–59. Recent Research in Biblical Studies 1. Sheffield: Sheffield Phoenix, 2008.

———. "Write or True? A Response to Ellen Frances Davis." In *Signs and Wonders: Biblical Texts in Literary Focus*, edited by J. Cheryl Exum, 239–47. Semeia Studies. Atlanta: Scholars, 1989.

Davis, Ellen F. *Swallowing the Scroll: Textuality and the Dynamics of Discourse in Ezekiel's Prophecy*. Bible and Literature Series 21. Sheffield: Almond, 1989.

Delitzsch, Franz. *Commentary on the Old Testament*. Vol. 6, *Proverbs, Ecclesiastes and Song of Solomon*. Edited by Karl Friedrich Keil and Franz Delitzsch. 1875. Reprint, Grand Rapids: Eerdmans, 1980.

De Vries, Simon J. *1 Kings*. Word Biblical Commentary 12. Waco, TX: Word, 2003.

Dietrich, Walter. *Nahum, Habakkuk, Zephaniah*. International Exegetical Commentary on the Old Testament. Stuttgart: Kohlhammer, 2016.

Doan, William, and Terry Giles. *Prophets, Performance, and Power: Performance Criticism of the Hebrew Bible*. New York: T. & T. Clark, 2005.

———. "The Song of Asaph: A Performance-Critical Analysis of 1 Chronicles 16:8–36." *Catholic Biblical Quarterly* 70 (2008) 29–43.

Downer, Alan S. *The Art of the Play: An Anthology of Nine Plays*. New York: Holt, 1955.

Eagleton, Terry. "J. L. Austin and the Book of Jonah." *New Blackfriars* 69/815 (1988) 164–68.

Eaton, John. *Festal Drama in Deutero-Isaiah*. London: SPCK, 1979.

Engnell, Ivan. "The Ebed Yahweh Songs and the Suffering Messiah in 'Deutero-Isaiah.'" *Bulletin of the John Rylands Library* 31 (1948) 54–93.

Evans, Craig A. "Dead Sea Scrolls." In *Dictionary of the Old Testament: Prophets*, edited by Mark J. Boda and J. Gordon McConville, 143–52. Downers Grove, IL: IVP Academic, 2012.

Fohrer, Georg. *Die Hauptprobleme des Buches Ezechiel*. Beihefte zur Zeitschrift für die alttestamentliche Wissenschaft 72. Berlin: Töpelmann, 1952.

———. *Die symbolischen Handlungen der Propheten*. Abhandlungen zur Theologie des Alten und Neuen Testaments 25. Zürich: Zwingli, 1953.

Foley, John Miles. *How to Read an Oral Poem*. Urbana: University of Illinois Press, 2002.

Giesen, Bernhard. "Performance Art." In *Social Performance: Symbolic Action, Cultural Pragmatics, and Ritual*, edited by Jeffrey C. Alexander et al., 315–24. Cambridge Cultural Social Studies. Cambridge: Cambridge University Press, 2006.

Giles, Terry. "Performance Criticism." In *Dictionary of the Old Testament Prophets*, edited by Mark J. Boda and J. Gordon McConville, 578–83. Downers Grove, IL: IVP Academic, 2012.

Giles, Terry, and William Doan. "Performance Criticism of the Hebrew Bible." *Religion Compass* 2 (2008) 237–86.

———. *The Story of Naomi—The Book of Ruth: From Gender to Politics*. Biblical Performance Criticism Series 13. Eugene, OR: Cascade Books, 2016.

———. *Twice Used Songs: Performance Criticism of the Songs of Ancient Israel*. Peabody, MA: Hendrickson, 2009.

Gottwald, Norman K. "Tragedy and Comedy in the Latter Prophets." *Semeia* 32 (1984) 83–96.

Greenberg, Moshe. *Ezekiel 1–20*. Anchor Bible 22. Garden City, NY: Doubleday, 1983.

Gunkel, Hermann. *The Psalms: A Form-Critical Introduction.* With an introduction by James Muilenburg. Translated by Thomas M. Horner. Facet Books: Biblical Series 19. Philadelphia: Fortress, 1967 [1930].

Habel, Norman. *The Book of Job.* Old Testament Library. London: SCM, 1985.

———, ed. *The Earth Story in the Psalms and the Prophets.* The Earth Bible 4. Sheffield: Sheffield Academic, 2001.

Hagedorn, Anselm C. "Nahum—Ethnicity and Stereotypes: Anthropological Insights into Nahum's Literary History." In *Ancient Israel: The Old Testament in Its Social Context,* edited by Philip F. Esler, 223–39. Minneapolis: Fortress, 2006.

Halperin, David J. *Seeking Ezekiel: Text and Psychology.* University Park: Penn State University Press, 1993.

Hauser, Alan J., ed. *Recent Research on the Major Prophets.* Recent Research in Biblical Studies 1. Sheffield: Sheffield Phoenix, 2008.

Hauser, Alan J. "Introduction and Overview." In *Recent Research in the Major Prophets,* edited by Alan J. Hauser, 1–77. Recent Research in Biblical Studies 1. Sheffield: Sheffield Phoenix, 2008.

Hazleton, Lesley. *Jezebel: The Untold Story of the Bible's Harlot Queen.* New York: Doubleday, 2007.

Heschel, Abraham J. *The Prophets.* 1962. Reprint, New York: Perenniel, 2001.

Hornsby, Teresa. "Ezekiel Off-Broadway." *The Bible and Critical Theory* 2/1 (2006) 2.1–2.8.

Horsley, Richard A. *Text and Tradition in Performance and Writing.* Biblical Performance Criticism Series 9. Eugene, OR: Cascade Books, 2013

House, Paul R. *The Unity of the Twelve.* Bible and Literature Series 27. Sheffield: Almond, 1990.

———. *Zephaniah: A Prophetic Drama.* Bible and Literature Series 16. Sheffield: Almond, 1989.

Houston, Walter. "What Did the Prophets Think They Were Doing? Speech Acts and Prophetic Discourse in the Old Testament." *Biblical Interpretation* 1 (1993) 167–88.

Hyman, Frieda Clark. "Elijah: Accuser and Defender." *Judaism* 39 (1990) 282–95.

Iverson, Kelly R. "Oral Fixation or Oral Corrective? A Response to Larry Hurtado." *New Testament Studies* 62 (2016) 183–200.

Jones, Barry A. "The Seventh-Century Prophets in Twenty-First-Century Research." *Currents in Biblical Research* 14/1 (2016) 129–75.

Joubert, Annekie. *The Power of Performance: Linking Past and Present in Hananwa and Lobedu Oral Literature.* Trends in Linguistics: Studies and Monographs 160. Berlin: Mouton de Gruyter, 2004.

Kutner, Eric. *Shot in the Name of Art.* Op-Docs. Opinion. *New York Times,* May 20, 2015. https://www.youtube.com/watch?v=drZIWs3Dl1k/.

Landes, George M. "The 'Three Days and Three Nights' Motif in Jonah 2:1." *Journal of Biblical Literature* 86 (1967) 446–50.

Lang, Bernard. *Monotheism and the Prophetic Minority: An Essay in Biblical History and Sociology.* Social World of Biblical Antiquity 1. Sheffield: Almond, 1983.

———. "Street Theater, Raising the Dead, and the Zoroastrian Connction in Ezekiel's Prophecy." In *Ezekiel and His Book: Textual and Literary Criticism and Their Interrelation,* edited by J. Lust, 297–316. Bibliotheca Ephemeridum theologicarum Lovaniensium 74. Leuven: Leuven University Press, 1986.

Lash, Nicholas. *Theology on the Way to Emmaus*. 1986. Reprint, Eugene, OR: Wipf & Stock, 2005.

Levitt Kohn, Risa. "Ezekiel at the Turn of the Century." In *Recent Research on the Major Prophets*, edited by Alan H. Hauser, 260–72. Recent Research in Biblical Studies 1. Sheffield: Sheffield Phoenix, 2008.

Levy, Shimon. *The Bible as Theatre*. Brighton: Sussex Academic, 2000.

Lundbom, Jack R. *The Hebrew Prophets: An Introduction*. Minneapolis: Fortress, 2010.

Lust, J. "A Gentle Breeze or a Roaring Thunderous Sound?" *Vetus Testamentum* 25 (1975) 110–15.

Mackenzie, Ian. "Improvisation, Creativity, and Formulaic Language." *Journal of Aesthetics and Art Criticism* 58 (2000) 173–79.

Mathews, Jeanette. "Deuteronomy 30: Faithfulness in the Refugee Camps of Moab, Babylonia, and Beyond." In *Bible, Borders, Belonging(s): Engaging Readings from Oceania*, edited by Jione Havea et al., 157–70. Semeia Studies 75. Atlanta: Society of Biblical Literature, 2014.

———. *Performing Habakkuk: Faithful Re-enactment in the Midst of Crisis*. Eugene, OR: Pickwick Publications, 2012.

———. "Translating Habakkuk as a Performance." In *Translating Scripture for Sound and Performance*, edited by James A. Maxey and Ernst R. Wendland, 119–38. Biblical Performance Criticism Series 5. Eugene, OR: Cascade Books, 2012.

Matthews, Victor H. *Social World of the Hebrew Prophets*. Peabody: Hendrickson, 2001.

Matthews, Victor H., and Don C. Benjamin. *Old Testament Parallels: Laws and Stories from the Ancient Near East*. 3rd ed. New York: Paulist, 2006.

Maxey, James A. *From Orality to Orality: A New Paradigm for Contextual Translation of the Bible*. Biblical Performance Criticism Series 2. Eugene, OR: Cascade Books, 2009.

Meyers, Carol, et al., eds. *Women in Scripture: A Dictionary of Named and Unnamed Women in the Hebrew Bible, the Apocryphal/Deuterocanonical Books, and the New Testament*. Grand Rapids: Eerdmans, 2000.

Mowinckel, Sigmund. *He That Cometh*. Translated by G. W. Anderson. Oxford: Blackwell, 1956 [1951].

———. *The Psalms in Israel's Worship*. 2 vols. in 1. Translated by D. R. Ap-Thomas. 1962. Reprint, with new foreword by James L. Crenshaw. Biblical Resource Series. Grand Rapids: Eerdmans, 2004.

Nelson, Robin, ed. *Practice as Research in the Arts: Principles, Protocols, Pedagogies, Resistances*. New York: Palgrave Macmillan, 2013.

Niditch, Susan. *Oral World and Written Word: Orality and Literacy in Ancient Israel*. Library of Ancient Israel. Louisville: Westminster John Knox, 1996.

Nogalski, James D. *The Book of the Twelve*. 2 vols. Smyth & Helwys Bible Commentary. Macon, GA: Smyth & Helwys, 2011.

———. *Interpreting Prophetic Literature: Historical and Exegetical Tools for Reading the Prophets*. Louisville: Westminster John Knox, 2015.

———. *Redactional Processes in the Book of the Twelve*. Beihefte zur Zeitschrift für die alttestamentliche Wissenschaft 218. Berlin: de Gruyter, 1993.

O'Brien, Julia. *Nahum, Habakkuk, Zephaniah, Haggai, Zechariah, Malachi*. Abingdon Old Testament Commentaries. Nashville: Abingdon, 2004.

O'Connor, Kathleen. "The Prophet Jeremiah and Exclusive Loyalty to God." *Interpretation* 59 (2005) 130–40.

Odell, Margaret S. *Ezekiel*. Smyth & Helwys Bible Commentary. Macon: Smyth & Helwys, 2005.

Olley, John W. "YHWH and His Zealous Prophet: The Presentation of Elijah in 1 and 2 Kings." *Journal for the Study of the Old Testament* 80 (1998) 25–51.

Page, Hugh. "Performance as Interpretive Metaphor: The Bible as Libretto for Research, Translation, Preaching and Spirituality in the 21st Century—Moving from Theory to Praxis." *Memphis Theological Seminary Journal* 41 (2005) 34–56.

Paul, Shalom M., and S. David Sperling. "Prophets and Prophecy." In *Encyclopaedia Judaica*, edited by Fred Skolnik, 16:566–80. 22 vols. 2nd ed. Detroit: Macmillan Reference USA, 2007.

Perlitt, Lothar. *Die Propheten Nahum, Habakuk, Zephanja*. Das Alte Testament Deutsch 25/1. Göttingen: Vandenhoeck & Ruprecht, 2004.

Perry, Peter S. *Insights from Performance Criticism*. Insights Series. Minneapolis: Fortress, 2016.

Petersen, David L. *The Prophetic Literature: An Introduction*. Louisville: Westminster John Knox, 2002.

Peterson, Eugene H. *The Message*. Colorado Springs: Navpress, 2002.

Pritchard, James B., ed. *The Ancient Near East in Pictures Relating to the Old Testament*. Princeton: Princeton University Press, 1954.

Queen-Sutherland, Kandy. *Ruth and Esther*. Smyth & Helwys Bible Commentary. Macon, GA: Smyth & Helwys, 2016.

Rabinowitz, Louis Isaac. "Prophets and Prophecy in the Talmud." In *Encyclopaedia Judaica*, edited by Fred Skolnik, 16:580–81. 22 vols. 2nd ed. Detroit: Macmillan Reference USA, 2007.

Redditt, Paul L. *Introduction to the Prophets*. Grand Rapids: Eerdmans, 2008.

Rhoads, David. "The Art of Translating for Oral Performance." In *Translating Scripture for Sound and Performance*, edited by James A. Maxey and Ernst R. Wendland, 22–48. Biblical Performance Criticism Series 6. Eugene, OR: Cascade Books, 2012.

———. "Performance Criticism: An Emerging Methodology in Second Testament Studies—Part I." *Biblical Theology Bulletin* 36/3 (2006) 118–33.

———. "Performance Criticism: An Emerging Methodology in Second Testament Studies—Part II." *Biblical Theology Bulletin* 36/4 (2006) 164–84.

Rofé, Alexander. *The Prophetical Stories: The Narratives about the Prophets in the Hebrew Bible; Their Literary Types and History*. Publications of the Perry Foundation for Biblical Research in the Hebrew University of Jerusalem. Jerusalem: Magnes, 1988.

Ruiz, Jean–Pierre. *Readings from the Edges: The Bible and People on the Move*. Studies in Latino/a Catholicism. Maryknoll, NY: Orbis, 2011.

Ryu, Chesung Justin. "Silence as Resistance: A Postcolonial Reading of Jonah 4:1–11." *Journal for the Study of the Old Testament* 34 (2009) 195–218.

Schechner, Richard. *Performance Studies: An Introduction*. 2nd ed. New York: Routledge, 2006.

Schmidt, W. H. "רָבַד, *dābhar*." In *Theological Dictionary of the Old Testament*, edited by G. Johannes Botterweck and Helmer Ringgren, 3:84–125. 16 vols. Grand Rapids: Eerdmans, 1978.

Schneiders, Sandra M. *The Revelatory Text: Interpreting the New Testament as Sacred Scripture*. San Francisco: HarperSanFrancisco, 1991.

Segal, Alan F. "Mysticism." In *The Eerdmans Dictionary of Early Judaism*, edited by John J. Collins and Daniel C. Harlow, 982–86. Grand Rapids: Eerdmans, 2010.

Seitz, Christopher R. "Isaiah 1–66: Making Sense of the Whole." In *Reading and Preaching the Book of Isaiah*, edited by Christopher R. Seitz, 105–26. Philadelphia: Fortress, 1988.

———. *Prophecy and Hermeneutics: Toward a New Introduction to the Prophets*. Studies in Theological Interpretation. Grand Rapids: Baker Academic, 2007.

Shelton, Pauline. "Making a Drama out of a Crisis? A Consideration of the Book of Job as a Drama." *Journal for the Study of the Old Testament* 24 (1999) 69–82.

Sherwood, Yvonne. "Prophetic Performance Art." Editorial. *The Bible and Critical Theory* 2/1 (2006) 1.1–1.4.

———. "Prophetic Scatology: Prophecy and the Art of Sensation." *Semeia* (1998) 183–224.

Shusterman, Richard. "Art as Dramatization." *Journal of Aesthetics and Art Criticism* 59 (2001) 363–72.

Smith-Christopher, Daniel L. "Ezekiel on Fanon's Couch: A Postcolonialist Dialogue with David Halperin's *Seeking Ezekiel*." In *Peace and Justice Shall Embrace: Power and Theopolitics in the Bible; Essays in Honor of Millard Lind*, edited by Ted Grimsrud and Loren L. Johns, 108–44. Telford, PA: Pandora, 1999.

Sommer, Benjamin D. Review of *Deutero-Isaiah: A Commentary on Isaiah 40–55*, *Review of Biblical Literature* 4 (2003). http://www.bookreviews.org.

Sowden, Lewis. "Theater." In *Encyclopaedia Judaica*, edited by Fred Skolnik, 19:669–85. 22 vols. 2nd ed. Detroit: Macmillan Reference USA, 2007.

Stacey, David. *Prophetic Drama in the Old Testament*. London: Epworth, 1990.

Stulman, Louis, and Hyun Chul Paul Kim. *You Are My People: An Introduction to Prophetic Literature*. Nashville: Abingdon, 2010.

Sweeney, Marvin A. *I & II Kings*. Old Testament Library. Louisville: Westminster John Knox, 2007.

———. *The Prophetic Literature*. Interpreting Biblical Texts. Nashville: Abingdon, 2005.

Tiemeyer, Lena-Sofia. "Recent Currents in Research on the Prophetic Literature." *The Expository Times* 119 (2008) 161–69.

Trible, Phyllis. *Rhetorical Criticism: Context, Method, and the Book of Jonah*. Guides to Biblical Scholarship: Old Testament Series. Minneapolis: Fortress, 1994.

Troxel, Ronald L. *Prophetic Literature: From Oracles to Books*. Oxford: Wiley Blackwell, 2012.

Turner, Victor. "Liminality and Communitas." In *The Performance Studies Reader*, edited by Henry Bial, 79–87. London: Routledge, 2004.

Twycross, Meg. "The Theatre." In *The Blackwell Companion to the Bible and Culture*, edited by John F. A. Sawyer, 338–64. Blackwell Companions to Religion. Oxford: Blackwell, 2006.

Utzschneider, Helmut. "Drama (AT)." https://www.bibelwissenschaft.de/stichwort/200072/.

———. "Is There a Universal Genre of 'Drama'?" In *Literary Construction of Identity in the Ancient World*, edited by Hanna Liss and Manfred Oeming, 63–79. Winona Lake, IN: Eisenbrauns, 2010.

———. *Micha*. Zürcher Bibelkommentare. AT 24/1. Zurich: TVZ, 2005.

Vanhoozer, Kevin J. *The Drama of Doctrine: A Canonical-Linguistic Approach to Christian Theology*. Louisville: Westminster John Knox, 2005.

Watson, Wilfred G. E. *Classical Hebrew Poetry: A Guide to Its Techniques.* Journal for the Study of the Old Testament Supplement Series 26. Sheffield: JSOT Press, 1984.

Watts, John D. W. *Isaiah 1–33.* Word Biblical Commentary 24. Waco, TX: Word, 1985.

———. *Isaiah 34–66.* Word Biblical Commentary 25. Waco, TX: Word, 1987.

Weiser, Artur. *The Psalms: A Commentary.* Translated by Herbert Hartwell. Old Testament Library. London: SCM, 1962.

Wellhausen, Julius. *Prolegomena to the History of Israel.* Translated by J. Sutherland Black and Allan Menzies. 1885. Reprint, Scholars Press Reprints and Translations Series. Atlanta: Scholars, 1994.

West, Travis. "The Art of Biblical Performance: Biblical Performance Criticism and the Genre of the Biblical Narratives." PhD diss., Free University of Amsterdam, 2018.

Wilks, John G. F. "The Prophet as Incompetent Dramatist." *Vetus Testamentum* 53 (2003) 530–43.

Williams, Rowan. "The Literal Sense of Scripture." *Modern Theology* 7 (1991) 121–34.

Wolk, Samuel J. B. "Mysticism." In *The Universal Jewish Encyclopedia,* edited by Isaac Landman, 8:73–76. 10 vols. New York: Universal Jewish Encyclopedia, 1942.

Wright, N. T. "How Can the Bible Be Authoritative?" *Vox Evangelica* 21 (1991) 7–32.

Wurzburger, Walter S. "Prophets and Prophecy: Modern Jewish Thought." In *Encyclopaedia Judaica,* edited by Fred Skolnik, 16:585–86. 22 vols. 2nd ed. Detroit: Macmillan Reference USA, 2007.

Yamasaki, Gary. *Perspective Criticism: Point of View and Evaluative Guidance in Biblical Narrative.* Eugene, OR: Cascade Books, 2012.

Young, Frances. *The Art of Performance: Towards a Theology of Holy Scripture.* London: Darton, Longman & Todd, 1990.

Zimmerli, Walther. *Ezekiel: A Commentary on the Book of the Prophet Ezekiel.* 2 vols. Translated by Ronald E. Clements. Hermeneia. Philadelphia: Fortress, 1979–1983.

Author Index

Scripture Index

Daniel

Hosea

Joel

Amos

Obadiah

Jonah